WITHDRAWN

THE DISABLED & THEIR PARENTS

THE DISABLED & THEIR PARENTS

A Counseling Challenge

REVISED EDITION

LEO BUSCAGLIA, Ph.D.

author of *Living, Loving & Learning* and *Love*

Also by Leo Buscaglia, Ph.D.:

Love

Because I Am Human

The Way of the Bull

Personhood

Living, Loving & Learning

The Fall of Freddie the Leaf

Library of Congress catalog number: 83-050284

SLACK Incorporated ISBN: 0-943432-13-8

Holt, Rinehart and Winston ISBN: 0-03-064176-4

Published in the United States of America by

SLACK Incorporated
6900 Grove Road
Thorofare, New Jersey 08086

In the United States, distributed to the trade by:

Holt, Rinehart and Winston
383 Madison Avenue
New York, New York 10017

In Canada, distributed to the trade by:

Holt, Rinehart and Winston, Limited
55 Horner Avenue
Toronto, Ontario
M8Z 4X0 Canada

Printed in the United States of America

10 9 8 7 6 5 4 3 2

SLACK INCORPORATED ISBN 0-943432-13-8

HOLT, RINEHART AND WINSTON

ISBN 0-03-064176-4

This book is dedicated to individuals with disabilities and their parents who, often alone, confused, misinformed and lonely, have wrestled with disillusionment, disappointment, despair, and seemingly insurmountable obstacles, and have emerged victorious — turning their dillusionment into renewed vigor, their disappointment to new courage, their despair to fresh hope, and discovering that what had seemed like insurmountable obstacles were merely "stepping stones" on their journey.

In so doing, they have confirmed for all of us the great potential and wonder in being human.

THE DISABLED & THEIR PARENTS

Contents

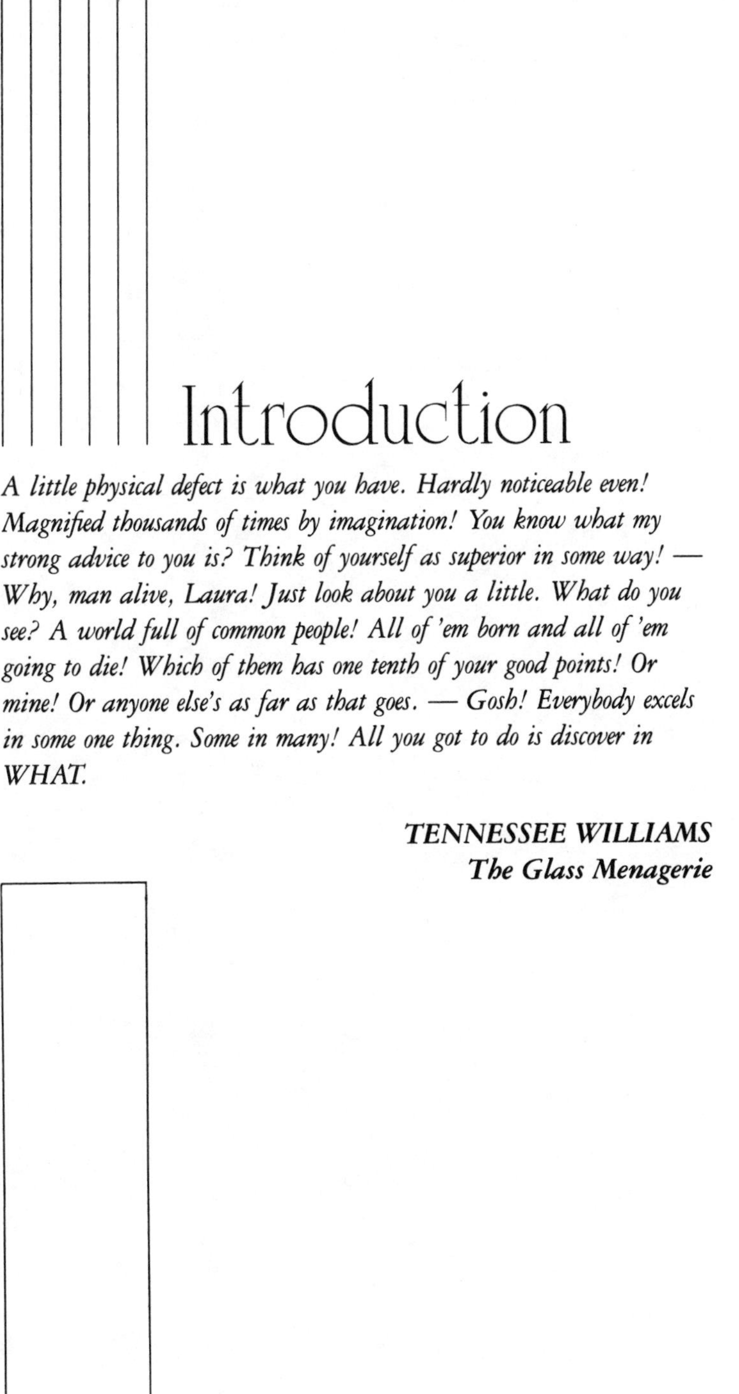

Introduction

A little physical defect is what you have. Hardly noticeable even! Magnified thousands of times by imagination! You know what my strong advice to you is? Think of yourself as superior in some way! — Why, man alive, Laura! Just look about you a little. What do you see? A world full of common people! All of 'em born and all of 'em going to die! Which of them has one tenth of your good points! Or mine! Or anyone else's as far as that goes. — Gosh! Everybody excels in some one thing. Some in many! All you got to do is discover in WHAT.

TENNESSEE WILLIAMS
The Glass Menagerie

When I think of how much heartache and despair could have been avoided if someone had sat down with us years ago and given us some counseling, some hope, some support, some knowledge relating to our child, I get white with rage! Are other families who have handicapped kids like ours treated in the same way?"

Silence.

"Then why the hell don't you do something about it?"

This challenge was presented to me over five years ago. I guess I have waited all this time for "someone else to do something about it." To my knowledge, it still hasn't been done.

For decades, almost all systemic studies relating to disabled individuals and their parents have stressed the need for more and better work in the field of counseling for them. The failure to help the disabled and their families to understand the nature and implications of a disability often causes everyone concerned more pain and suffering than the disability itself. Yet, so few have taken up the challenge. Too many of us professionals who work in this area have continued to hide our own interpersonal inadequacies in test results, medical jargon, case histories, new labels and the educational "wisdom" of the past. We have, in this way, abandoned the disabled and their families to their own resources. They have been left to discover their own solutions, suffer their own confusions and fears and experience their own despair. It is no wonder that so many of them have found only surface adjustments or have given in to overwhelming anxiety or hostility.

Their stories are always so similar. I hear them repeated again and again.

Their child is born with a disability. They are offered only a bit of medical information and less comfort and hope. The child is sent home. When they ask for "help" even the doctor, nurses or social workers seem inarticulate, embarrassed and inadequately prepared to deal with their "misfortune." Then begin years of confusion, fear, self-accusation, self-pity, self-hate. The hours in doctors' offices. The waiting. The continual tests, diagnoses, rediagnoses. The lack of thorough information. The interpretive generalities. The misinformation. The contradictory information. The continual pressures with no release. Not even baby sitters willing to sit for a few hours of relief. The growing family problems. The worries over money and bills. The rising tensions. The arguments. The uncertainty. Feelings which confuse and frighten them. All the frustrations of any family and so many more. Their feelings of inadequacy as they must stand by and watch their children, whom they love so much, slipping further and further away from the "normal" world they want to give them so badly. But what to do?

Then, the school battles. Admissions. Labels which are never explained. More re-evaluations! Mounds of records concerning their children in inaccessible files, shrouded in mystery. Anxiety as to whether or not they will be allowed to stay in school. Threats from school officials, stated and implied.

And the children, what will happen to them as they grow? Concern over their fears, their feelings of isolation, their mounting loneliness, their growing confusion, their sexual fantasies and frustrations, their questions regarding their feelings, their future, their tomorrow. Worry over their mounting anger. Rejection by a world that fears them and which they are more and more coming to fear. Frustration over the fact that they are learning so much about the wonders of Egypt, the magic of Renaissance Italy and the grandeur of the court of Louis IV, but so little about their empty feeling and the growing despair which is devouring them. Special needs, concerns, pressing issues which need to be dealt with at once...but no one to help, no one to talk to, no one who seems to understand.

So go their stories.

Though the problems which arise with a disability are often all-consuming, devastating and complex, it is possible for the disabled to reach adulthood without guidance being received by either the parents or the individual.

For six years of my professional life I spent eight to ten hours a day in counseling the disabled and their families. During this time I gained much insight into them and their very real and unique problems. I found them to be, for the most part, strong, persistent, sensitive, intelligent persons. I shared their frustrations, their hopelessness and their feelings of helplessness. I also experienced their joys, their triumphs, their growth, their wonder and their personal discovery. I developed a deep respect for them. They taught me a great deal about human strength and dignity.

This was a time of great frustration and questioning for me. Almost daily I asked the same questions. "Why had these people been made to carry their burden alone, for so long?" "Why had we professionals been so insensitive to their very human needs?" "Why had we actually created barriers for them along the way?" "Why had we offered such limited support, so few creative alternatives, so little praise?" "Why had we approached them telescopically for so many years, seeing them only as *problems, parts,* rather than as the total individuals they were?" "How could we forget that the meaning a part has can only be found in its relationship to the fully realized whole?" It is regrettable that time has not offered many answers to these questions or improvements to this sorry situation.

It is appalling how little attention is given, still, by medical doctors, psychologists and educators to the counseling of disabled persons and their families. This fact becomes even more astounding when one investigates the available literature and pertinent research in this field. With the exception of a few books, mostly of dated readings, works which deal in a very general way with the field of rehabilitation counseling, some inconclusive and often contradictory research, one is hard pressed to find meaningful literature in the field of counseling the disabled.

Surely, this book is not *the* answer. It is not meant to be an end, but rather, a modest beginning. It is, for me, acceptance of a challenge. In a larger sense it is a challenge to parents, medical doctors, psychologists, counselors, educators, physical and occupational therapists, social workers, psychiatrists and all those in the helping professions, to become more cognizant of the desperate need disabled persons and their families have for good, sound, reality-based guidance, and the tremendous resultant despair and loss of human potential when it is not forthcoming. It is an attempt to view counseling the disabled in its broadest and most human sense as a multidisciplinary process of rehabilitation, the prime concern of which is to help the disabled and the family through the complicated processes necessary to meet the unique mental, physical and emotional adjustments confronting them, as well as to acquire the necessary hope, insight and strength for them to take up, as their own, the greatest of all human challenges, the inalienable right of every person, disabled or not, to self-actualization.

Section I:

The Overall Challenge

Chapter 1:

A Handicap Is Made, Not Born

There is another and perhaps greater danger involved in this matter of accepting the limitations of others. Sometimes we are apt to regard as limitations qualities that are actually the other person's strength. We may resent them because they are not the particular qualities which we may want the other person to have. The danger lies in the possibilities that we will not accept the person as he is but try to make him over according to our own ideas.

ELEANOR ROOSEVELT
You Learn By Living

omewhere, even as you read this, a child is being born with a limitation. It may be blindness which will make the grandeur of a far-off mountain range a life-long mystery. It could be deafness, precluding the child's ever knowing the splash of the surf or the wonder of a Bach cantata. Perhaps cerebral palsy or spina bifida will deny the individual the experience of running through the wind or becoming an athlete. The brain may be damaged which will have a more disguised and subtle effect upon future behavior and learning or could bring about seizures or irreparable mental retardation. But birth defects are not solely responsible for these disabilities. At this moment, too, a child or adult is being involved in an accident. One may be cruising along in a car on a beautiful Sunday afternoon, and suddenly, in an unguarded second, find oneself permanently limited, with the brain crushed, limbs mangled, and mind devoured. One may slip in a shower, be struck by a golf ball, hit by a surfboard or slip on a door mat. No one is immune from possible irreparable disability.

These persons may have wealth or have no worldly possessions. They may be educated or unschooled. Their emotional lives may be healthy or tenuous. The one thing these individuals all will have in common is that each will be faced with a new, unexpected, possibly devastating adjustment. This adjustment may require them to drastically change their way of life, their profession, their hopes for the future and their plans for achieving their dreams.

A disability is not a desirable thing and there is no reason to believe otherwise. It will, in most cases, cause pain, discomfort, embarrassment, tears, confusion and the expenditure of a great deal of time and money. Still, with every passing moment, handicaps are being made as well as born.

Though they may not be aware of it at the time, the infant born with a birth defect and the adult who is crippled later in life will be limited not so much by the actual disability as much as by society's attitude regarding the disability. It is society, for the most part, that will define the disability as a handicap and it is the individual who will suffer from the definition.

Dr. Sol Gordon (1974) puts it well when he states:

> Society creates handicaps. While most disabilities are products of birth and accident, the debilitating impact on the person's life often results not so much from the "disability" as from the manner in which others define or treat the person. We incarcerate hundreds of thousands of people with special needs in custodial institutions; even those fortunate enough to receive services in the community usually find them in segregated and consequently stigmatizing settings such as sheltered workshops and special schools. These stereotypic means of serving people with special needs, through institutionalization and isolation, reflect the assumption that people with disabilities have neither interest nor ability to interact with the larger society.

There is an amusing, but rather disarming, Spanish story which tells of a land where the inhabitants, one by one, find that they are growing tails! Much to their horror, the first to sprout these monkey-like appendages do their utmost to hide them. They awkwardly stuff their tails in baggy trousers or flaring skirts in order to hide their *strangeness*. But as they discover that everyone is growing tails, the scene drastically changes. In fact, the tail proves to be very useful for carrying things, for quicker mobility, for opening doors when arms are full. Clothes designers begin to create clothing to accommodate, indeed, accentuate and liberate the newly grown tails. Soon, adornments are being used to call attention to these most novel appendages. Then, all at once, those who have not grown tails are seen as freaks. They frantically become engaged in finding means of hiding the fact by buying artificial tails or retreating from the tail-filled society altogether. How embarrassing! No tail!

In our culture, we continuously encounter examples of such attitudes. What is to be considered normal or beautiful is constantly being defined or redefined. In one era it is considered desirable for a woman to be as slim and shapeless as possible. Her body is molded and squeezed into confined, corseted lines. Breasts and buttocks are flattened and hips are hidden under designer patterns which will disguise her natural contours. Shortly thereafter the *style* changes. Now breasts are freed, even padded and left partially exposed, hips and buttocks are glorified and women are encouraged to revel in their shapeliness.

Standards of beauty, like standards of physical perfection,

may differ not only within a society, but also among societies. While the standards for the United States, at one time, may be the slim, boyish look for the female, the Italians, for instance, may continue to admire the more *Titian-like* ladies — pink, soft, round, ample, satisfying their age old desire to "have something to hold on to."

In Western cultures, large, long ears may conveniently be tucked behind well-designed hairdos. In various African and Polynesian cultures, the ears are often pulled in all manners of torturous ways to deliberately elongate them, and thus, make them attractive and more desirable to the individuals in their community. Lips are pulled, feet are squeezed, noses are smashed, and accommodations are made to suit society's will.

How individuals define physical beauty or normalcy will be determined to a large extent by what their cultures have taught them about perfection and beauty. They are, in this way, preconditioned to standards of physical perfection from childhood, long before they are able to decide for themselves and create their own individual standards.

Often, as we mature, our personal criteria for perfection changes and may become counterculture. There were those men, for instance, who rebelled against the clean-shaven look and as a result, lost their jobs or the respect of friends and families. Women who first took to short skirts scandalized their parents and friends and were often excluded from *decent* society. Then, a few years later, the societal trends changed. Beards, long hair, and short skirts became acceptable. Then a crew-cut hair style or a long skirt was considered strange.

This influence of society upon expectations of physique and beauty may be observed in the behavior of very young children. They do not seem to be much disturbed at their early age by cultural standards of physical beauty or normalcy. They play freely and joyfully, equally at ease with the pock-marked little girl, the skinny boy, the lame child or the young athlete. It is only later, after they have learned and incorporated the cultural standards of perfection and beauty, that we hear them taunt Mary for her *crossed eyes,* call Pete a *retard,* mimic Fred's *stutter* or pantomime Anna's *palsy.*

The media is a strong force in influencing attitudes of perfection and beauty. Seldom, if ever, do we see an obese woman advertising deodorants; she is used for Italian spaghetti ads. It would be a shock, indeed, to see a shirtless, underdeveloped young man in a canoe used for a cigarette commercial or a model with uneven teeth showing toothpastes. Rather, the models are the currently accepted versions of the *idealized* perfect specimens, the concept being that if one uses the product, one can be that way, too.

Horror films continue to enhance and influence our attitudes regarding beauty and physique by suggesting fright when depicting the physically different. Monsters always seem to have a disfigured face, a hunched back, a clubfoot or a twisted limb which they drag menacingly behind them.

It is no wonder that our attitudes toward the people we encounter are often formed by the initial response we have to their external physical attributes. Everyone wants to be, and be seen with, a *perfect physical specimen.*

On the first day of teaching my university class in the Education of Exceptional Children, I frequently ask the students to complete an interesting questionnaire. It is a short check list which asks how far they would go in a personal relationship with disabled individuals of their own age.

One side of the questionnaire lists such problems as deafness, cerebral palsy, mental retardation, blindness, and epilepsy. On a graded distancing scale they are to check (1) I would have them as a friend, (2) I would invite them to my home, (3) I would date them, (4) I would marry them, (5) I would be parent to their child. It is not surprising that very few students go beyond the second level of relationship with any of the mentioned individuals. This is a simple, but striking example of attitudes regarding disabilities and differences.

There is little doubt that the human physique influences behavior, and to a large extent, then, determines human interaction, communication and relationships. In addition, individuals often equate outward physical characteristics with the inner nature of the person, his or her general personality and mental ability. It is not uncommon for people to correlate a physical disability such as cerebral palsy, blindness or deafness, and even certain speech impediments with subnormal intelligence.

My students are given another exercise each semester which they find most distasteful, but often quite enlightening. They are asked to go somewhere in the community and feign stuttering. The purpose of the experience is made quite clear. It is to help them to *feel* the social effect of a disability, the trauma it can create for the possessor and the observable responses and reactions it elicits.

The *insight* most often mentioned by the students who perform the experiment is that in most cases the speech problem produces a dual effect upon the listeners. Not only do they seem to "fear" the stutterers, but they also tend to treat them as if they were simple-minded. It is not uncommon for the stutterer to be led by the hand to the object requested or to be given simplistic directions, accompanied by child-like gestures, or shouted responses in exaggerated, mouthed syllables.

People with physical defects are often treated in a like manner, even though there has never been a systemic investigation which offered any meaningful support to a disabled body-disabled mind connection. Yet this generalized response is made by many of us daily. "Sound mind in sound body." "What can you expect from a fat slob?"

Much of the psychology of the disabled is essentially a social psychology. It is based primarily upon interaction with others in the individual's particular and personal environment.

It is an easy leap then from the opinions and impressions society has and sends off regarding physical disabilities, to physically disabled persons assuming these as a part of their behavior and personality. This phenomenon is often referred to as *somatopsychology*. This is the study of how society's response to disabilities will affect disabled persons' actions, feelings and interactions. It suggests that society may influence persons with physical or mental problems to limit their actions, change their feelings about themselves, as well as affect their interactions with others. The degree to which they are influenced will depend upon the strength, duration and the nature of the judgmental stimulus.

This is well illustrated in a story related by a sensitive young lady with athetoid cerebral palsy. As an adolescent, she had learned quite well how to hold a spoon in her hand, but in *her* way, with her elbow planted firmly on the table. In this manner, she could very efficiently bring the food from her plate to her mouth, in a more controlled fashion, without too much spillage. A real accomplishment for her! Her parents continually reprimanded her with "proper young ladies did not eat with elbows on the table." It was made quite clear that until she learned to eat *properly*, she would not be taken out to dinner with the family. Without the support of elbows firmly on the table, her food was usually catapulted about the room with little respect for man or animal.

In this case, the family was insisting that what was *normal* for society was to be used as the standard for all, even a daughter with athetoid paralysis.

Another classic case in point was presented beautifully by Christy Brown in a small but important book called *My Left Foot*. Severely involved with cerebral palsy, he was given up for hopeless by those in his environment. But in spite of this, his keen, alert mind was eagerly seeking expression through any avenue available. After many frustrations and trials he found that he could use the toes on his left foot to write and to draw. All those about him, except his mother, were appalled and dissuaded him—assuring him it wasn't *right*. People didn't eat, paint, write, type, with their feet! It was grotesque! With the persistence of one whose need for expression far exceeded cultural limits and approval, he not only used his left foot to write, but produced several books, including a magnificent biographical best-seller called *Down All The Days*.

Included in the domain of somatopsychology is also the factor of semantics. Johnson (1946), Korzybski (1951), Whorf (1947), Lee (1947), and Sapir (1931) have all studied and expounded upon the power of words and syntax to affect an individual's personality and self-image. They have suggested that language does not only *convey* ideas and feelings one has regarding those ideas, but it can also *shape* the ideas and feelings of the listener. For instance, Johnson considers language a powerful enough force to *create* a disability such as stuttering in a child and serious neuroses of all kinds in adults. It is well known that if we are told enough times that we *are* something, we are likely to believe it, as well as become it.

I recall an incident which occurred in a class for physically disabled children which serves as an illustration of this power of words. The teacher and the physical therapist were trying to help a paraplegic child in braces walk with a stroller. The child kept saying "I can't! I can't!" Finally the teacher asked, "Sally, who said you can't?" "My mother said so. She said I can't ever move without my wheelchair so I might as well accept it! She knows because the doctor told her!" The physical therapist smiled and hugged her softly, "What do *you* think?" she asked. Sally looked firmly at the therapist, then the teacher.

"I don't know," she answered. "Would you like to try?" the therapist asked. A long pause, "I think so," the child replied. Sally now walks with a stroller.

We often define disabled persons in terms of limitations. "You can't" is a phrase they learn early. No one seems too much concerned with what they *can* do. Taken as *total* humans it is safe to suggest that they *can* do more than they *cannot*. Too often they define their disability during an entire lifetime in terms of the words which are used about them. How often have we seen two parents discussing their children in the supermarket with the children at their side. "This is the stupid one," one mother states, "but he has a nice way about him." In a pointed manner, unconsciously, she is telling her child who he is.

Beatrice Wright, in her excellent book, *Physical Disability—A Psychological Approach* (1960), suggests rather persuasively that people should be quite concerned with terminological issues especially relating to the disabled. For instance, she feels we should always refer to a *person who is physically disabled,* rather than a *physically disabled person,* for the former phrase suggests that the individual is a person *first,* and secondarily, disabled. She continues, and it is difficult to disagree, that though this may seem insignificant, it has powerful effects. Dr. Wright goes so far as to reject even the word *handicapped.* She quotes from Hamilton (1950) who sees the word *handicap* as dealing more with the cumulative obstacles with which the person with a disability must cope, both in terms of physical limitation and cultural, societal, and interpersonal problems. It is well, then, to remember that a *disability* is more of a *medical condition.* On the other hand, it may or may not become a *handicap* to the extent to which it does or does not debilitate the individual emotionally, intellectually, and physically.

In this sense, Christy Brown's cerebral palsy is not a handicap to his communicating. He is able to express his creative genius by substituting his left foot for his right or left hand. It would have become a handicap if he had been prevented from using his foot and allowed himself to be persuaded by his doctor, parents, family, friends or society, that his dream of making his unique, personal statement was unrealistic. Christy Brown, then, may be said to be less *handicapped* in terms of communicating than a young teenager who has a simple protrusion lisp, but who refuses to recite in class because the speech impediment is embarrassing.

In this book, for the most part, the word *exceptional* (in the sense of rare, or forming an exception to the statistical norm), disabled, impaired or limited will be used, rather than *handicapped*. If the term *handicapped* is used, it will refer to those particular individuals who, because of some force—social, personal or otherwise—have allowed their disability to debase or debilitate them sufficiently so as to prevent them from achieving some desired goal, or preclude their faring for themselves.

Wright (1960) states this well in summing up her discussion. She concludes:

> A physical attribute is a physical handicap only when it is seen as a significant barrier to the accomplishment of particular goals. This means that, in the individual case, a physical disability may or may not be a physical handicap. This is also true of a physical attribute that is not a deviation. Moreover, a physical attribute may become handicapping not because it is physically limiting, but because it adversely affects social relationships.

Pearl Buck tells us in her book, *The Child Who Never Grew,* that while her daughter, born severely mentally retarded, lived in China, she was not recognized as handicapped. The Chinese, at the time, accepted the disabled as simply a fact of life and cared for them as they would any child. It was not until Mrs. Buck brought her child back to a Western culture that she began to see the stigmatization and prejudice toward the disabled. Then, even she began to perceive her daughter as handicapped and as a result, to treat and respond to her differently.

It seems almost simplistic to belabor the points made so far. Suffice it to suggest that the child with a physical or mental disability, born in our society, is not, as yet, handicapped, simply disabled. Doctors, parents, teachers, psychologists, friends, relatives, all, no doubt, well-meaning, will be responsible for convincing these children, or helping them to learn, that they are handicapped. It is a difficult thing to avoid, for our own fears, misunderstandings, apprehensions, and prejudices will come out in thousands of different ways, mostly unconscious. They will be disguised in medical mumbo jumbo, educational jargon, psychological testing, parental protection, familial over-concern, all disguised under the mantle of love.

It is imperative, then, for those of us who care about disabled individuals to be constantly on our guard to be certain that we are not aiding and enhancing the process of their becoming handicapped as well.

It might be well for us to consider the following guidelines. Some of these will be elaborated upon later but are stated here, merely for the purpose of reminding us that *handicaps are made, not born.*

- ★ Remember that the disabled are their own persons, not yours. They do not belong to you, to your family, your doctor or to society.
- ★ Remember that each person who is disabled is different, and no matter what label is attached for the convenience of others, is still a totally "unique" person. There are no two retarded children who are the same, or no two deaf adults who respond and react in a similar fashion.
- ★ Remember that persons with disabilities are *persons* first and disabled individuals secondly. These persons have the same right to self-actualization as any others—at their own rate, in their own way, and by means of their own tools. Only *they* can suffer their nonbeing or find *their* "selves."
- ★ Remember that the disabled have the same needs that you have, to love and be loved, to learn, to share, to grow and to experience, in the same world you live in. They have no separate world. There is only *one* world.
- ★ Remember that the disabled have the same right as you to fall, to fail, to suffer, to decry, to cry, to curse, to despair. To protect them from these experiences is to keep them from life.
- ★ Remember that only those who are disabled can show or tell you *what is possible for them.* We who love them must be attentive, attuned observers.
- ★ Remember that the disabled must do for themselves. We can supply the alternatives, the possibilities, the necessary tools—but only they can put these things into action. We can only stand fast, be present to reinforce, encourage, hope and help, when we can.
- ★ Remember that the disabled, like ourselves, are entitled to life as we know it. They, too, must decide to live it fully in peace, joy and love, with what they are and what they have, or to sit back in lacrimal apathy and await death.
- ★ Remember that persons with disabilities, no matter how disabled, have a limitless potential for becoming—not what *we* desire them to become, but what is within *them* to become.
- ★ Remember that the disabled must find their own manner of doing things — that to set our standards (or the culture's standards) upon them, is to be unrealistic, even destructive. There are many ways of tying shoes, drinking from a glass, finding one's way to a bus stop. There are many ways of learning and adjusting. They must find the best way for them.

- ★ Remember that the disabled also need the world, and others, in order to learn. All learning does not take place in the protected environment of the home or in a classroom, as many people believe. The world is a classroom. All of personkind are teachers. There is no meaningless experience. Our job is to act as loving human beings with emotional Band-Aids® always ready after a fall, but with new road maps at hand for new adventures!
- ★ Remember that all persons with disabilities have a right to honesty about themselves, about you, and about their condition. To be dishonest with them is the most terrible disservice one can perform. Honesty forms the only solid base upon which all growth can take place. And this above all—remember that the disabled need the best *you* possible. In order for them to be themselves, growing, free, learning, changing, developing, experiencing persons—*you* must be all of these things. You can only teach what you are. If you are growing, free to learn, change, develop and experience, you will allow *them* to be.

Chapter 2: A Child Is Born

The first cry from my heart, when I knew she would never be anything but a child, was the age old cry that we all make before inevitable sorrow: "Why must this happen to me?" To this there could be no answer and there was none.

PEARL BUCK
The Child Who Never Grew

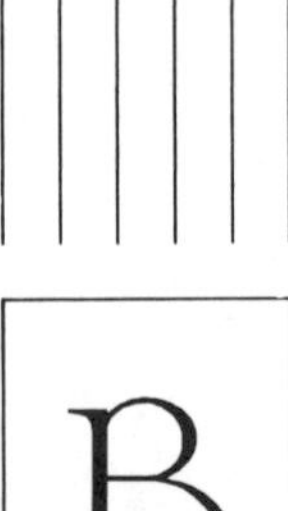

Birth is a miracle, for each person born has limitless potentials and possibilities. Each individual has the power to create, to share, to discover new alternatives, and to bring fresh hope for humanity. Birth, for most families, is a time for rejoicing, for pride, for gathering together loved ones and sharing with them in the celebration of a renewal of life.

For other families, birth may not be as joyful an occasion. On the contrary, it may be a time for tears, despair, confusion and fear. It may demand a totally new life style of all involved, full of mysterious and unique problems.

One such example occurred several years ago, in a small community hospital in a suburb of Los Angeles, where Mrs. T., a twenty-nine-year-old woman, gave birth to her third child. Her other two children were girls, both active, growing and intelligent. She and her husband had been happily married for twelve years. They had always hoped for a boy. They had planned to call him Jedidiah. They got their wish. Jedidiah was born. He was born disabled. Her story from that point on was similar to so many!

Right from the start, through her semi-drugged state, Mrs. T. sensed that something had gone wrong. It was different from the previous times when she had given birth to her daughters. This time she felt a sense of panic, of fear, of tension. She could not account for these ominous feelings but they were there.

Her anxiety grew as time passed. She wondered where her husband was, her doctor, and especially her child. Why were they delayed so long? Why were the nurses moving about so quietly and efficiently, whispering and avoiding her glance? Or was she just imagining this? Most mysterious of all—why had she been moved from her previous double occupancy and put in a single room, alone?

When her husband finally appeared, the pain on his face was obvious to her. (Hadn't they been together for twelve years? Couldn't she read him "like an open book"?) He was with the doctor. The doctor's face was more confusing for her to comprehend than her husband's. It seemed torn between false confidence and bewilderment. Her first fears were answered.

The baby was not dead.

But what then?

Complications.

What complications?

They would be discussed later, when she was stronger. But she wasn't to worry.

Worry! Of course she'd worry! What complications?

Your child was born with a handicap.

My God! What kind of a handicap? (Trying to hold back tears of panic.)

Some type of a neurological problem that would produce paralysis.

How serious? (Hold back the cry of pain.)

It's impossible to say at this time.

Is the child going to be all right? (More tears.)

He's going to have to be in intensive care.

Can I see him?

Not now. Later. Rest.

Rest! Oh God!

Jedidiah lived. His condition was serious. Jedidiah would never walk. There was some question about how much he would learn, though he appeared bright. He was brain damaged and one could *never tell*.

It would be a long time before Mrs. T. would *rest* again.

This may appear, to some, overly dramatic, but it is repeated daily in maternity wards all over the world. Each hour of each day, children are born who are blind, deaf, have some form of cerebral palsy, some degree of mental retardation, or some minimal brain damage that will later cause a learning disability. Some will be only mildly involved, so that the problems will be hardly noticeable until the child is faced with specific stresses brought on by society or school. Others will be so seriously disabled that they will either die shortly after birth or have to be institutionalized. But a larger number of these children will survive, be educated, and grow into adulthood. It is estimated that there are seven million disabled children in the United States today. This does not include the thousands of children who are being diagnosed as *learning disabled*. What kind of life and future these children will have when they grow up will largely depend upon them—but it will also be influenced by the sensitivity, attitudes, knowledge and general personality of their parents and families. Their societies will also have a great deal to do with what kind of human beings they will become, for it will stipulate what will be demanded of them, how they will be helped, and if they will be accepted or rejected.

It does not take long for mothers, like Mrs. T. for example, to learn about attitudes regarding disabled children. The reaction to Jedidiah's birth, right from the beginning, informed her. The response to the birth of her son was not accompanied by joy and congratulations, as in the case of her earlier children but rather with whispering nurses, quiet, halting explanations by her doctor, embarrassment by her family and friends, awkwardness by everyone. She learned early that there was something very "wrong" about having a disabled child. It was an occurrence that had to be discussed in whispers. She had always felt that birth was a joyous gift to be shouted about in pride. She remembered the great feeling she had when she presented her two healthy daughters to her husband, her parents, her neighbors and friends—to the world. There was something not quite right about presenting an imperfect gift. Who would want to accept it? And what would people say when they couldn't say, "What a beautiful baby," as they cooed and tickled him? She prayed they wouldn't say, "I'm sorry." Sorry for whom? Sorry for her? For her child? Sorry for society?

It was easy for her to see what this implied!

But there was no escape. The child was there. He was real. He was hers. She couldn't give him away, though years later it was possible for her to confess that she had wished she could. She even fantasied that there had been some mistake. They had brought "someone else's child." Though she felt foolish, she had wanted the doctor or nurse to recheck, make sure. This couldn't be happening to her. She had heard of it happening to others but not to her!

Many painful hours later when the child was brought to her, she couldn't wait to be left alone with him. As with her previous children, she wanted to "really" look at him—examine his feet, his head, his back. Her initial shock was great. She had never seen a baby like this one. She was fearful of her own child!

After being with him a while she discovered, to her surprise, that, like her other children, he, too, cried, cuddled, nursed, slept, reacted. He even smiled and cooed.

Yes, he wasn't like other children, but he was a child—her child. He seemed so helpless but cute in his way. He seemed more in need of her than her other children. He appeared weaker, more sensitive to light and dark, to sounds. His body tonus was different. His sleeping rhythm was different. He was unique.

At this point he was still primarily a medical label. She even forgot what the doctor had called his condition but she trusted the doctor. He had skills. He knew his job and would save the child who would, in the past, have died at birth. But she was not a medical doctor. She knew nothing of reciprocal muscle movement, spasticity, brain dysfunction. No one seemed to feel that it was important for her to know anything beyond the label. She felt afraid and ill-prepared for her new role. But, no matter, she had to embrace this strange, new being. Jedidiah was her child, after all.

Giving birth to a disabled child happens quickly. There is no forewarning, no time for preparation. Educational or psychological counseling at this crucial time for this mother or other such confused parents is almost nonexistent, either in or out of the hospital. So much of what they will do for their children must come from instinct, or trial and error. As to their feelings, their fears, their anxieties, their confusions, their despairs, they will have to handle them as best they can.

In an unpublished survey done in 1974, the author with two assistants sent out a brief questionnaire to maternity wards in large city hospitals, as well as small community hospitals across the country. It requested information regarding the routine procedures, if any, for giving either medical information or psychological guidance to parents of children who were born disabled in their hospitals. In most cases the responses stated that there were no such *routine* procedures. Whatever medical information or counseling was given was at the discretion of the individual physician in charge. Formal psychological guidance or counseling for the parents was nonexistent through the hospital, though they explained that it was often recommended when the mother was "unduly disturbed." A similar questionnaire was sent to the parents of disabled children to ascertain their perception of the help they were offered. The parents responded that there was no formal, routine plan which they could discern for helping them in the hospital. Most of the parents stated that they were given some knowledge of their child's special medical problem, but none felt that it was specific enough or adequate. They felt that new questions were constantly arising in the early days, after the child was released from the hospital, but they *feared* bothering the physician too much, that "he was always so *busy* and there never seemed to be time to *just talk*." Psychological counseling for them was not available, seldom suggested as a possibility. These parents stated that they had to work their own way through their fears, anger, despair, and confusion. A few, who could afford it, felt a strong need for, and obtained, some professional counseling, "Just to keep myself and my family from falling apart!"

So, in the crucial periods of birth and infancy when both child and parent need the most help, little, if any, is offered. Yet it is during this period when the parents will be the key to helping their children develop the basic trust or mistrust which will follow them throughout life. There is, perhaps, no more relevant period for disabled children's future than this, for it is a time when they will be helped to form basic attitudes concerning future optimism-pessimism, love-hate, growth-apathy, security-frustration, joy-despair and general learning. It is urgent, then, that parents be made aware of the importance of these early months of life and the special and unique problems and concerns they may create. They must be informed and cognizant of their responsibility and what the profound and lasting effect of what they will, or will not do, can have on their children's continual growth and development. This is just another way of saying that it is during this vital time that counseling for disabled children and their parents must begin.

During the period from birth through infancy, parents of disabled children must be made aware that they are often so harassed by the many physical demands of their children, their very real pain, their physical discomfort, their needs for special diets, their frequent doctor's appointments and special medications, that they may fail to realize that, like other children, they have normal needs as well. They will require the same cuddling, the same love, the same rocking, the same linguistic stimulation, the same opportunities to explore themselves and their environment. In other words, all of those simple things which will reveal to them that they are loved, cared for and safe; things which will show them that they are a part of the greater world and that it is possible for them to use their environment for continual growth and discovery.

Too often, during these early years, physically and mentally disabled children are required to spend much of their time in and out of hospitals. This creates an almost continual separation from the physical closeness of the family and the warmth and security of the home. So important is the parent-child affective relationship during these early days and so closely is it correlated with the child's physical, mental and psychological well-being, that many hospitals have created mother-child live-in units, where they can be together during prolonged hospital care.

But hospitalization is not the only kind of isolation that may be incapacitating. Even when home, much time will be spent being held, locked into braces, imprisoned in casts or caged, even tied into cribs. An entire infancy may be spent within a limited *safe* environment, where their children can be *guarded* but also which will prevent them from exploring the new world. This protection may continue for years.

I recall visiting a class for physically impaired infants. At the time I visited, teachers and aides were engaged in removing the children from their wheelchairs only to instantly lock them into a standing position at a desk.

I asked if they were ever freed to play in the dirt or sand. The teachers responded in surprise.

"Freed? Why these children can't walk!"

"Can they lie on their stomachs?" I asked.

"Of course!" was the curt reply.

"Then why can't they be occasionally placed face down on the grass?"

Some of these children, for the first time, became the friends of grass. It was a joy to experience. They shrieked with infant wonder! They discovered the smell and taste and shape of a blade of grass. One child even caught a glimpse of an earthworm as he wound his laborious way through the green!

These early explorations are vital to an infant's growth. To learn, a child must be free to explore. It is the infant's world with which we must have empathy, not ours. This does not mean that parents and teachers must be constantly dashing about meeting the infant's every need. But it must be remembered that infants have no time perspective, are totally dependent and only we can give them, at this stage, the opportunity to discover and enlarge their world. This is difficult for them to do when they spend most of their lives confined or isolated.

Understanding the great importance of the infant's need to explore is not easy for the parent who is unschooled in growth and development, and as a result of this lack of knowledge, many children acquire additional disabilities which can be prevented. The nondisabled child will usually find a way to meet the needs of the normal day-to-day environmental groping. Disabled children will, in many cases, not be able to do this. They are not free to discover for themselves. Therefore, because of these reality limitations, they may also become sensorily deprived by being kept from the world of sounds, feelings, stimulations, sights, and the vital sensorial information which can only be conveyed through experience. Only through these experiences will they learn to differentiate themselves from mama and papa and the pet dog, or learn simple forms and shapes and how to relate to and with them. Continual normal growth and development will depend upon being constantly exposed to the world.

Recent research has revealed that this environmental manipulation and organization is so vital for future learning that there is a whole discipline emerging for toddlers and infants referred to as "Programs for Cognitive Enrichment." These programs are designed specifically to compensate for and counteract any sensory deprivation found among children who are deprived due to environment or impairment. If children cannot go to the stimulus, it must be brought to them if they are to develop properly. Receptors deprived of stimulation early in life atrophy and many even fall into disuse.

Disabled infants, too, often are not talked to in the manner of other children. They are not exposed to modes of language development. It is true that no child has ever been taught language. In fact, we are not really sure how a child learns this most subtle and exclusively human phenomenon. We do know, though, that a child who is not exposed to language during the early years of life will never again learn it as effectively, as efficiently, nor as successfully. We know that language has a developmental sequence, or pattern, which all children follow and that all which seems to be needed for learning to speak is the proper stimulus, a sound-language-filled environment, and receptors which are intact. As infants encounter sounds and language in the environment, they will proceed through periods of babbling, echolalia, words, sentences, and on into the more complex syntactical structures. But all through these periods their being stimulated in a spontaneous and rich language environment is most significant. Since their early linguistic world is mostly made up of parental stimulation, they will often learn to talk precisely as do their teachers, in this case, their parents. Studies have been done (Hess and Shipman, 1965; Ortar, 1966) regarding the influence of parental stylistic language codes upon language learning in children. These studies illustrate dramatically the import and effect of language stimulation upon children in their early years. The language they hear in their homes during infancy and childhood will affect their future language learning, cognitive, and problem-solving abilities. It is, therefore, imperative that disabled children be talked to, communicated with, and verbally stimulated even more than their nondisabled siblings, who will have the benefit of more outside stimulation. Language will also be the main tool for their continual conceptual and perceptual growth. The more linguistic symbols children have, the more varied and wondrous will their words become.

Parents must be helped to understand that their own feelings about their child's impairment during infancy can stand in the way of the child's opportunities for growth to adulthood. Often these feelings are unconscious. It is not uncommon for the mother of a disabled child to say, "I'd rather not go out, even to the market, than to have to take my child. It's such a physical hassle!" To a very real extent this is true. But she may fail to add that "It's embarrassing. People point and stare. Children comment, 'Look mama, at the funny baby!' " It is a well-known fact that how we treat our child is, in some measure, a product of the child's own qualities, physical and emotional, actual or perceived. In other words, the children act as a stimulus to those in their environment. Work by Bell (1968, 1971), Schaffer and Emerson (1965), and others have illustrated this phenomenon. When children are healthy, beautiful, and responsive, we tend to react to them in a positive manner, we want to spend time with them and show them off to others. On the other hand, if the child is irritable, physically unattractive, or continually demanding, as many disabled infants, of necessity, may be, our response is often negative and we tend to avoid extensive contact with them.

There is a saying which is appropriate to this discussion: "To love the seemingly unlovable is the real virtue." It is easy to love bouncy, cuddly, beautiful children. People are eager to pick them up, play with them, and *make over* them. The disabled infant may lack the physical beauty to entice attention, response, and love, but has the identical emotional needs for these as any child. It is understandable that it might be difficult to accept an infant who, because of a disability, is almost constantly whining, crying out in pain, forever demanding attention and who gives so little joyful reinforcement to us in return, but it is just as necessary as with any child.

It is also well known that infants respond to the feelings of those with whom they interact. Those who fear infants, handle them grudgingly, are hostile or anxious about them are better to leave them alone. Impaired children, like all children, perhaps even more so, will sense this. They will need attention that expresses security and confidence, along with loving experiences that will open the world for them.

No parent is perfect, but no child demands perfection. In the early stages of learning the requirements of their unique role, the parents will feel irritations, anxieties, and fears. They may be immersed in their own concerns and problems, and momentarily be unable to respond to those of the infant. But this is no cause for concern. What is important to the infant, in early years, is the reliability of the parents' love, manner with which it is usually expressed over the long period of time, and the consistency of its general tone and expression. Primarily, it must be remembered that in matters of learning to live and to love, infants are infants no matter what their physical limitations.

Parents of disabled children need to be counseled about disciplining their disabled children. They are often reluctant to reprimand disabled infants and toddlers, to train them, as they do their other children, to teach them realistic limits. Their rationale is that these children already have enough to contend with. Perhaps so, but they must also learn to live with the family and in the world. During their infancy they must learn, as other children, to avoid injuring themselves and others as well as to gain a respect for another's life space. They must, unless for some special dietary reason, be put on the same feeding-sleeping schedule as normal children. Later they, too, must be helped through the process of toilet training. It is not uncommon to have children with disabilities, for whom there is no reasonable excuse, come to school without having been toilet trained and with no knowledge of a sense of self or others.

I recall a blind seven-year-old child whose parents were still diapering him at nine years old and kept him from school because "he rebelled to being trained or going to school and we didn't want to cause him more problems." Two days after being at school with other children the child trained himself.

Most discipline training is common sense, backed with real concern and love. It is a knowledgeable compromise between parent and child with mutual concern, trust and respect. All human beings need some realistic limits. Disciplining impaired infants, realistically, within their unique limits, is not cruel, but rather can be one of the most meaningful kindnesses.

Perhaps one of the greatest, and most painful problems parents who have disabled infants will have to be prepared for is that of the social deprivation which their impairment may create. Most people are very hesitant to treat children with impairments as they would other infants. They are fearful of handling them, rolling them about, tickling them, tossing them into the air or involving themselves in activities which they would enjoy with any *normal* infant. This may take the form of almost total social isolation for these children and deprive them of the first normal interactions in fun with others which eventually will lead them to the learning of the many normal more complex social interactions required of them as they mature.

The problem is a very real one, not only with adults but with children. I have heard many parents of disabled children decry the fact that other children are often not allowed to play with their disabled child. Regrettably, this is a very real fact, but since the social growth of the child will depend upon these contacts and communication with other infants and children, it is imperative that social interaction occur. This may mean ingenious, creative manipulations on the part of parents. One mother, for example, baked cookies for the neighborhood children and soon found that her backyard became very popular—her disabled child had plenty of playmates.

So, Children are Born. In this case, they are infants who are disabled. But they are first and foremost infants. In a real sense, they are more like other nondisabled infants than different. As such, they will have to go through the same social experiences, the same developmental processes, the same psychological learning, as other infants. Their impairment may cause problems which may interfere with the process to some extent. They may cause them to develop certain skills and attain required experiences later than other children their age. But, attain them they must. If they are allowed to be infants—experience, learn, feel and think as infants—they will continue on to more mature growth and development. Much of how this will occur will be determined by the feelings, the attitudes, the values of their parents and families during their very early life. Their hope-filled motivations, positive responses and loving interactions will give them the strength to grow on their way.

But infants will learn only what they are taught. Their parents are their first teachers. It is necessary for them to know the *how* and the *what* of early mental, physical and emotional development. This will be discussed in some detail in later chapters. For now, let it suffice to say that one is born first an infant and only secondarily an infant with a disability. Children are born to live. To the extent to which their parents consider them infants who have limitations, but who, like all other children, have the right to equal experience and opportunities, so they will realize themselves.

Section II:

As The Researcher Sees The Challenge

Chapter 3:

Counseling The Disabled And Their Parents — A Review Of The Literature

But understanding alone is not enough. When I understand something but do not put it into action, nothing has been accomplished either in the outside world or within myself.

BARRY STEVENS
Person to Person

JIM LEIGH, Associate Professor in the Department of Special Education at University of Missouri – Columbia, contributed this searching examination of research. He discovered that although much research in counseling the disabled and their families has been done, we have barely scratched the surface of this complex field....

SUSAN MARSHALL is a doctoral student in Reading at the University of Missouri – Columbia. Her experience includes teaching in Special Education and Remedial Reading programs for seven years and teaching College English for three years.

Since the passage of PL 94-142 in 1975, an increasing awareness of the importance of counseling exceptional individuals and their parents has resulted in a proliferation of articles and books pertaining to the topic. Prior to 1975, Gowan (1965) had characterized theory and practice in this aspect of counseling as being in a "primitive state," while Wyne and Skjei (1970) maintained that exceptional children had been "virtually ignored" by the counseling profession. Unfortunately, as many parents and exceptional individuals can attest to, the volume of professional literature in a field does not necessarily correlate highly with the availability and quality of services within that field. Nevertheless, the quantity and variety of studies reviewed in this chapter suggest that professionals in the counseling area are compiling significant amounts of information which, hopefully, will contribute directly to the actual practice of counseling disabled individuals and their parents in the near future.

A comprehensive review of the literature in the area of counseling exceptional persons and their parents is considerably beyond the scope of this chapter. Moreover, despite the impressive amount of available literature, the specific results from many of the studies reviewed must be described as inconclusive, due partly to the nature of research in general and partly to the lack of quality which characterizes many studies in this facet of counseling. The purpose of any experimental research is not to prove theories or to establish unequivocal knowledge, but rather to investigate objectively stated hypotheses and obtain results which tend to support or negate the hypotheses. In order to accomplish this goal, the research must conform to certain rigorous criteria. Unfortunately, much of the counseling literature fails to attain the necessary high standards. In many cases, it is impossible to evaluate the significance of the results of the research due either to use of a poor research design or to inadequate reporting of the essential facets of the research. In other words, although many researchers have reported success in using various counseling approaches and techniques with exceptional individuals and parents, the utility of the reported results is limited by the failure to describe specifically and in detail exactly what, when, where, how, why, by whom, and with whom something was done. Without this vital information, it is not possible to reproduce the study or program to determine if the reported techniques and approaches actually do work.

Many variables exist which contribute to the success or failure of any counseling method in any study. A number of studies fail to report essential characteristics of the subjects, such as age, sex, and even the exact nature of the disability. Another factor which greatly influences the effectiveness of any form of counseling is the skill of the counselor. The characteristics and qualifications of the individuals who provided counseling are largely ignored in many studies; such individuals are often identified only by a brief title such as *therapist, psychologist,* or *counselor.* Quite often, even the counseling approach or technique is not adequately described. Of course, any approach or technique may be valid, but before it can be applied it must be understood, and understanding is dependent upon a precise description of the procedure.

Possibly the most serious deficiency of much of the research is caused by the lack of control groups and objective measurement devices. A control group enables the researcher to evaluate more precisely the effects of the treatment, or experimental variable. Even when control groups are used, which is seldom, the researcher often fails to report sampling procedures or criteria for matching subjects. Moreover, while objective measures of results are occasionally employed, too many studies merely report that the behavior of children "improved" or that parents derived "benefit" from the counseling. Although all of these criticisms certainly apply to much of the literature which will be reviewed in this section, many other studies had to be omitted altogether because the poor quality of research or reporting made the results virtually useless.

Although research certainly is not the only way in which knowledge may be established in a field, the literature which will be reviewed in this chapter, with a few exceptions, is primarily research-based. It has already been pointed out that the field is too broad to cover the general literature thoroughly. Only relatively recent research will be presented, since most important findings from older research have already been interpreted and reviewed elsewhere. Finally, essentially only studies performed specifically with exceptional persons or their parents will be included. To state that the results of other counseling research using different subjects is applicable to exceptional individuals and parents is largely an assumption which has yet to be investigated.

ROLES AND RESPONSIBILITIES OF SCHOOL COUNSELORS

School counselors in many programs have assumed major responsibilities for implementation of the provisions contained within PL 94-142. Humes (1978) identified the following duties related to special education frequently performed by school counselors: 1) participating in multidisciplinary staffings, 2) assisting in the development of Individualized Education Plans, 3) monitoring the progress of students in relation to established goals and objectives, 4) counseling parents, 5) planning extracurricular activities for students with handicaps, 6) consulting with classroom teachers, 7) providing inservice education, and 8) maintaining records.

Through a survey of 275 school counselors in Florida, Lombana (1980) investigated the demands on counselors' time due to their involvement in fulfilling requirements stipulated within PL 94-142. Results indicated that 36% of those surveyed allocated up to 10% of their time to students with handicaps, 23% spent from 11% to 25% of their time with the handicapped, 27% devoted 26% to 50% of their time to the handicapped, and 14% spent more than 50% of their time providing service to exceptional students. Given the extensive amounts of time that many counselors are expected to allocate to students with handicapping conditions, Lombana expressed concern that many counselors lack sufficient coursework and training in the field of special education.

With the recent emphasis on mainstreaming exceptional students, Parker and Stodden (1981) contend that the school counselor can help with the integration of disabled students into the "regular" school classroom. They describe the counselor as being in a key position to aid with the acceptance of disabled students by nonhandicapped students, to assist disabled students in accepting themselves and their "new" environments, and to lead teachers, parents, and administrators in discussions of attitudes toward and needs of students with handicaps. Other researchers see the counselor's role as being an advocate for the handicapped (Kameen & McIntosh, 1979), a career counselor and career educator (Bowe & Razeghi, 1979; Brolin & Gysbers, 1979; Sinick, 1979), and a "link" between students, parents, teachers, and administrators (Bowe & Razeghi, 1979; Brolin & Gysbers, 1979; Connolly, 1978; Parker & Stodden, 1981; Perosa & Perosa, 1981).

In order to fulfill any of these roles effectively, the counselor must be able to *relate* to the handicapped student. Nathanson (1979) suggests that the effective counselor must first examine his or her own prejudices and biases and be able to recognize and acknowledge them even if they cannot be entirely eliminated. The effective counselor also must be able to refrain from both pitying the student and dwelling upon the handicap. The student must be viewed as capable rather than incapable, a person with both abilities and limitations rather than a "fragile" being requiring protection. To illustrate these principles, Nathanson provides a series of vignettes which can be used for counselor education on the "wrong way" to counsel the handicapped.

Using a simple but most appropriate method to investigate essential characteristics of counselors, McDavis, Nutter, and Lovett (1982) asked thirty students with handicaps to list the qualities in a school counselor which they found to be the most helpful. When the students were given a list of the qualities they named and asked to rank them, the top five qualities identified were 1) giving information, 2) listening, 3) being available, 4) helping to examine alternatives, and 5) exhibiting respect. However, on further investigation, McDavis et al found that many of the disabled students considered the special education teacher to be their counselor and many did not even know the school counselor's name. The authors recommended that school counselors need to spend more time working with handicapped students, initiate more contacts with handicapped students and their parents, consult more often with special education teachers, and provide more career information to students with impairments.

COMMUNICATING DIAGNOSTIC INFORMATION TO PARENTS

Regardless of the nature of the counseling, the process usually begins when the parents take the child to a professional person or clinic for initial diagnosis. Although the purpose of this first visit is to obtain an accurate diagnosis of the child's condition and to communicate this information effectively to the parents, quite often the parents are more confused and upset after the session than before.

A number of studies have been conducted which document this dissatisfaction. For instance, Abramson, Grovink, Abramson, and Sommers (1977) conducted a study involving 215 Connecticut families with retarded children under age six, which was designed to measure parental reactions to services which their children had received. The researchers found that 94% of the families had sought professional advice from a physician. Only 18% of the parents had received what they perceived as informative and sympathetic advice. Twenty-eight percent of the families received an objective clinical portrayal of the situation; 24% were referred to another source; and in 14% of the cases the families felt that the physician attempted to minimize the symptoms. Nine percent of the families believed that they received a very "bleak prognosis," five percent were given misinformation, and three percent were merely told to love the children and treat them as "normal." Fifty-one percent of the families reported that they were either very dissatisfied with, dissatisfied with, or uncertain about the advice which they received; 19% reported being very satisfied; and 30% said they were satisfied.

A study conducted by Williams and Darbyshire (1982) revealed similar results. When parents of hearing disabled children were asked about their experiences with the professional who diagnosed their child, the majority revealed a lack of understanding of what a hearing loss meant and a reticence to question the physician even though they did not understand the information given to them. Eighty-four percent reported that they were not able to understand the information given to them; 72% did not realize what a hearing loss would mean to the child; and, according to Williams and Darbyshire, 64% did not have a "realistic appreciation" of how the loss would affect their own lives.

Anderson and Garner (1973) interviewed twenty-three mothers of retarded children to determine the kinds of professionals visited by mothers from the time of birth of the retarded child onward and the degree of the mothers' satisfaction with these visits. The 23 mothers studied made a total of 453 visits to various professional people and were satisfied with 75% of these visits.

Many of these contacts occurred before a mother suspected that something was wrong with her child. The degree of satisfaction with these visits was very high, indicating that the mothers were not initially negative toward professional help when invoked for the usual injuries and illnesses of childhood. However, there was a large decrease in satisfaction with further diagnostic and later nondiagnostic visits to professionals. The most common complaints were that 1) although it was obvious that something was wrong with the child, the mother was often told that nothing was wrong; 2) the professional seemed to become disinterested in the mother and child after several visits; and 3) the amount of time spent by the professional in examining the child was felt to be insufficient or the professional did not take adequate time to explain the diagnosis to the mother. Quite often the mother was offered no guidance in dealing with immediate problems, and sometimes left the interview feeling no hope for the future. It was reported that professionals had curtly instructed some parents of older children to institutionalize their child. Many mothers also stated that the doctors did not seem to be as interested in the injuries and illnesses of their retarded children as they were in those of normal children. Pediatricians and general practitioners were the professionals most often visited, and mothers were satisfied with about 75% of these visits. Psychologists were consulted only after an abnormality was suspected, and mothers were satisfied with only half of these visits, possibly because psychologists were primarily involved in diagnosis, which received a low degree of satisfaction regardless of the profession involved. Anderson and Garner concluded that although the mothers were generally satisfied with the majority of all visits, professionals should remember that certain visits require "unusual knowledge, skill, wisdom and humanity, and more than a little time spent with the parent."

The Alexander Graham Bell Association for the Deaf obtained information from 260 parents regarding the counseling received. Fellendorf and Harrow (1970) reported that only half of the parents were satisfied with the diagnostic information received from the initial visit to a professional. Similarly, Dembinski and Mauser (1977) found that only one-third of 234 sets of parents of learning disabled children felt confident when interacting with a professional.

Various researchers have speculated on the reasons for parent dissatisfaction. Abramson et al (1977) see physicians asking limited questions due to their inadequate training of and exposure to the handicapped. Wolraich (1982), in a study of professionals and parents of mentally retarded children, found that not only do physicians receive little training in handicapping conditions but are poorly educated in child development. In addition, physicians were found to be more pessimistic than professionals in other disciplines about the expected levels of functioning of mentally retarded individuals. The parents felt that the physicians exhibited a generally negative attitude and had difficulty understanding the language which the physicians used to relay their diagnoses.

Sonnenschein (1981) identified several reasons for problems in communication between professionals and parents. Often, the physician wishes to maintain a "professional distance," and, therefore, seems to show no empathy for the parents. Some parents come to the professional either blaming themselves for the child's condition or assuming that the professional believes that it is their fault. In addition, parents may be seen as being less observant, less perceptive, or less intelligent by the professional and their parental concerns may be dismissed. The professional also may inaccurately label parents as being "unreasonable," "irrational," "resistant," or "pushy" when they do question or contradict a professional opinion. Consequently, the professional sometimes views parents as adversaries rather than partners in the treatment of the child.

Anderson (1971) has described the "shopping behavior" of parents which may result from ineffective communication between professionals and parents. According to the author, *shopping behavior* refers to "parents making visits to the same professional or to a number of different professionals or clinics in such a manner that one visit follows another without resolution of a resolvable problem." Anderson points out that a great deal of the parents' time, energy, and money may be expended by this process. Shopping behavior may be caused by various reasons. As time passes, it may become obvious that the initial diagnosis was inaccurate or incomplete, and the parents may decide to visit another professional or clinic. The most common reason, though, is that although the diagnosis was accurate, the parents either refuse to accept the results or the professional fails to explain adequately the results to the parents. In either case, the consequent fear and anxiety or confusion of the parents may result in a visit to another professional, who will hopefully provide a less threatening, or possibly a clearer and simpler, explanation of the child's problems. Anderson states that, in some cases, only one parent will attend the initial informing interview and will later have much difficulty in conveying whatever information was gained to the spouse. The spouse, in turn, will suggest another visit to a different source for confirmation or explanation, and the shopping behavior starts. Anderson suggests ways in which shopping behavior may be decreased. If possible, it is desirable that both parents attend the initial interview to avoid later misunderstanding due to failure or unwillingness to communicate the information. Anderson also discusses the importance of an effective initial professional contact to prevent the shopping behavior from becoming firmly established. In many cases, the child will make some progress with or without professional help over a period of time, and this progress may be attributed by the parents to the contacts with many professionals. Accordingly, the reinforced shopping behavior continues in the future.

In a study conducted at the UCLA Neuropsychiatric Institute, Keirn (1971) investigated the prevalence and reasons for shopping behavior. A shopping parent was defined as one who seeks a third professional evaluation after having received at least two others on previous occasions. Of the 218 families surveyed, only three percent could be classified as shopping parents according to this definition. Further, the parents who were shopping were not searching for a "magical cure," as often suggested, but rather were seeking help for severe problems which had become increasingly difficult to handle in the home over a period of years. Keirn concluded that the term "shopping parent" is a misnomer, since very few parents travel from one professional to another, rejecting recommendations and information. Most of these parents, according to Keirn, are simply requesting services different from those they have previously received, and should be helped rather than stereotyped and criticized.

Stephens (1969) stated that the way in which handicapping conditions are interpreted to parents is a primary indication of the quality of any diagnostic clinic. He discussed two methods of conducting sessions with parents. In the *virtuoso model*, a team of highly trained specialists meet with the parents, providing detailed and thorough information on all facets of the handicapping condition. Although this method may facilitate communication between professionals, it is often inadequate to convey information to the parents. Stephens pointed out that parents are usually not impressed by a group of professionals who are trying to impress each other with their diagnostic skills. Furthermore, parents probably gain very little understanding or insight into the problem from hearing detailed laboratory reports and test results. Moreover, to convey the information effectively, several interpretation sessions are more desirable than a single meeting. Stephens suggested that the *interaction model* of interpreting diagnostic information to parents is preferable to the virtuoso model. In contrast to a formal, structured presentation by a number of specialists, the interaction model utilizes the questions asked by the parents to establish the format and guidelines for the session. Information which is given on the basis of the parents' needs and interests is usually better understood and more useful. Generally only one or two professionals will meet with the parents to discuss a variety of problems over a period of time.

Morgan (1973) stresses that professionals should realize that even the most intensive and thorough diagnostic efforts will be almost useless to the retarded child unless the results and implications are adequately explained to the parents. According to Morgan, "Certain terms glibly used by professionals to describe general levels of retardation are meaningless to most parents."

In a 1970 study, Marshall and Goldstein found that the method of presentation and type of handicapping condition may influence the amount of information understood by the mother. Three consultation methods were used to give information to forty-five mothers of speech-impaired mentally retarded children and to forty-five mothers of speech-impaired children with normal intelligence. The three procedures were routine diagnostic consultation, videotape replay of the consultation, and audio-tape replay of the consultation. Although there appeared to be no significant difference between audio-tape and video-tape results, the mechanical reproduction of the consultation did promote understanding of the information, especially with the mothers of speech-impaired normal children. Much more research is needed to determine the conditions under which audio-visual equipment may facilitate the interpretation of information; it does seem, however, that mechanical reproduction may be beneficial in certain situations.

McDavis, Nutter, and Lovett (1982), in a study of the counseling needs of thirty handicapped students and their parents, found that the professionals most highly valued by parents were those who gave them accurate information, demonstrated concern, provided encouragement, exhibited respect, supported the parents' efforts to care for their children, helped them to make decisions, and did not pity them. More specifically, in a study of 234 sets of parents of learning disabled children, Dembinski and Mauser (1977) discovered that parents had their own recommendations to professionals:

- ★ use clear language,
- ★ provide a warm, open atmosphere which allows the parents to feel free to ask questions,
- ★ include both parents in visits,
- ★ provide nontechnical reading materials or references to help the parents better understand the child's problem,
- ★ provide written reports,
- ★ provide for communication among the disciplines to decrease the number of professionals who have to be consulted,
- ★ provide educational assistance to parents, and
- ★ provide information on social behavior as well as academic behavior.

Additionally, Williams and Darbyshire (1982) found that the majority of parents in their study expressed a desire for better counseling at the time of diagnosis and subsequent counseling in relation to educational and behavioral problems. In relation to this desire, Abramson et al (1977) suggest that physicians act as counselors when diagnosing handicapping conditions and provide information on agency and community services in order to shorten the time between diagnosis of a problem and the initiation of specialized services.

It would appear feasible to attempt to identify some of the factors which influence the results of meetings between parents and professionals. For example, in 1969 Davidson and Schrag investigated the variables which determine whether recommendations made during child psychiatric consultations would be carried out or not. In this study it was found that 52% of the recommendations from the initial consultation were not carried out. Recommendations were more likely to be followed if both parents were present rather than a mother or father alone. The age of the child also was a significant factor, since more recommendations were followed for children under the age of nine than for children over age thirteen. It was discovered that parents who had discussed their child's problems with others were more likely to follow the recommendations than those who had not discussed the problems with anyone else. A very significant finding was that parents were much more inclined to follow recommendations if they agreed with the professional's diagnosis and evaluation of the problem. The authors pointed out that unless the parents understand and accept the information which is presented, very little can be done for the child. Since no significant relationship was found between the reactions of the child to the consultation and the implementation of the recommendations, the great importance of the attitudes and reactions of the parents must be emphasized. Even seemingly insignificant factors which are usually ignored may influence the effectiveness of the consultation. For example, if families had to wait more than an hour to see the professional for an appointment they were much less inclined to follow the recommendations than were those families who waited a half hour or less. Perhaps the particular techniques for conducting diagnostic interviews will someday be determined by an awareness of these and other factors which may exert significant influences. At present, the format and content of initial consultations seem to be based more upon the convenience and opinions of the professionals than upon the unique needs of the parent and child.

Unfortunately, the initial diagnostic encounter is often the only form of counseling which the exceptional individual or parents receive. Whether because of a lack of facilities and resources or a lack of genuine concern, the parents of an exceptional child often find themselves alone with nothing but a new label such as *mentally retarded* or *learning disabled* for their child. There may be special education programs available in which the child can learn self-care skills or academic skills depending on his or her capabilities, but relatively few of these programs also provide truly helpful guidance regarding the many problems and difficult situations with which the child and family must contend. In addition to facilitating cognitive and intellectual achievement, most special education classes purport to be working toward emotional and social development. However, it is usually assumed that the child will naturally achieve these secondary goals through interaction with teachers and other children. In many cases as long as the child learns basic academic skills and conforms to the class rules, the program is considered successful. For the child who needs special counseling with certain problems or special guidance to grow emotionally and experience life more fully, help is often absent.

COUNSELING EXCEPTIONAL INDIVIDUALS

A limited number of studies pertaining to individual counseling techniques with disabled persons have been conducted. In a 1970 study, Anthony suggests that it is not sufficient for a counselor merely to be warm and caring when dealing with physically disabled persons. Quite often it is necessary to confront the individual concerning his or her negative self-concept and inappropriate behaviors and attitudes which have developed. Anthony found in examining an established rehabilitation counselor training program that many prospective counselors did not possess the necessary skills to facilitate the attainment of certain counseling goals. Since some previous research has shown a positive relationship between the frequency of confrontation and the ability to facilitate a client's progress, Anthony contends that counselor training programs should give greater emphasis to the development of confrontation skills.

In 1968 Gardner and Ransom described a counseling approach called *academic reorientation* to be used with remedial readers. This approach contains several important features to help children develop more desirable behavior. An explanation is given to children about their learning problems to reduce misconceptions and self-doubt. Whenever the child makes positive statements about school, social reinforcement is provided in the form of smiles and increased attention. The counselor and child work together to understand in what situations certain types of behavior usually occur. In addition, the child is made aware of the negative or aversive consequences of continuing the undesirable behavior, while alternative ways of behaving more appropriately are developed. Emphasis is also placed on the ability to label and understand feelings. The counselor's attitude and a working relationship between the counselor and teacher are also considered essential facets of academic reorientation. In a study conducted at the University of Southern California, sixteen subjects with serious learning and behavioral problems were involved with academic reorientation. The children displayed increased cooperation, fewer inappropriate behavior patterns, and greater achievement in reading skills as a result of the counseling. The authors pointed out that although academic reorientation may be very beneficial in some situations, it is not a substitute for more intensive and long-term counseling techniques when they are necessary.

Ottens and Ottens (1982) see crisis intervention as an effective treatment approach for use by the counselor who works with retarded students, since, according to the authors, retarded individuals will often allow what to the average person is a typical or minor problem to become a catastrophic situation. The Ottens suggest that counseling sessions for the retarded should be brief and begin as quickly as possible after a problem begins. As necessary, others involved with the retarded youngster, such as parents, teachers, and other students, should be included in the counseling process. The Ottens suggest that the counseling be "reality-oriented" and, like Anthony, maintain that the counselor should directly confront the student with the inappropriateness of behaviors or thoughts. The counselor should be positive and supportive while helping the student to refrain from acting impulsively. The Ottens also suggest that the counselor should use the problems that arise as a basis for teaching the retarded person how to act in related situations which might occur in the future.

Techniques of group counseling seem to have been investigated more than individual counseling techniques. In a study involving fifty adolescents receiving psychiatric treatment at a hospital in New York City, O'Connell, Golden, and Semonsky (1972) identified factors which influenced the decision of adolescents to continue or drop out of group psychotherapy. Age, sex, race, social class, and diagnosis were not significant factors in this decision. It was found that adolescents who failed to utilize group psychotherapy had low normal intelligence, poor verbal skills, and a tendency toward impulsive acting out. The authors suggested that minimal cerebral dysfunction may prevent effective utilization of group psychotherapy. Adolescents who best utilized group psychotherapy were characterized as having a poor home situation. With these adolescents, group psychotherapy seemed to fill the family's role of providing support and direction for solving problems.

In 1974 Gumaer and Myrick used behavioral group counseling with twenty-five disruptive elementary school children. During eight sessions of counseling, the children themselves identified behaviors which needed improvement (eg, talking out and leaving one's chair during class). Behavioral data were collected and charted, and candy and praise were employed as reinforcers for appropriate behavior. Furthermore, group discussions enabled the children to share feelings and gain personal feedback from one another. Teachers were trained to use the behavioral techniques and were complimented by the counselor for their positive efforts. During the eight weeks of counseling sessions, the disruptive behavior was almost entirely extinguished, while appropriate behavior increased in the classroom. However, after group counseling and systematic reinforcement were discontinued, some of the children's behavior returned to the original level. The authors stated that continued systematic reinforcement in the classroom after counseling might have resulted in more permanent effects.

Two methods of group counseling involving fifty-two emotionally disturbed students were compared by Maynard, Warner, and Lazzaro in 1969. The method of verbal reinforcement counseling involved several topics for discussion (eg, being in a special class, relations with others, and classroom behavior) which were presented by the counselor. During the discussions, the counselor verbally reinforced all remarks which were considered to be positive, appropriate, and helpful in understanding the situation. The second method of counseling enabled the groups to choose and discuss their own topics within a nondirective, client-centered approach. The results indicated no significant differences between groups that received the two different methods. Both methods were effective and beneficial when compared to a control group that received no counseling at all.

In 1970 Humes described an eclectic approach to counseling educable mentally retarded adolescents. Twelve weekly one-hour sessions were divided into three facilitative sessions and nine problem-oriented sessions. During the facilitative sessions, acceptance, understanding, and warmth were stressed as the counselor used a nondirective, unstructured approach. During the remaining problem-oriented sessions, specific difficulties in areas such as school adjustment, family and peer interaction and heterosexual relationships were explored. Certain pictures from the Thematic Apperception Test and Symonds Picture-Story Test were used to stimulate ideas and discussion. Humes reported that this approach resulted in an increased level of socialization and interpersonal relationships, and suggested that other exceptionalities besides educable retarded adolescents might benefit from the combination of unstructured and structured techniques.

DeBlassie and Cowan (1976) also found group counseling to be effective for the educable mentally handicapped, stating that problems were revealed more quickly and feelings of inadequacy were dealt with more readily than in individual counseling. Vance, McGee, and Finkle (1977) feel that group counseling is often the method of choice for mentally retarded students because of its past effectiveness, its economy in terms of time and money, and its emphasis on social interaction and consequent effectiveness at building self-concept and improving interpersonal relations. The authors see group counseling as providing opportunities 1) to identify maladaptive behavior, 2) to increase feelings of acceptance and belonging to a group, 3) to make new friends and build new interests, 4) to correct misconceptions about self and others, 5) to release anxiety and tension, and 6) to learn to cope with social situations similar to ones which might be encountered outside the group. Vance et al also gave specific guidelines for activities, composition of the group, length of meetings, and counselor behavior.

COUNSELING PARENTS OF EXCEPTIONAL INDIVIDUALS

The area of parent counseling is currently receiving increased attention due to PL 94-142 mandates and as professionals realize that even outstanding educational and therapeutic programs often provide little benefit to the exceptional child without support and assistance from the parents. Radin conducted a study in 1969 in which three matched groups of twelve disadvantaged, high ability students who had formerly attended a preschool program received different types of kindergarten experiences. While one group attended a standard kindergarten only, another group participated in the Supplementary Kindergarten Intervention Program (SKIP) in addition to standard kindergarten. The SKIP class emphasized development in cognitive areas discussed by Piaget, such as classification and representation. The third group also participated in standard kindergarten and the SKIP class, but in addition utilized a parent counseling program. Mothers became actively involved in the educational program of their children, and became valuable resource persons for learning in the home. The results of the study indicated that the factor which caused the highest performance by the children on cognitive tests and also a more stimulating home situation was the parent counseling program.

Millman (1970) described open-ended group meetings in which ten to twelve parents of children with minimal brain dysfunction attended 60- or 90-minute sessions each week for as long as they desired. The purpose of the sessions was to provide knowledge concerning cerebral dysfunction and how it affects the behavior of children and to enable parents to discuss their own attitudes and feelings toward their children. Millman stated that parents reported both greater understanding of brain dysfunction for the first time and better effectiveness in handling the behavior problems of their children.

Success with groups for parents of children with learning disabilities was reported by Bricklin in 1970. In his procedure, new parents are first seen individually, then with other new parents, and finally as part of an existing group. Usually parents of children with similar difficulties and age are placed together. Initial sessions are highly structured with much leader participation, but parents gradually assume more responsibility for the group discussion. During the meetings, parents become more knowledgeable about the particular learning problems of their children, and have the opportunity to share feelings and ideas. Bricklin pointed out that certain aspects of the counseling sessions may be difficult for parents since it is hard to change established ways of perceiving and responding to children. However, Bricklin contends that both parents and children have the capacity to change.

According to Lewis, even though group counseling techniques have been investigated, most reports of these procedures do not include either control groups for comparison or the use of objective tests. In a 1972 study, to investigate the results of a group procedure on sixty-two parents of mentally retarded children, Lewis used a control group, which did not participate in the group counseling, as well as two objective tests. Schaefer and Bell's Parent Attitude Research Instrument (PARI, 1955) was used to measure attitude changes, and a true-false test of information about mental retardation constructed by Lewis was used to measure knowledge gained. During ten weekly 90-minute sessions for each of three groups, parents introduced and discussed topics in an open, nonstructured atmosphere. Data collected at the end of the study indicated that the parents' attitudes toward children were improved for two of the three groups, while parents who did not participate in group procedures had "less enlightened attitudes" with the passing of time. All groups of parents who experienced the group procedure demonstrated a greater knowledge of retardation after the ten sessions, but the control group showed no significant change. Lewis also found that no significant difference regarding either child-rearing attitudes or knowledge of retardation existed between mothers and fathers in any of the groups. In addition to the objective data, Lewis subjectively reported that parents seemed to acquire increased self-direction, confidence, and optimism, all of which typically are general counseling goals.

Yura, Zuckerman, Betz, and Newman (1979) reported on a school Parent Involvement Project which utilized group counseling and education of parents of handicapped students. Both parents and school personnel participated, with parents interacting with each other and the group leaders and the teachers offering "moral support," information on the functioning of individual children, and explanations of classroom procedures. The group met for eight sessions, each of which dealt with a separate topic. By using behavioral checklists for pre- and post-testing and other recorded observations, the authors determined that the parents had a more positive attitude about their children's capabilities and that disruptive behavior by the children decreased in frequency after the parents had participated in the project. In addition, school personnel noted that the parents showed more support for the school program after completion of the eight sessions.

Much of the current literature on counseling for the parents of the handicapped calls for the counselor to help the parents deal with negative feelings about the disability and to provide them with emotional and psychological support (Williams and Darbyshire, 1982). Kronich (1978) described the group as a forum in which parents can safely express anger and disappointment and hear what other parents feel. Huber (1979), in his experiences with group counseling, found that parents often expressed a sense of relief upon finding that they were not unique in their responses to their child's handicap.

Numerous articles have discussed the stages (eg, denial, anger, bargaining, depression, acceptance) through which parents of handicapped children progress (Opirhory & Peters, 1982; McDowell, 1976; Perosa & Perosa, 1981; Prescott & Iselin, 1978; Prescott & Hulnick, 1979; Christensen & DeBlassie, 1980). Although none of the recommendations is based specifically on experimental data, the authors strongly suggest that it is the counselor's major task to assist the parents in moving through the stages. Perosa and Perosa (1981) suggest that without acceptance of the child's disability the entire family structure will be affected. The parents may begin to compete with each other for the affection of the child or each parent may blame the other for the disability. In other cases, parents may blame the child for the tension in the household. The author also reports that sometimes one parent may disengage from the family and the other parent may become very overprotective.

Although much of the literature dealing with counseling of parents of the handicapped suggests that the major challenge for the counselor is to help the family work through stages in order to adjust to the reality of having a disabled child, some researchers question whether the parents ever actually do totally "adjust." Wikler, Wasow, and Hatfield (1981) conducted a study to determine whether parents of mentally retarded children actually "adjust" to having a retarded child or whether their sorrow is chronic. The authors also compared the predictions of social workers concerning the extent of the parents' grief at eight specific and two non-specific points of development in the child's life to the parents' actual reported feelings of sorrow at those points. Wikler et al found that the parents do indeed feel chronic sorrow. The sorrow was not continuous but rather periodic in nature. The social workers markedly overestimated how upsetting the parents' early experiences with their mentally retarded child were and significantly underestimated how difficult the parents' later experiences with their mentally retarded child were. Burggraf (1979) found similar experiences of chronic sorrow among parents of the handicapped. She stated that many parents report feelings of grief, disbelief, or anger even after living with a disabled individual for twenty years.

Even when the importance of providing counseling is acknowledged, the question arises: is it more effective to counsel the children, the parents, or the teachers? A small amount of research has investigated the relative effectiveness of providing counseling for different groups. Taylor and Hoedt (1974) compared the effects of direct intervention by counseling children to the effects of indirect intervention by counseling parents or teachers. In this study, 372 elementary school children with behavior problems were divided into four groups that received different treatments. In one group the mothers of the children received an Adlerian type of group counseling; in a second group the teachers of the children received the same form of counseling. Children in the third group were directly involved in group counseling, and children in the fourth group received no special counseling either for themselves or for their teachers and parents. Teachers and parents who were counseled were taught to identify children's behavior problems and then to apply the appropriate principles of encouragement. Children who were counseled were involved in whatever approach seemed most comfortable to that particular group. After a ten-week period, results indicated that counseling with significant adults such as parents and teachers was more effective in reducing behavior problems than directly working with the children.

In another experiment in 1972, Love, Kaswan, and Bugental compared the effectiveness of three interventions with ninety-one elementary school children who had emotional and behavioral disorders and came from different socioeconomic levels. With one group of children, direct child therapy based on psychoanalytic theory was used. The parents of another group of children received counseling which was also psychoanalytically oriented. A new intervention called *information feedback,* in which interpersonal information was gathered on each child through questionnaires, behavior observations, and video recording of family interactions, was used with the third group. This information was then given to both parents and teachers for discussion and decision-making. The researchers concluded that interventions which focus on parents are more effective in improving children's school performance than is time-limited psychotherapy for the child. It was discovered that information feedback produced improved grades for children in upper socioeconomic levels, parent counseling resulted in higher grades for lower socioeconomic levels, and child therapy was associated with lower grades for all levels. The authors stated that although all three methods produced some improvements in behavior, possibly due primarily to attention, the comparative weakness of the effect of child therapy indicated that the parents rather than therapists are the most important source of attention.

FACILITATING PARENT-CHILD INTERACTIONS

Many professionals would argue that it is futile to attempt to determine *who* (ie, parents or disabled individuals) should be the recipient of counseling, since an *ecological* approach to intervention is generally preferable. For example, Perosa and Perosa (1981) view the child as part of the family system and therefore see effective counseling for the handicapped child as being impossible without the involvement and support of the family. They report that the child's disability often affects the entire family structure by causing a myriad of problems within the family. Thus, efforts to address those problems must necessarily include all family members who are affected.

In 1974 Seitz and Hoekenga focused on parent-child interactions in a program in which parents observed and imitated models interacting with their children. Four pairs of parents and mentally retarded children participated in the program for an hour each day, three days a week for eight weeks. Parents first observed therapists working with their children, while receiving explanations of what was being accomplished. The parents gradually assumed the responsibility for working with their own children, until they substituted completely for the therapists during the last two sessions. Progress was measured in terms of increased verbal interactions between parent and child. By the end of the program, all children had increased the average length of verbal utterances, and three children increased the actual number of utterances per session significantly. In addition, the verbal behavior of parents changed substantially. For example, more questions were asked and more commands were given by some parents when appropriate. The authors reported that the altered verbal behavior of the parents produced an increase in positive responding by the children. The most important consequence of these changes in the verbal behavior of parent and child, according to Seitz and Hoekenga, was that the child became an active participant in the communication process rather than merely a passive receptor of verbal stimulation.

Ray (1974) discussed another program which placed emphasis on improving the parent-child relationship rather than providing counseling for either parent or child alone. At the Family Training Center in Tennessee, parents and retarded children between the ages of three years and fourteen years participated together in an intensive residential behavior modification program for a month. The parents first observed the staff interacting with their child, and received explanations and descriptions of the various behavioral techniques and principles being used. As the parents demonstrated increasing knowledge and skill in behavior management, the child spent more and more time back in the home, with a parent trainer available for home consultations and support. Ray described family training as a departure from traditional methods of counseling and therapy which are often implemented after negative behavior patterns are firmly established. Family training emphasizes prevention of more serious disabilities by teaching both parents and children new ways of behaving and interacting.

SUMMARY

Considering the amount of literature which has been published on counseling exceptional children and their parents, it would seem that much knowledge now exists in this area. However, possibly the only conclusive statement which can be drawn from this review of literature is that the results of the research and the opinions stated in the articles are quite inconclusive. Even though unquestionable facts and truths have not emerged from the literature, certain findings do provide important and hopefully useful information. It is obvious, for example, that professionals need to devote much more attention to the format and content of initial diagnostic interviews with parents. The results of existing research clearly demonstrate that parents are often confused and dissatisfied with the information, or lack of information, about the problems of their child. One study indicated that the term "shopping" behavior as applied to parents who visit many professionals is both overused and misused, since the very few parents in the study who did qualify as "shopping" parents were seeking valid assistance and not merely a different diagnosis. Even if a great number of parents do engage in this behavior, perhaps professionals should view it as a reflection of the quality of the services offered rather than as an indication of the parents' denial of reality. Although opinions differ concerning how the initial consultation should be conducted, there is agreement that the presence of both parents and an emphasis on interaction rather than a structured, formal presentation enhances the amount of information gained. The literature also emphasizes that a greater chance exists that recommendations will be carried out if parents understand and agree with the diagnosis. Although this may seem to be an elementary statement based on common sense, research indicates that professionals often underestimate the importance of the parents' attitudes.

Perhaps the least amount of research has been done in the area of counseling exceptional individuals themselves. Although certain individual counseling techniques, such as facilitative confrontation and academic reorientation, have been described, most of the current literature is concerned with group counseling techniques. Almost all of the individual and group counseling approaches which were discussed reportedly produced various improvement and benefits. However, the lack of replication of research and the failure to control important variables in many of the studies prevent firm conclusions concerning the effectiveness of any specific technique.

Parent counseling is receiving an increased amount of attention as studies have indicated that parents must play an essential role in efforts to remediate their child's problems. In fact, the results of many studies indicate that parent counseling may be more beneficial in many situations than direct therapy or remediation with the child. Virtually all of the reported parent counseling has been conducted in groups in which parents receive information about their child's disabilities and often discuss and share feelings and attitudes about their child and themselves. Both structured and nonstructured approaches have been employed, as well as a combination of various approaches.

One of the most significant directions emerging from the literature pertains to the focus on parent-child interactions and relationships. Instead of counseling either children or parents in isolation, some approaches, such as those involving modeling and behavioral techniques, emphasize the development of new patterns of behaving and interacting for both parents and children together.

In conclusion, an increasing awareness of the importance of counseling exceptional individuals and their parents must continue, and this awareness must be reflected by more and better research. The areas of needed research are as numerous and diverse as the many facets of counseling mentioned in this section, in addition to the many other counseling aspects not discussed. Several basic questions must be answered. Are there certain counseling approaches and techniques which are more or less successful with certain exceptionalities? Under what circumstances are group counseling approaches more appropriate than individual counseling approaches? What effect do the qualifications, attitudes, and personality of the counselor have on the effectiveness of counseling? Should all counselors receive highly specialized training and education and be required to meet certain qualifications before they work with exceptional children and parents, or can teachers, parents, or anyone who cares and has the ability to communicate empathically, be a counselor? How important are variables such as age, sex, race, and socioeconomic status in the counseling situation? The number of questions which could be asked is limited only by the imagination and diligence of those currently working with exceptional individuals and parents.

Perhaps a central issue which must first be resolved concerns the goals of the counseling process. Counseling approaches which are directed toward the exceptional individual's conformity to the behavioral and educational standards of "normal" society may produce different results than the approaches which focus upon developing an awareness of the vast human potential of every person, whether intellectually retarded or physically impaired or gifted. Before researchers can investigate if and how counseling goals are being met, they must identify the goals. Only when these goals are realized and pursued through systematic and rigorous thought and research will exceptional individuals and their parents begin to receive the guidance and counseling they need and deserve.

Section III:

The Family Meets The Challenge

Chapter 4: The Role Of The Family

Life is so daily. Parenthood is an endless series of small events, periodic conflicts and sudden crises which call for a response. The response is not without consequence: It affects personality for better or for worse.

HAIM G. GINNOT
Between Parent And Teenager

hat is a family? For better or for worse, everyone has experienced a family and felt its influence. For some this influence has been very productive, meaningful, and positive, for others it has been traumatic, and in some instances, even destructive. Opinions vary as to the efficacy and value of the family as a social system. There are those who feel that our culture's very existence will depend upon the return of the *extended family,* wherein large groups of people with common ancestry live together in some defined and structured unit. This may include parents, grandparents, great-grandparents, children, grandchildren, and even in-laws. Under a common roof, these people support each other, love each other, plan together and share the process of life in a cooperative fashion for the benefit and fulfillment of all.

There are others such as Cooper (1970) and Laing (1967) who see the family as we know it today, as the single most destructive force to individuality, human growth and personality, and would do away with it entirely. They would recommend rearing children apart from parents and any structured family and placing them into the hands of competent people who are professionally trained for the subtle and complex task of childrearing.

Even the noted psychologist, Bruno Bettelheim, has suggested that if we want all children to have equal opportunity to develop their intelligence then we will have to free ourselves from a few of our most widely held prejudices—that children are all the private property of their parents to do with as they please.

No matter to which of the two beliefs one subscribes regarding the family's value, or even if one finds good and bad in each, there is no question that the family, as it now exists, is a powerful force. It plays an important part in determining human behavior, building personality, influencing the course of moral, mental and social evolution, shaping the culture and its institutions. As a powerful social force, it cannot be ignored by anyone who is seriously engaged in any study of human growth, development, personality, or behavior.

In the past, the mother-child relationship within the family inevitably was seen as having the greatest import and was considered the first social dyad; therefore, the most significant in shaping behavior and personality. For this reason it was the most often studied. Though this relationship is still considered a core one, it is becoming increasingly clear that individual or small group relationships become significant dynamically only as a part of a larger social context. These findings have caused researchers to shift their attention from the mother-child relationship in the family to the study of the interactions within the entire family unit, as a group.

THE ROLE OF THE NORMAL FAMILY

Sociologically, the family is defined as a small, interdependent social system within which may be found smaller subsystems, depending upon the family size and defined roles.

Usually the father and mother form the central and most significant unit as *head* of the household, but there are also many other intrafamily relationships such as father-son, father-daughter, mother-son, mother-daughter, brother-sister, and each will affect the other. It is known that the complex interrelationships among all family members, and subgroups which form within the family, and any modification therein, will work their influence upon each member individually and on the group as a whole. Any change in behavior such as a sudden withdrawal from or addition to the unit will change the entire unit. This is commonly illustrated when there is either a divorce or a birth or death in the family.

Most families have a reasonably stable alignment, clearly defined family roles, their own agreed upon norms and value definitions. Generally, when these are consistent, it has been found that problems are reduced, the amount of decision making is lessened and basic changes in family structure are not often necessary. All family members in the unit know their roles and how they are expected to fulfill them. But even in such healthy families, a violent occurrence such as serious prolonged illness, natural disasters, unforeseen financial difficulties, will often necessitate that all members redefine their roles, and learn new values and patterns of behavior to conform to the altered life style. In other words, with each new striking occurrence, the family must be restructured. The extent of the restructuring will be determined by the strength of the causal stimuli, the closeness or interrelatedness of the total unit and the depth of emotional responses involved.

Though a significant social unit in itself, the family does not live in a social vacuum. It is actually a part of a greater social unit, the immediate community and total society in which it exists. In a sense, it is a small culture within a larger culture in which it acts and is acted upon. Any sociopathologic occurrence within the greater society will also have its effect upon the family unit and that of all of its members. Social prejudice, for example, on the part of the larger community toward all or any member of the family will take its toll upon each. This prejudice may be directed toward the family's race, color, religion, economic condition, social status, and even physical and mental differences. It will be a potent, influential force upon the family's behavior.

All of these factors will determine what is referred to in psychological literature as the family's *emotional tone* or *emotional climate.* This term refers to the subtle but generally consistent atmosphere created by the interaction of the members within the family unit. Though research has more often been directed to the correlation between child-rearing techniques and their effects upon personality characteristics of children within the family, there is still some question regarding the positiveness of this correlation as stated by Behrens (1954) and Johnson and Medennis (1964). There is, on the other hand, meaningful and positive support for the greater import of the theory of "family climate" as it affects the growth and development of each member (Sears, Maccaby, and Levin, 1957; MacGregor et al, 1964; Satir, 1964; and Rogers, 1939).

It is common these days in both lay and professional literature to blame the family for all of society's ills. It is blamed for the rising crime rate, drug addiction, and the alarmingly escalating suicide rates. Educators blame the family for school failures. Law enforcement officers blame the family for spoiling children and creating defiant rebels. Psychologists blame parents for causing permanent and crippling learning and emotional problems in their children.

These accusations are only partly founded in fact. Problems are also created by schools, by unreasonable and antiquated laws and inadequate law enforcement procedures and by a confusing, unstable, and radically changing society.

It is true that the family must take its share of the responsibility, for it is mainly within this social unit that the child will learn how to be the kind of human being society stipulates as normal. But, in addition, it is also here where one can be helped to maintain uniqueness, develop individuality, and emerge a creative, self-actualizing human person. This is a tall order for family members, who themselves are the products of other families, who have, in most cases, inadequately prepared them for these demanding tasks.

It is said that "having a child doesn't make you a parent." Anyone who is physiologically and anatomically normal can have a baby. To be an outstanding parent requires skill, knowledge, sensitivity, and wisdom—qualities which are not readily available to all. It is not that parents need to be perfect, it is merely that they must be aware, sensitive, and human. It is not perfection that seems to be the key to being a successful parent, but humanness. Happily, this quality is far easier to attain, since being human is what we can do best. It is the parents who feel that they must convince their children that they are perfect who seem to create family disturbances. It is the parents who must always be right, must always know the best way, must always have the last word, who must at any cost, be worshipped (love is not enough) by their children, who create disillusionment. It is the parents who feel they must hide all of their problems from their children, disguise their fears, internalize their longing, worries, and *appear* always as totally well-integrated people, who eventually alienate themselves from their children. "Truth will out." This symbol of perfection is too difficult to maintain. Consider the disillusionment and the feelings of insecurity brought upon children when they discover (often not until adolescence) that their parents are not the constantly emotionally healthy, problem-free individuals that they have been led to believe.

The best things stable parents can be is human, in all the meanings of the word. Striving, growing human beings must let it be known that they are lonely at times, cry when they are hurt, become angry when they are frustrated, forget, and do all of the wonderful things the human person does. Parents must also know how to laugh at themselves, love, care, dream, need and share. In other words, parents must know that they are *human* and not *gods*, and therefore are very happy to do what they can do best, be human beings! What better model for children?

Basically, the family serves its members as a training ground. It affords infants a place where, while assured of having the physical needs met for food, water, and housing, they may experiment with the repertoire of behavior that is available. In this way they will discover those behaviors which are congruent with their growing feelings and needs and those of the *small unit* society in which they are being raised. Though, as yet, they are not aware of it, this smaller unit, the family, is a miniature, in most cases, of what they will encounter when they become a part of the greater unit, society. The key to the growth process lies in the opportunity which the family affords children a safe place to find themselves and others in their world. In essence, the family is the first significant training ground for newborn infants.

The child finds that this training ground is inhabited by people—father, mother, sisters, brothers, grandparents, and others. Each has grown into an assigned role in the family, but each, according to unique experiences and an essential personality, has also developed into a *different* person. Each has strengths and weaknesses, each has fears, loves, attachments, needs, desires, and dreams. It is from this multitude of possibilities for personality development that the child will be free to select, while all the time trying to find and maintain a personal self. Their first relationship, or dyad, within the family unit will be with the mother. It is upon her that the child will depend for food, comfort, and joy. Her voice will be heard, her body warmth felt, her responses sensed more than anyone else's. The child will need her for existence and will have this real need for her for a longer period of time than any other living creature. It is with her that the process of imprinting will occur. She will become a model, the first human attachment. The child will strive to be like her. As she meets needs, there will be reciprocity and the child will try to meet hers. In a sense, they will condition and shape each other. It is from her that the child will first learn to be human. To be sure, as time passes, each family member will have a share in this process and the child will both give to and take from each.

For the most part, unconsciously, children learn about the world outside and of life from each person in their family. If they are fearful, the child will learn to fear. If they are suspicious, the child will become so. If they are optimistic, so will the child know optimism. If they love, so the child will love. This, of course, is an oversimplification of the process of personality growth and development—but in general we *learn* to be human and the family members are our first teachers.

To a greater or lesser extent, the family members will not only respond as conscious teachers to children, but they will also have unconscious feelings about them. It is partly through these disguised and unconscious feelings, along with more expressed feelings, that they will sense who they are. Their self-concept will be born. If the family members as a group respond positively to them, they are likely to see themselves in a positive light. They may learn that they are beautiful, capable, alert, and that they have great hope for the future waiting outside the family. On the other hand, if their responses are negative, they may learn that they are limited, unattractive, embarrassing, and dull, with a dim future.

To some degree each family member tells each other who they are and whether or not they are likely to succeed, even before they have come into contact with the larger society outside of the home.

Jean Paul Sartre (1956) goes so far as to say that "Before the children are born, even before they are conceived, their parents have decided who they will be." It is difficult for a helpless child, who has no other alternatives at that point in time, to disagree.

The family continues to play its part even after children are able to interact with the environment outside the family. Children experience new growing and sometimes frustrating periods as they become a part of the larger social structure. Their playmates will make new demands of them, perceive them differently from their family and offer them new insights into themselves. Their teachers and schools may create additional demands of them and force them into more formal restricted structures where they will be expected to meet certain expectations of behavior and achieve certain prescribed goals. "You can't always do what you want," they will hear. "The world doesn't belong to you, you know!" "Conform or get out!" Often, they are not offered many alternatives. This, in contrast to home and family. As Robert Frost said, "Home is a place that when you go there, they have to take you in."

The healthy family assumes an additional role, mainly that of support, of understanding, of acceptance. It is the environment that remains somewhat constant—even while all other situations seem to be continually changing. And so it will be as the child grows into adulthood.

Basically, then, the role of the stable family is to offer a safe training ground for young children to learn to be human, to learn to love, to build their unique personality, develop their self-image and to relate with, and to, the changing greater society of which and to which they are born.

To varying degrees, families succeed or fail in aiding children toward the realization of these vital functions. Nevertheless, children will grow into adulthood with or without these learnings and will have to deal with the results. They may never be able to adjust to society or they may learn the necessary skills later, relearn them, or unlearn them, depending upon the pressures they are capable or willing to deal with in the processes involved in their self-actualization.

THE ROLE OF THE FAMILY OF THE DISABLED

All things that are true regarding the role of any family are true for the family of the disabled. But, there is evidence that indicates the problems will be intensified within the family in which a member is disabled.

From the moment a disabled child or adult is brought home from the hospital, the all important emotional tone of the family changes. Of course, this phenomenon occurs even when a normal child is born or a visitor arrives to stay even for a brief time. Emotional tones will vary and change with external stimuli. But in a home now faced with a disabled individual, family members, who, up until this time, have been quite secure in their role definitions, will be required to change drastically. Mother, for instance, who went away to the hospital in joy and expectation, will usually return to a very different ambiance. Father has already been forced into his new role and the feeling adjustments it requires. He has already, in his way, brought these into the family.

As we related earlier, birth is usually a time for rejoicing, for celebration. But it is different now. The family will, by the time the child is brought home, have already felt the impact of the strange and mysterious news. A family member is disabled.

Much of the initial response to this news will be determined by what kind of information is given, how the information is presented and the attitude of the person who is communicating. In the case of the birth of a disabled child, since the mother is usually in the hospital, the job of first explaining often falls to the father. Most fathers have neither the knowledge nor the ability to present such emotionally laden information in an adequate fashion to children and relatives. This is understandable. He may want a hospital social worker or family doctor to help him. So much of how the disabled child will be accepted into the family and the resultant emotional tone within the home will depend upon the initial explanation.

It is wrong for parents to disguise the facts that they present to the family or relatives. This is often done to lessen the blow, but most often it is an unconscious way of shirking an unpleasant responsibility. The rationalization will be that "children will not understand at their age anyway." It is amazing how well children will understand and accept if they are included in both the intellectual and emotional content of family problems. It is only when facts are disguised and emotions denied that fears, confusion, and impotence take the place of right action.

Information is vital, but equally as vital is the emotional tone of the explanation. It is useless to *pretend* with one's feelings. Children have had years to *psych-out* their parents and for the parents to disguise their true feelings from themselves or the children, is the worst, most destructive type of deception. This deception inevitably produces an atmosphere of mystery which, in turn, creates anxiety and fear. Though all the facts may not be known at the time, anxiety and fear can be avoided with truth, a sharing of the problem, its possible effects upon the family and what it will mean for each individual.

Usually, in the early days of a disability it is impossible to know the extent of the problem, or to determine its future implications. But there is a great deal of security in deciding what can be done *now*.

A parent of a child with Down's syndrome (mongolism) related to me that she and her husband had decided not to tell the children anything before she brought her retarded child home, perhaps in the secret hope that the disability would go unnoticed. When the family finally gathered to see the baby, the physical characteristics of the child caused great curiosity, anxiety, and even fear among its siblings. The smallest child shouted in tears, "I don't like that baby. It's not pretty. I hate it! Take it back!"

The parents agreed that the tears, pain, and negative effect of such an outburst was much greater than what it would have taken to prepare the children adequately.

Clinical research has repeatedly shown that the greatest influence upon whether the disabled child is either accepted or rejected in the family is the attitude of the mother. If she is able to deal with the occurrence with reasonable acceptance and assurance, in a well-integrated manner, the family will do so also. Banish (1961) found that children in the family take on the parents' attitudes toward the disabled in the family. If mother is despondent, tearful, disappointed, awkward, and wanting, so too, will be her husband and children.

There are other factors, of course, which will affect the family's role in accepting or rejecting a disabled member. It has been found, for instance, that the manner in which the family has dealt with serious problems in the past will be directly correlated with how they will deal with new problems. If the family has met special conflicts in the past with organized, well-executed group solutions, they are more likely to be able to work out appropriate alternatives and answers to future problems.

Children who have been protected from conflicts in the family and whose parents have considered these conflicts to be their personal problems, to be discussed behind closed doors, will find coping with any new such instances a most difficult task. If, on the other hand, the children have always been included in family decisions, both pleasant and unpleasant, they will have greater coping powers when presented with any new conflicts. If the children are secure within the family and have a cooperative, growing and meaningful relationship with parents and siblings, they will feel less threatened by the new and different. They have been allowed to be a part of the solution or the plan for change, and it seems logical, then, that this new occurrence will be handled in the same manner.

What is being implied here, simply, is that if the family has, in the past, been functioning as a healthy unit, it is questionable and improbable that any single crisis will cause it any great devastation. Most healthy families will meet problems in a realistic and productive manner, even discovering that the dynamics of group problem solving serves the function of making the family a closer, more meaningful unit.

Having a disabled person in the home will continue to arouse problems which will require role redefinitions and changes from each family member, even after the acceptance of the initial impact. Exceptional demands will constantly be encountered. Demands for time, for family restructure, for changing attitudes and values, and for new lifestyles will be made. Most of these demands will not be imagined but will be very realistic, indeed. Perhaps, at first, the child will require constant nursing, special medications, unique treatments and special diets. As the sole nurse in most cases, the mother will often have to give inordinate amounts of attention to the child and have less opportunity for relaxation and personal interaction with other members of the family. Her husband and children will be required to readjust, to help and support her during this demanding period. These added responsibilities may continue for weeks, months, even years. It will not be easy for anyone. It will be especially difficult for the husband and children who have been accustomed to being the "center of mother's life."

A poignant play, *Joe Egg* (1967), deals dramatically and devastatingly with this period of adjustment. It relates the slow disintegration of a marriage in which the birth of a disabled child demands extreme emotional and environmental change. For the first time, both husband and wife are forced to look squarely at themselves. The consequence in this case is the discovery of fears, disguised hostility, inadequacy, even hate. The result is tragedy.

A professional man, father of an upper-middle-class family in Southern California who had two severely disabled children, as well as two physically normal children, became so despondent over his inability to deal with the accentuated social and psychological family adjustments to disability that he committed mass murder—his wife, his four children, and finally himself. His short note of explanation was full of the pain and confusion of one whose everyday problems have so fogged-in his perception that he becomes lost and is unable to find any more satisfactory way out!

Worry, too, will take its toll upon the family. Realistic concerns about the child's well-being, the added personal responsibility, the financial burden, the constant uncertainty, the physical exhaustion which grows into irritability and ends in frequent tears. Unreasonable outbursts of temper may result, which seem to lead to a desire for isolation and escape.

At a recent interview a husband talked about his concerns regarding the changes in his wife since the birth of their defective child. He said, "Since the baby was born handicapped, she's changed. She's lost her sense of humor, her interest in me and the kids, in everything. She shouts at us all the time and she never did before. She's moody. She cries a lot and doesn't want us to help her. She wants us to leave her alone. She never wants to go anywhere or do anything. It's as if she wants to isolate herself, with the baby, and exclude the world."

These may be rather extreme cases for illustrative purposes, but in every situation in which there is a drastic change required within the family, there will be some demands for role changes and life styles made upon the mother, father, and children. The extent of these role accommodations and the flexibility with which they will be made will be determined by the previous experiences, learnings, and personalities of those involved. The healthy person makes the healthy adjustment. Those who are functioning on the brink of despair will usually find that any such catastrophic happening will push them over into neurosis and possibly bring forth heretofore successfully repressed feelings, anxieties and fears.

Families will not only have to deal with internal pressures, but also with pressures exerted by outside social forces. Relatives, well-meaning friends and casual acquaintances often create additional problems. Unconsciously, they may, by their attitude, exert pressures upon the family of the disabled by suggesting that there are better doctors for the child, better clinics, or new remedial techniques which should be tried at once. These well-meaning remarks are often interpreted by the over-sensitive, over-worked families as critical, cruel and questioning of their abilities and decisions as mature individuals.

Often the implication is made that if the mother had been more careful during pregnancy or taken better care of herself or even not married her husband, there would have been no disabled child. These thoughts can be devastating for the families who are already wrestling with these notions, consciously or unconsciously.

Society finds it difficult to cope with differences. It will express this in many subtle, covert, or even unconscious ways in the manner in which it segregates the physically or mentally disabled, stares at them in public, or avoids contact with them whenever possible. Impaired individuals can usually offer a list of a thousand verbal and nonverbal occurrences in which the society reveals its insensitivity, lack of knowledge, rejection, and prejudice toward them. These societal feelings will have their effect upon the total family and its relationship with the disabled member. Stories are common regarding neighbors who have the attitude, "There is a handicapped child in that house and there must be something very wrong with a family if they can have such a baby."

One mother expressed her anxiety over the change of attitude of one of her own nondisabled children who was in elementary school. She told of how her child had stopped wanting to play with or even see her disabled brother. "She refused to be seen with him in public. Previously, she had been very close to her brother, then, all at once, this wish to totally avoid him. She even told some of the neighbors that he was not really her brother at all."

The role of the family of the disabled person, then, can best be understood in a sociopsychological context. It is one, as with the normal family, in which there are continual reciprocal effects, family-child, family-culture-child, each upon the other. Any change in any one family member affects each in turn, depending upon the psychological state of the family. The major difference in the family with the child who is disabled is that their problems are intensified by the many special needs, attitudes and requirements which are put upon them, due to the presence of the disability.

The family of the disabled can act in a most positive manner as a mediator between the society in which their children will have to function and the more loving and accepting informed environment it can afford them. But to do this each family member must adapt to their own feelings about the disability and the child who is disabled. They must understand that only in this way can they help the child adapt to their feelings regarding their disability and finally, themselves, as total persons.

The import of the family role cannot be minimized, for it is within this *safe* proving ground that disabled persons will first learn and continually experience that, even with severe limitations, it is permissible for them to be themselves.

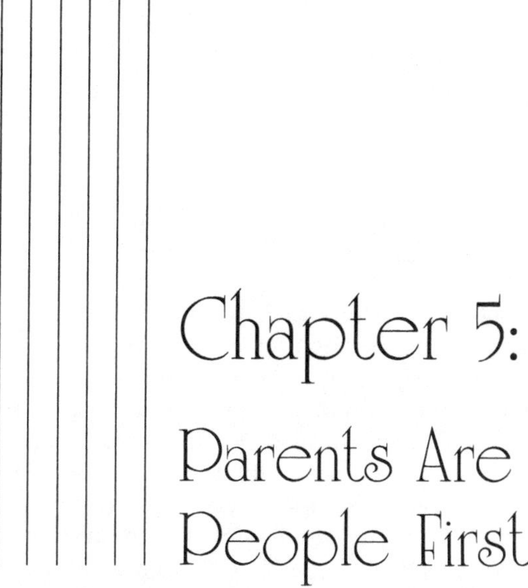

Chapter 5: Parents Are People First

Almost every doctor who saw and examined me, labeled me a very interesting but also a hopeless case. Many told mother very gently that I was a mental defective and would remain so. This was a hard blow to a young mother who had already reared five healthy children. The doctors were so very sure of themselves that mother's faith in me seemed almost an impertinence. They assured her that nothing could be done for me.

She refused to accept this truth, the inevitable truth—as it then seemed—that I was beyond hope. She could not and would not believe that I was an imbecile, as the doctors told her. She had nothing in the world to go by, not a scrap of evidence to support her conviction that, though my body was crippled, my mind was not. In spite of all the doctors and specialists told her, she could not agree. I don't believe she knew why—she just knew, without feeling the slightest doubt.

CHRISTY BROWN
My Left Foot

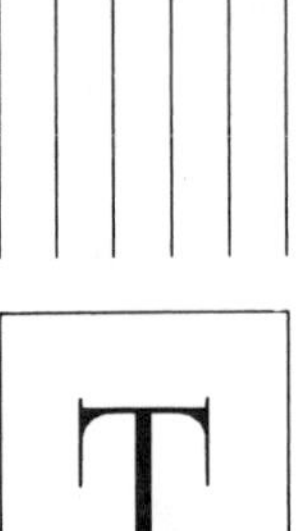

Two individuals marry, have a child and become, by definition, parents. The idea of *parent* puts them into a role as accepted and defined specifically for them by their society as well as, to some extent, by themselves. Parenthood suggests a certain group of requirements, traits, responsibilities, responses, and characteristics. In many cases, parenthood, for the woman, may be a product of labor and fulfillment, for the man a sign of manhood, potency, and virility. For both, it can be an acceptance of responsibility, of adulthood, the attainment of a certain status, a realization of selfness, as well as togetherness. Parenthood is in a very real sense a uniting of uniquenesses, a presentation to the world, through this uniting, of another unique product.

As is often the case, when individuals have labels imposed upon them or agree to accept certain labels, preconceived notions of behavior and feelings go along with the label. Let us remember that until we acquire our own personal definition and feelings for these labels, which are but words, they are merely meaningless phonetic symbols put in an agreed-upon order, but, in themselves are only air put into vibration. We bring our own meaning to the words we use. The word *mother* for instance, has a dictionary meaning, cold and clinical, "a female parent." But, depending upon our real experiences with *mother,* we bring to the word some strong emotional responses as well as role definitions. So it is with the word *father* or *parent.*

The power in a word such as parent is obvious. The very mention of the word can put a glint of pride in the eyes of a man or a woman, or can put public school officials preparing for open house in a turmoil. "The Parents are coming!" It may cause a young lover to experience fear and trembling with the possibility of, "I'm meeting her parents tonight for the first time," or the young bride-to-be to sigh, "When I marry him I have to take his parents, too!"

When words are commonly associated with specific expectations and role functions, the words often create a reaction and become a stereotyped *set* which further act as a stimulus for certain preconceived attitudes and emotions. It follows, therefore, that parents are often seen en masse as certain specific *things.* The danger lies in our very human desire to simplify by generalization. If they can be grouped, it becomes easier to analyze them, accuse them and often even abuse them without having to deal with each as a separate entity. One often hears many professionals, who should know better, sigh, "Parents are always the cause of all their kids' problems," forgetting that they themselves are parents. They may be unaware that just a few miles away there could be another professional sighing the same lament about *their* children!

A parent is always a person first. He or she cannot be separated from parenthood, of course, but an individual is also much more than just a parent. Having a child is merely one part of a complicated role as a person. The parent is also a son or daughter, a husband or wife, a worker, a citizen, a consumer, and many other things.

Only in rare instances does becoming a parent drastically change the *person* that one is. Most generally, a thoughtful person will make a thoughtful parent. A loving person will be a loving parent. On the other hand, a confused or neurotic person will also make a confused and neurotic parent.

Persons who bring a disabled child into the world acquire a new role, becoming, in addition, *special parents,* who are often forced to look more deeply and evaluatively into the interactions of this new role. They must try to understand feelings and attitudes brought about by a new situation for which there are few guidelines or definitions. The birth of an imperfect child will confront them with a unique challenge which would never have been faced had the child been *perfect.* Whereas previously they would have been able to raise their children with well-defined role expectations, this will no longer be the case, for new questions will be raised. These questions may never have had to be asked. Disturbing questions as, "Why did this happen to me?" "Will I be able to be a good parent in spite of my child's disabilities?" "Will I be able to meet my child's unique needs?" "Will I be able to deal with the social pressures?" "Will I be able to meet the financial burden?" "Will I have the emotional strength?"

Many parents of disabled children may never get beyond the questioning stage, since most of the questions they will ask of themselves can have no specific answers. "Why did this happen to me?" Who can say? "Will I be able to be a good parent to my disabled child?" One will have to wait and see. "Will I be able to meet my child's needs?" Who can predict? "Will I be able to deal with the social prejudice I am feeling?" Who can tell? "Will I be able to meet the financial burden?" "How much will it take?" "Will I stand up under the emotional drain, the special demands?" It is impossible to say what hidden strength one has until situations demand it. There can be no definitive answers, only personal ones. In most cases, and for most parents, the answers will be "yes." But they will never know until they cease asking the questions and begin to live the answers, in action. To continually live with unanswerable questions is to court impotence and frustrated inactivity. To avoid this will require that they gain special knowledge and insight into the dynamics of human behavior, the phenomena of change, and the psychology of everyday life. Only through their expanded knowledge and feelings which bring along with them *hope* will they be able to move to creative action. As Norman Cousins (1970) states, "Hope is the beginning of plans. It gives men a destination, a sense of direction for getting there, and the energy to get started. It enlarges sensitivities. It gives proper value to feelings as well as to facts."

Since parents are but people, there will be times when hope disappears and personal problems seem too monumental to deal with. They, then, may desire to receive counseling. For the most part, parents who are helped with some knowledge and insight into themselves and their exceptional child will be able to deal with and solve their problems in their own way. Though all parents of an exceptional child should be offered some guidance and counseling, not all of them will require continuing psychological help.

There are many insights and much knowledge which will aid parents of children who are disabled toward a better and more growing adjustment for themselves and their child.

They will need to understand their special feelings regarding their children and their impairments. So important is this that a whole chapter will be dedicated solely to a discussion of these feelings. But, in addition, they will need to know more about themselves as unique individuals. They must understand that they are largely the product of their culture, that this culture has taught them not only how to be the human beings they are, but also their specific human responses, reactions, and attitudes.

It is important that they know that the human being that they have become was not determined by their human anatomy. (In fact, it has been found that when we have no human models, we may use our anatomy to accommodate the discretion of our surroundings. We may again become naked apes.) What makes them *human* are their habits, their learning, the beliefs they acquire, the love they know, the fears they have, their dreams and hopes for the future.

As they mature, there are many forces which will continue to help them to learn who they are. Primarily, the greatest effects will be from family and culture, but to some extent, they will also be affected by their unique self along the way.

Studies of animal behavior are continually used to relate to human behavior. It does not seem pertinent to the researchers that our brain, the center of our consciousness, is not a dolphin's brain, a monkey's brain, or the brain of a pigeon. It is an organ that is unique only to us.

Even though developmental studies which equate animal and human behavior follow different patterns, they inevitably seem to reach the same conclusions. The animal develops quickly. Some species, in a few hours or days, become fully functioning creatures. Humans, on the other hand, remain helpless. They must be fed, fondled, and protected, or they will surely die. But very shortly animals will reach their capacity for animalness. Humans, on the other hand, will continue to grow. We will find means to influence our own environment. We will develop empathy with others and pick up subtle changes in interactions. We will be able to study, observe, and learn about others and ourselves. We will form values and ideas and react to them. We will gain language as we know it (the only living creature who can). We will be able to go out of ourselves and create beauty from what we are. We will not only react and take from the world, but will learn to experience it and bring it new creations. Though our central nervous system is so designed as to help limit and modify our environment, we may use our consciousness to enlarge our world. We will discover, analyze, label and assimilate what we experience in a never-ending process of self-discovery. There seems to be no end to our abilities. Our optimal capacity for growth has never been measured. Every teacher worthy of the title knows that no matter how much anyone is aware of something, one can never know everything about it. However advanced we are with anything, it may freely be said that we are only just beginning! *The process seems to be one of the greater the consciousness, the more there is of self. The more there is of self, the more one is aware. The more one is aware, the more one will find!*

Since we essentially learn to be the persons we are, learn to feel, learn to perceive the world, there is always the possibility, of course, that the perceptions may be wrong. Essentially, we will know this if we are in touch with our honest feelings about ourselves. Often, too, it is the response and reaction of others in our environment that will act as a mirror to our behavior. If we remain in touch, we will learn that what we are seeing may not be an accurate perception of what there is. We may find that what we are feeling may not be an indication of what the stimuli suggested. We may even discover that we are only hearing what we will to hear and not the message that is being sent at all. If we desire to be more accurate in our feelings and perceptions, we will learn from these experiences that we must change. The birth of an exceptional child may indicate to us, for example, that our present self is not enough, that we need more information, more accurate perception of our feelings, more understanding for and empathy with others. There will be new demands which the unique situation creates. We are experiencing a new type of subculture where fresh insights, keener knowledge, more subtle feelings are required. We are, thus, driven to change. Resistance to this change may only bring frustration and despair. It may seem easier to remain the self that we are but we will soon find that this is not so. Resistance to change can bring pain. The decision to change will not be an easy one to make for it will require a deep investment in self, a great deal of personal energy, and a disciplined dedication. But it becomes easier if we understand that anything that is learned can be unlearned, within both the conscious and the unconscious self. Research has shown that given the proper stimuli and motivation we can continue to learn and adjust to new patterns of behavior for the remainder of our lifetimes. But, it always entails a degree of uncertainty, of fear and struggle.

Herbert Otto has often stated that change and personal growth will only occur when individuals are willing to risk themselves and experiment with their own lives. The keys to the process of change suggested by Otto lie in his words *risk* and *experiment*. Change is always a risk. We can never be certain that we are making the right decisions. We are never sure that we are not better off as we are. But, certainly we will never find out unless we are willing to *experiment* with our lives, discovering new ways, new paths, new alternatives. It is not that these ways, paths, alternatives are not already within us, it is only that we do not realize them until we undertake to find them. All things are, to some degree, already in all people, but we need the world and others to help us to recognize and actualize them.

Sidney Jourard (1971) said, "Growth is the disintegration of one way of experiencing the world, followed by a reorganization of this experience, a reorganization which includes the new disclosure of the world. This disorganization, or even shattering, of one way to experience the world is brought on by new disclosures from the changing being of the world, disclosures which were always being transmitted, but were usually ignored."

What Jourard is implying is that our solutions are already possibilities within us but to find these we must first shatter previous conceptions which serve to fog our present perceptions, and let in the many new possibilities. This sounds more simple than it is, of course, but it can only be realized when it is put into action. Change also can be invigorating, joyful, satisfying and full of wonder.

Parents of exceptional children are in no sense more "ready" than any other parents for the demands for change and adjustment which confront them with the birth of their child. Still, they are often expected to be superhuman beings, and with little or no guidance, to suddenly cope with strange and confusing feelings regarding themselves and their child. In addition, they are asked to understand complex medical problems which relate to the child's disability. And, in the matter of a few short days, to assimilate and integrate all of these things so that they can accept and assume the added responsibilities of the new, mysterious role this physical disability will play in their day-to-day functioning. Often, the only help they will receive toward accomplishing this will come from their physician who will usually take the necessary time to explain any anatomical abnormalities. But most physicians are not trained as humanistic counselors—the role of the old country doctor, long lost in our mechanistic, efficient, time-ridden society. In the present day busy doctor's office, there is little time allotted for listening, explaining, assuring and reassuring. Even when time is made, an unprepared doctor may feel awkward and inadequate in a role for which he has had little preparation. For instance, to one distraught mother, a neurologist explained her child's inability to read by saying, "Mrs. Smith, your child has developmental dyslexia due to minimal brain dysfunction." Pause. "Do you understand?" Then, he chuckled to himself and added gently, "Forgive me. How the hell would you understand?"

Being the parents of a child who is disabled will be a complex new role. To take on this inordinate task, the parents must be afforded the dignity of an understandable medical diagnosis, some reassurance regarding feelings of guilt, uncertainty and fear, some vague idea about what the future will hold for them and their child, and most of all, a great deal of hope and encouragement toward helping them to accept the challenge before them. No matter how many professionals will help with assurances and explanations, in the final analysis the major responsibility will fall to them, the parents.

A teacher of preschool deaf children put the situation well when she said, "It is easy for me to criticize these parents and tell them what to do. I have their children for only a few hours a day, a few days a week. They live with them and their problems for twenty-four hours a day, every day. I love to work with deaf children, but I'm not sure I'd be able to do the job these parents are doing if I had to be with them, day and night, for seven days a week!"

Professionals often forget that giving birth to a child who has a disability does not alter the fact that the parents are still people just like other people. They impose inordinate demands upon them. They threaten them with statements such as, "unless you stop rejecting this child, we will not be able to do anything to help." Or even less realistically they insist that the parents "at once, accept their exceptional child!"

One mother's response to such a statement was an angry "How the hell can I?" A poignant reply.

Another parent told how she had to find her own strength to raise two children, both born blind. She rationalized that she had been uniquely chosen by God to have disabled children because He knew that she was a good mother and would do well by them. "I know that was pretty far-reaching," she said later, "but it got me over the hump."

It is imperative that we see, and help, parents of children who are disabled to see themselves as people first, like all people, with the same mental and physical strengths and limitations and variations thereof. They need not, at the start, accept *anything* except the challenge that comes with taking on the responsibility to grow, to realize their potentials, to learn, and to become greater human beings, along with their special child. All else will surely follow.

To raise an exceptional child in our culture will demand the best parents have to give. In fact, it will perhaps become their life's second greatest challenge. The main challenge to any person will always be *personal* growth, development, and self-actualization. Parents can only give to their children, or anyone else, what they themselves have and know. For parents the main responsibility will always be to themselves. This may sound selfish but it becomes less so when one considers that ignorance only creates more ignorance, while only wisdom can create wisdom. No dead person has ever taught life, as no loveless person has ever been able to teach love. One must have these qualities first, before sharing them with others.

The first step, then, in the complex process of dealing with the exceptional child lies in accepting the obvious fact that the parents of these children are only human. As such, they will have to face their own special needs. They will need to become aware of their real feelings and become fearless of them. They will have to accept what they are now. They will have to accept the challenge of their own emotional and intellectual growth. They will need to accept the risks involved in the process and be willing to experiment with change.

There will be moments of doubt and even failure. But as parents grow in wonder and discovery, and if they are able to revel in the fact that they are not expected to be perfect, only human, these moments become fewer. They will find that as they become more aware of and concerned about themselves, they will become more aware of and concerned about others. They will discover that as they experiment and drop preconceptions, new alternatives will appear. As they risk becoming involved with and trying out new-found alternatives for feelings and behavior, they will see their unlimited selves and world expanding.

Verda Hiesler ends her helpful book, *A Handicapped Child in the Family*, with the following statement:

> In talking with you as the parent of a handicapped child, I have tried to focus your awareness on the opportunity for growth as

> a person available to you by seeking the meaning within yourself of the difficulties you experience in this task of parenthood. In life, it is healthy to reach for joy and to build for fulfillment. But when life brings you sorrow, that also has value which can be utilized in your quest for wholeness.

In this growing process, individuals find that they are not alone. Everyone has similar problems to some extent and must find their own unique answers, their own creative solutions. There will be strength in the knowledge that in our time the Kennedys had to do it, the Humphreys had to do it, many John and Mary Does had to do it, and that most emerged from what had seemed, at the time, to be tragedy, into what seemed later on to be a significant human victory—the triumph over despair.

One such person, as mentioned earlier, was the renowned author, Pearl S. Buck. In *The Child Who Never Grew,* she recounts her own personal conflicts—no different from yours or those of John and Mary Doe. In the opening of the book, she shares with her readers the reason for finally deciding to write of her personal struggles. She tells of the many letters she received pleading for help. In her skillful and touching way, she relates the following:

> They write to ask me what to do. When I answer I can only tell them what I have done. They ask two things of me: first, what they shall do for their children; and, second, how shall they bear the sorrow of having such a child?
>
> The first question I can answer, but the second is difficult indeed, for endurance of inescapable sorrow is something which has to be learned alone. And only to endure is not enough. Endurance can be a harsh and bitter root in one's life, bearing poisonous and gloomy fruit, destroying other lives. Endurance is only the beginning. There must be acceptance and the knowledge that sorrow fully accepted brings its own gifts. For there is an alchemy in sorrow. It can be translated into wisdom, which, if it does not bring joy, can yet bring happiness.

To grow as a parent is, in a meaningful sense, to help all things to grow. A disabled child may be the key to one's continued, accelerated, unique *becoming*. In a sense, as a unique person, each of us must grow independently in order to grow with others, but parents can only do this if they are willing to accept the fact that they are people first, parents second, and only then the parents of a child with a disability.

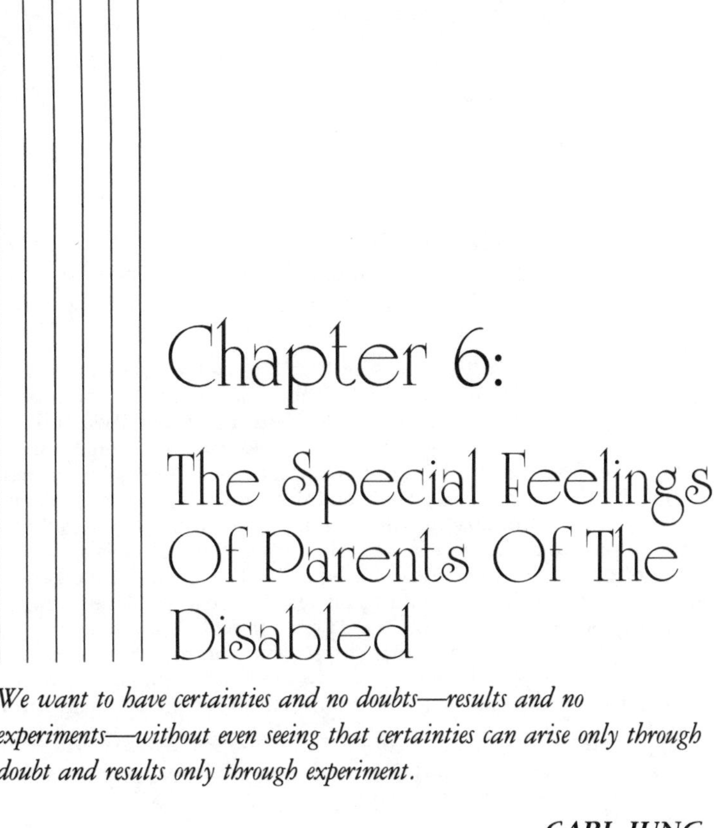

Chapter 6: The Special Feelings Of Parents Of The Disabled

We want to have certainties and no doubts—results and no experiments—without even seeing that certainties can arise only through doubt and results only through experiment.

CARL JUNG
The Stages of Life

n *The Child That Never Grew* (1950), Pearl Buck describes her initial feelings upon learning that her daughter was born irreparably mentally retarded.

> To learn how to bear the inevitable sorrow is not easily done. I can look back on it now, the lesson learned, and see the steps; but when I was taking them they were hard indeed, each apparently insurmountable. For in addition to the practical problem of how to protect the child's life, which may last beyond the parent's, there is the problem of one's own self in misery. All the brightness of life is gone, all the pride in parenthood. There is more than pride gone, there is an actual sense of one's life being cut off in the child. The stream of the generations is stopped. Death would be far easier to bear, for death is final. What was is no more. How often did I cry out in my heart that it would be better if my child died! If that shocks you who have not known, it will not shock those who do know. I would have welcomed death for my child and would still welcome it, for then she would be finally safe.

In a lifetime it is rare that one can escape sorrow. As with the yin and the yang, joy and sorrow move together, one with the other. More often than not, the sorrow we experience is a momentary one, passing as quickly as it comes. It is but another conscious event which one has come to expect in the normal process of living. As such, it is experienced, then let go. It is possible though, that many persons can live their entire lifetime without knowing real despair, the type of inescapable despair that will not let go but must be lived with. The type of despair that cannot be changed. The person will have to change lifestyle and feelings to accommodate it, for it will always be there; it is inescapable. Permanent disability can produce such despair.

Of course, there are as many patterns of coping with emotion as there are adults and children who are forced to live with it. The processes may vary; there will be those who realize at once that nothing can be done about the problem, that it is real, and that it is there. They accept it as a matter of fact. In a realistic, well-integrated manner, they will meet it face to face, as they have other past stresses. They will choose alternative ways of coping, and look for new constructive ways to deal with this inescapable despair.

At the other extreme will be those who will spend their lives bathing in tears of self-pity and martyrdom, feeling lost, misunderstood and unloved, in self-imposed isolation.

Most parents who have exceptional children will find themselves either somewhere between the two extremes of adjustment or perhaps vacillating from one to the other.

No matter what the individual's strength, one is seldom truly ready to encounter real despair. A woman never enters the hospital to give birth to a child emotionally prepared for the advent of a child who is disabled. These thoughts may occur but are quickly dismissed. The odds for her having a healthy child, in her ideal image, are in her favor. She certainly is not prepared for the knowledge that her child will perhaps have to live a life with a disability which may impose permanent limitations to all activities, and which will require from her, as well as all the other family members, unusual expenditures of time, energies and monies.

The initial shock of this realization and its resultant feelings of disbelief will be charged, at first, to the degree to which the disability is clearly visible or irreparable. A disability in a newborn child such as spastic paralysis or missing limbs is more inescapable, a constant visible reminder of one's pain. As such, it is initially less easy to deal with than the problem of a child who is born seemingly perfect but whose damage is internal, less visible. In the latter case, the stress and anxiety arise from the fact that the actual extent of the problem cannot be ascertained and the parents must be constantly at the mercy of the unpredictable future, watching, waiting, hoping.

Most of the meaningful research done in the period of initial reaction has been concerned with the feelings and responses of the mother. But it seems safe to generalize, perhaps to a lesser degree, the initial reaction will involve the father and siblings. They are being asked to accept an unwelcomed reality. The perfect child they anticipated is not forthcoming. Instead, they will be required to accept less than their ideal expectation. This realization brings with it deep sorrow and disappointment for the entire family.

This sorrow and disappointment often results in a period of self-pity. "This cannot be happening to us!" It is a time for crying out, for mourning the reality of the lost dream of having a healthy, normal child. Solnit and Stark (1961) have stressed the importance of this mourning period in the process of working through feelings related to the disabled child. They state:

> In the mother's mourning reaction to the loss of the healthy child, her wishes for and expectations of the desired child are crushed by the birth of the defective child. Her anxious fears of having a damaged child are realized. These disappointed, highly charged longings for the normal child may be recalled, intensely felt, and gradually discharged in order to reduce the impact of the loss of the expected loved child. This process, which requires time and repetition, can liberate the mother's feelings and interests for a more realistic adaptation.

This mourning process, brought on by the first realization of disability, is mainly concerned with tears, disappointment and disbelief. Parents often express these feelings in terms of their wishing the problem away, wondering about the child's true identity, or even more drastically, as expressed by Pearl Buck, wishing the child dead. It is also a time of questioning. *Why me?* A time for finding an explanation. *Is God punishing us?* A period for blaming oneself. *If we had only gone to that other doctor . . . If I had only not taken those pills . . .*

Some mothers feel a personal responsibility for the condition in which their child comes into the world. They blame themselves for not having been more careful during pregnancy. They wonder if it is something they have done or have not done. Thoughts and emotions such as these give rise to strong feelings of self-recrimination and condemnation. These affect children by reducing their self-concepts and feelings of personal worth. The individual's level of anxiety is also raised and strong feelings of guilt are created.

Parents who have children with disabilities also feel shame. Feelings of shame are more other-centered than feelings of guilt. Here, the concern is with the attitudes of others. "What will people think?" "What will people say?" The parents feel that friends and relatives will point the finger, ridicule and accuse them of wrongdoing. They, like most of us, may have vague and uncertain notions as to the causal factors regarding disabilities. Some may feel that they are related to sins of the fathers, ignorance, poverty, filth, that "These things don't happen to good, God-loving families."

"I'll never forget the pain I felt," related one parent, "When my mother-in-law gave me the 'I told you so treatment.' She was convinced that my child was born disabled because I had continued to go to parties during my pregnancy.

We all knew that she was grabbing at straws. Even after the doctor assured me that it had no relationship to my child's problem, it continued to bother me. The implication was still there. The fault was *mine.* I should have known better. *I* was being punished for *my* frivolity, for not heeding her advice. Since there will never be a way of knowing for sure, the idea still gnaws at me and hurts! I guess feelings aren't always based on logic."

When feelings of shame become ever powerful they often cause the person to feel not only unworthy, but sinful and disgusting. So strongly may they feel these things that they refuse to see anyone. Wives have been known to refuse to see their own husbands and children for days, even weeks. This is understandable, for shame reaches to the very core of our being and touches the deepest levels of our emotional lives. When people become parents they see their offspring as extensions of themselves. They hope that their children will become in some way a reflection of their *best* selves. They are ashamed when they are not. When all hope for their becoming so is seemingly taken from them, they will feel helpless, hopeless and ashamed. They find it difficult to deal with this cruel reality. They are often tempted to retreat from it.

Fear is another emotion common to parents of exceptional children. We are naturally fearful of what we do not understand. We have all had some experience with children. We have known children of friends or have related to them as a part of our immediate family. We have cuddled them, played with them, responded to them and known a sense of pleasure in their presence. Few of us, on the other hand, have experience with or understand disabled children. We know little of their problems and are embarrassed and suspicious of them. We are ill at ease in their company. Often our knowledge of disabled persons is limited to frightful images of the blind man, with glass-like eyes, staring blankly into space, sitting on the street corner selling pencils. We remember the retarded boy in our hometown (there inevitably seems to be one) who was always so pitiable, unkempt and whom everyone made fun of. We recall the lady with the braces on her legs who struggled so hard to get out of her car, while the many curious eyes, including our own, watched. We fear that this is what is in store for our child. Pity, pain, ridicule. We fear about our child's future and safety. We are afraid there will be no appropriate schools, no jobs. We are afraid of what our child will think and feel and whether we will be strong enough to cope with these special feelings and needs.

Fear is often depicted in cartoons as a group of dark clouds hanging menacingly over an isolated individual. Indeed, it has been depicted as such by many parents of disabled children. "I always seemed to be haunted by dark clouds of fear, which constantly interfered with any clear perception. These impenetrable clouds made decisions almost impossible for me, at the beginning. I just couldn't see through them."

Along with fear comes uncertainty. Uncertainty about the child, about the disability and its prognosis, about the doctor's abilities, about people's reactions to us and our child. Uncertainty about our function, our ability, our future and that of our child. We are also uncertain about what our children will think of us when they grow up. Will they accuse us? Hate us? This uncertainty, at the moment, seems overwhelming, intolerable.

It is not uncommon, then, that after the birth of the disabled child and the resultant onrush of devastating feelings for which one is ill-prepared, there usually follows a time of deep depression. This is sometimes described as a time of self-imposed exile, of physical and mental isolation. It is a time when one does not want to think, plan, feel or do anything. A time of escape, of apathy, of nothingness. It is a time similar to when physical pain becomes so unbearable that the person falls into unconsciousness, except in this case, the emotional pain becomes so acute and pervasive that the individual falls into a type of psychological unconsciousness. The mother goes through her hospital visits or home routines much like an automaton. The father goes off to work in a dream-like state. They know that they will have to face their pain and accept the challenge if they are to continue to function, but it is as if they know they must wait. There must be a period of retrenchment. Perhaps only tears, often seemingly senseless and inappropriate, flow of their own accord to prove that affect is still there and in time, one way or another, will surface.

There are other parents who will feign joy and well-being. They will want to prove to family and friends that they are strong and ready for whatever comes, that they love their child, regardless of the disability, and life for them will go on as usual. They will keep their pain and despair bottled up. Their tears will be private, allowed only in moments when they are alone. Their pain will be as intense, but they will keep it in check. "What's the use of tears?"

In actuality, they, too, are going through an affectless period of robot-like existence. Their feelings will have to be dealt with, too. They, like the first parents, are waiting, biding their time.

As human beings we have little choice. We can either face our problems and feelings, accept them and do something about them, or we can deny their existence and push them out of our consciousness. If we choose the latter, we repress these feelings and unconsciously create psychological patterns of defense to keep them in check. Often, we do this because, at the moment, it is the best way we have for coping with whatever pressures are upon us. There are many such mechanisms of defense against pain. We may rationalize and find good excuses for our actions, and our reactions. We may project our feelings by blaming others for our unhappiness and despair. We may seek out convenient scapegoats for these inadequacies. We may blame the doctor, our spouses or even God or society in general. We may sublimate these feelings of fear and inadequacy and overcompensate by striving to be the best parents ever.

These defense patterns are formed under great stress. In most cases, they represent a stopgap, not a permanent solution. As such, they will serve their purpose, but in the long haul, they will take their toll. Keeping emotions in check takes great energy. Playing an unreal role is not easy. Feigning well-being is often transparent and hollow. In most cases, at some time or other, the parents will be forced to face their true feelings regarding themselves, their family, the child who is disabled and the disability.

Defense mechanisms are not always bad. Most of us use them to some extent to maintain our everyday level of functioning. But it is the inordinate dependence upon such systems that will bring on added problems. When people cling tightly to established defense systems and show little or no sign of conflict and anxiety about them, it may be best to allow them this temporary adjustment, at least until they feel the need to deal with their more honest, inner feelings. In many cases it is the momentary respite and insight one gains through a defense mechanism which offers the way to finally enter the realm of emotion. In some manner or another, most mature adults will find a method of breaking through this often damaging system of defenses and deal with their true feelings and emotions.

This process of facing up to feelings and especially strong emotion is not an easy one. It will require strength, honesty, insight, intelligence, and sensibility. The price is high but the value is even greater. To do this, parents need to comprehend a few important facts.

★ The cruelly painful reality of being suddenly presented with a child who will be permanently disabled and the feelings of utter helplessness to change the physical problem are not easy things to accept. The feelings of fear, guilt, anxiety and pain which accompany this realization are *appropriate.* It would be rare human beings indeed who could, at once, with no question, accept their exceptional children.

★ The feelings of disbelief and shock are honest feelings, too. It is natural for parents to feel that they will give birth to a normal child. They will certainly be ill-prepared for the birth of a child who is impaired. Therefore, it is *normal* at first to question, to blame, to reject, even to hate themselves and their child.

★ To go through a time of self-pity and mourning is to be expected. All parents have a dream of a perfect child, a new life which will to some extent reflect their own but go beyond them. They have dreams of their child being the football hero or the belle of the ball. They have hopes that they will realize themselves, bring some new wonder to the world. These may be unconscious feelings, but they are known to be very human dynamics in the psychology of birth. They believe that these dreams have been permanently shattered. They pity the child. They pity themselves. They have a *right* to go through a time of mourning as they would mourn the death of a loved one—for to some extent, the reality of a disabled child is the death of a loved dream of the perfect child they hoped for. But tomorrow may also offer unexpected dreams; as beautiful as those which have been shattered.

★ Some self-recriminations and self-condemnations are normal. When things do not go as we would will them, we have been taught that it is mainly our fault. We are told to blame ourselves and no one else. To some extent, this is true and may be a sign of maturity, but it is wrong to condemn ourselves for things over which we obviously have no control. How can one blame oneself for retrolental fibroplasia, spina bifida, glaucoma, dwarfism, some severe forms of retardation, certain metabolic problems, brain damage, cerebral palsy, or muscular dystrophy? Strange, but even in cases where such *self-recrimination is mostly unrealistic,* parents still persecute themselves.

★ Intense feelings of guilt, shame and fear related to differences are very real indeed, as is the anguish they produce. Everyone, to some extent, knows these feelings, often experienced early in life and continued on, to some degree, throughout all periods of development. We want to be somewhat the same as others. We fear being labeled *oddballs* or *weird*. We know that obvious physical and mental differences are often seen as such. We feel the desire to hide these differences but are powerless to do so. We feel guilty about our inadequacy and inability to deal with differences. As behavior, this is *very understandable*.

★ It is normal to want to avoid pain. It is a *natural* response of human beings to protect themselves from sorrow and suffering. We will want to put it out of our mind, run from it or disguise it, anything to avoid knowing the agony of pain. It is natural that we will spend some time denying its existence, wishing it away, fantasizing its disappearance. We want to eradicate it from our experience so that we can again know joy. This is to be expected for it is pathology to cling to pain.

★ Parents will find that there will be inordinate demands made upon them for their time, their patience and their physical endurance. These demands will cause them great frustration and resentment. The nature of the child's helplessness and the special needs imposed by the disability will make them feel a sense of overwhelming responsibility.

★ They will often feel trapped and tied down. These feelings may build into resentments toward each other, their child and the disability that they will find disturbing but which they have a *realistic right to experience*.

★ Parents will feel helpless, stupid and confused at times in dealing with a disability but it must be understood that the disability they are dealing with is a new experience and like all new experiences will take time to become accustomed to. As with all new learning, they will be clumsy at first, awkward, and may perform inefficiently, but after many trials the tasks will become more simple and routine and be far less time and energy consuming. If parents feel at a loss at first, it is because in reality, they do not have the facts or experience, they do not know how to act appropriately and they should not be expected to do so. But this will come in time.

This is not a complete list of the special problems with which the parent of a child who is disabled must contend, but it is stated so that it may be realized that these are all appropriate feelings and responses and in no way abnormal. Disabilities are facts. They are real. Inability to meet all the demands they will incur is not an indication of being weak, inadequate or ignorant. It is rather an affirmation of being a human being like everyone else, not perfect.

Feelings and perceptions are often neither predictable nor logical and therefore not simple to deal with. In the beginning, most parents will need some help in trying to sort out their feelings, in determining what is real and what is hoped for or imagined. It is important to understand that information alone at this time cannot be the answer. It certainly will be a vital necessity and will clear up many misconceptions and confusions, but in itself, it can only be a beginning. Along with the intellectual content required for being a good parent of an exceptional child will be the need for an understanding of one's affective needs. Parents will need to study their feelings, fears, desires, anxieties. This does not mean a "six lessons to proficiency" type study, but will require them to "work at their feelings" over many years. It will be a long and arduous task. No two parents will be the same, deal with their feelings in a similar fashion or acquire the same insight. As previously noted, there will be no general rules or principles which will apply to all parents. Insights and help will only be appropriate as they apply to each individual person, for each is unique. It has been possible to generalize in this chapter only because the research indicates that the onset of a disability will bring about some of these conflicting feelings in most parents with enough consistency to warrant generalities.

It is a well-known psychological principle that what we feel, rather than what we know, will often have a greater effect upon ourselves and others. It becomes imperative, then, that we do not minimize the special feelings of parents who have disabled children for some degree of understanding and acceptance of these feelings must occur if the parent is to move on to more constructive and less self-defeating behavior.

This chapter was opened with a quote from *The Child Who Never Grew*. It seems appropriate to close with another statement from the same book in which Mrs. Buck describes her devastating struggle with this initial phase of despair; this period of inaction, yet action, numbness, yet overwhelming sensitivity, hopelessness, yet hope.

> The first phase of this process was disastrous and disorganizing. As I said, there was no more joy left in anything. All human relationships became meaningless. I took no more pleasure in the things I had enjoyed before; landscapes, flowers, music, were empty. Indeed, I could not bear to hear music at all. It was years before I could listen to music. Even after the learning process had gone very far, and my spirit had become nearly reconciled through understanding, I could not hear music. I did my work during this time: I saw that my house was neat and clean, I cut flowers for

the vases, I planned the gardens and tended my roses, and arranged for meals to be properly served. We had guests and I did my duty in the community. But none of it meant anything. My hands performed their routine. The hours when I really lived were when I was alone with my child. When I was safely alone I could let sorrow have its way, and in utter rebellion against fate my spirit spent its energy. Yet I tried to conceal my weeping from my child because she stared at me and laughed. It was this uncomprehending laughter which always and finally crushed my heart.

Chapter 7: The Rights Of The Family Of The Disabled

It is awesome and responsible to consider one's world as one's representation. Then I am responsible when the world gets mean and small, angry or guilty. I am not only my brother's keeper. I am my brother.

WILSON VAN DUSEN
Person to Person

Many families of the disabled, as a result of society's prejudices, feel themselves relegated to a minority status position with few or limited rights. These feelings are often reality based. They result mainly from their almost daily encounters with socially derogatory attitudes. They are expressed in patronizing inferences of friends and relatives, in the avoidance responses of strangers and often covertly implied in the attitudes and treatment given them by the very professionals who purport to be dedicated to the remediation of the physical and mental disabilities of their child. The professionals' impatience, condescension and skepticism toward them and their child, stated or imagined, and their insistence upon the relegating of their child into special categories and segregated schools and classes, seem to continually imply their inferior status.

Barker (1948) and Wright (1960), as well as others, have equated these prejudicial attitudes inflicted upon families of the disabled as similar in many respects to those imposed by society toward other minorities such as the poor and some ethnic and religious groups. These attitudes often covertly suggest that the family of the disabled should know its place, that to take such children into a public restaurant or impose them upon others is thoughtless, revolting and inconsiderate, that there must be something suspicious about a family with a disabled child.

"We'll never forget," one family related, "when we took our son, Tom, to a local restaurant for his birthday. He was ten. We were all dressed up in our Sunday best and were all set to have a real celebration! To say the least, Tom's palsy doesn't help to make dinner the neatest happening, but we've learned to live with it and it doesn't seem to matter anymore. What does matter is that he can eat by himself and that's a big thing. Aside from getting food all over his mouth and chin, and a little drooling, he does a pretty good job. Anyway, he was doing particularly well on this occasion and we were having a great time. Then, at one point, just during the main course, the people rose in the booth next to ours and stomped out. As the woman passed our table she looked directly at us and spat, 'DISGUSTING!' We heard her continue mumbling as she left, 'How do you expect decent people to eat with that sight going on?' When the cake finally came, the candles didn't seem so bright. Tom didn't care too much about blowing them out. That was his tenth birthday!"

A study done in 1956 by Cowin, Unterberg, and Verillo found an interesting correlation between attitudes toward the blind minority and those imposed upon other minority groups. In many respects both were treated in the same degrading manner and made to suffer the same indignities. The problem is further complicated for the family of the disabled since other minority groups can find reason for pride in their differences and uniqueness, as well as in their cultural and racial histories; the disabled person and the family can find little reason for pride or celebration for a disability.

It is not uncommon to find then that families of the disabled are often forced into making several adjustments to prejudicial attitudes. They may form a common bond of disability and retreat into themselves as much as possible. In so doing they endeavor to live with the impairment and do the best they can to protect the child and meet the child's needs within the family structure. On the other hand they may refuse to accept an inferior position and fight the society that imposes it. They may insist upon "things as usual," a family atmosphere as it was before the birth of the disabled child. Or, they may deny the impairment altogether. This may lead them to seek out numerous doctors until they encounter one who will give them the diagnostic label which best fits their fantasy or comes most close to *normal*. It is not uncommon, in this last adjustment, to find that a family has had as many as ten or more diagnostic workups made by at least as many doctors. No matter which of these solutions they choose, the family will have to suffer great pressure which can cause their feelings of internal honesty and family pride to depreciate and severely damage their family security and solidarity.

These adjustments to societal prejudices often result in the enhancement of their already present feelings of uncertainty, fear, avoidance and frustration. A type of vicious circle is thus created which can only be broken when the family understands that even as a minority it has some very basic rights, when it knows what its rights are and learns to exert them. Only then will they be able to progress beyond the almost devastating inferior status position to that of change agent, constructive actor and problem solver.

The basic rights of the family having a child with special needs might include, as a start, the following:

- ★ The right to sound medical knowledge regarding their child's physical or mental problem.
- ★ The right to some form of continual re-evaluation of their child at definite periodic intervals and a thorough, lucid explanation of the results of the findings.
- ★ The right to some helpful, relevant and specific information as to their role in meeting their child's special physical and emotional needs.
- ★ The right to some knowledge of the educational opportunities for a child such as theirs and what will be required for later admission to additional formal schooling.
- ★ The right to a knowledge of the community resources available for assistance in meeting the family needs, intellectual, emotional and financial.
- ★ The right to knowledge of the rehabilitation services in the community and the resources available through them.
- ★ The right to some hope, reassurance and human consideration as they meet the challenge of raising a child with special needs.
- ★ The right to some help in seeing their child's potentials instead of forever concentrating upon the imperfections.
- ★ The right to good reading material to help them acquire as much relevant information as possible.
- ★ The right to some interaction with other parents who have children with disabilities.
- ★ The right to actualize their personal rights as growing, unique individuals, apart from their children.

To most parents, a medical diagnosis is a mysterious thing about which they know little or nothing. Such terms as spina bifida, glaucoma, osteomyelitis, paraplegia, cerebral palsy are, to many parents, meaningless. Labeling a condition, as most professionals know, does little to describe a problem except in a most global way. It does even less for the parents. Stratton (1957) illustrated this with patients who had been hospitalized with tuberculosis. He found that they had little or no understanding of such common terms related to their condition as germ, lesion, function or sputum.

Terminology is often a major deterrent to communication. Even if parents understand the term, they are likely to believe that this term can be generalized to all who carry the label. They may, therefore, expect a common ability, response and reaction from the entire group. The result can lead to such misconceptions as—"all blind persons are totally dependent," "all deaf individuals will also be academically retarded."

The main purpose of knowledge is for behavior change. It is often the case that a professional will feel the need to impress the parents, perhaps unconsciously, with long, complicated verbiage and meaningless labels. Parents have a right to an explanation that is as concrete and appropriate to their understanding and experiences as possible. Care must be taken to use common, everyday illustrations and words which relate clearly to these personal experiences so it becomes behaviorally relevant.

It cannot be assumed that more educated, intelligent parents have a greater understanding of professional jargon than the less educated. In fact, it is possible that such parents could be more reluctant to question the meaning of a term, assuming that they should know it and thus feel that it would be demeaning to admit that they do not.

It is equally important that the parents not be talked down to. Parents are not stupid; they are, in this case, simply not informed. They will be most eager to learn technical terms and concepts for this will make them feel more a part of the situation. But these must be explained. The important factor is that *precise* language be used which will communicate best what is intended. Barker and his associates have suggested that so important is communication to patients' welfare, that professionals should be specifically *trained* in the precise use of language, language that will meet, directly, the comprehension and the emotional needs and levels of the individuals with whom they are working.

Equally important to the welfare of the parents, and to which they have a right, is information about the future. It is clear that professionals are not magicians. They can never be certain of the child's prognosis. Since the prognosis in each disability varies according to so many individual, physical and emotional factors, it is especially impossible to predict with any real degree of accuracy what the future holds. How often have persons, about whom a prediction is made based upon their present functioning, shown what their determination and the miracles of a dedicated rehabilitation team could perform? How often have we heard that Joe, for instance, would never walk again, or that

Mary would not be able to learn beyond the first grade level, only to discover that Joe is now walking and that Mary is working at the sixth grade level and looking forward to graduation? Still, this presents one of the major concerns of parents who, in most cases, want to know precisely what to expect regarding their child's future. This is a normal apprehension, and, as such, it must be dealt with. Most parents will understand if they are told that specific predictions are impossible. If they are educated as to differences which occur with growth and development and regarding each individual's responses to these physiological conditions, then they may understand the unpredictability of a specific prognosis. Much of their anxiety will, in this manner, be alleviated. They can be given authoritative information concerning the nature of the condition as it presently exists and some idea about the course of the planned treatment. Especially, they can be instructed *specifically* as to *their* role in the process.

It is well to let the parents know that through routine periodic checkups they will be alerted to any changes which may require treatment or prognostic adjustments. This will assure the parents that they will, as things change, be given new knowledge and guidance along the way. It is unwise, except in most unique situations, to withhold information. The child is mostly the responsibility of the parents, not the doctor, psychologist or educator. Thus, they must have the facts.

It is important, too, that professionals demonstrate to the parents, by their concern, that their child is in the hands of a competent specialist who is equally interested in their child's welfare. This releases parents from an already overtaxed sense of responsibility. Professionals will do well to constantly reassure parents that they are there to help. This assurance presupposes that though the parents are the key to their child's rehabilitation, the professionals are ready and caring helpers in the process.

Diagnosis too often takes the form of what is *wrong* with the child, what the *problems* are, with what they *cannot* do. This is so often the stress of medical and educational diagnosis that parents often return home with a limited, negative, pessimistic view of their child. It is equally necessary for the professional to emphasize the child's assets as well as liabilities. It is well to show what the child *can do,* or comment on those aspects that are functioning especially well. One parent mentioned that it was only when her paraplegic child had been called *beautiful* by her doctor that she had actually looked beyond the child's legs.

Indeed, her child was a pretty youngster!

If adjunctive rehabilitative personnel are to be used in treating the child, it will be necessary to explain what the specific functions of these professionals will be in the total helping situation. There are many persons who because of limited contact will not know the specific duties of the occupational therapist, the physical therapist, the psychologist, the speech and language therapist, the special educator, and many others who may form a rehabilitation team. So, the parents have a right to sound and thorough medical knowledge of their child's disability.

Parents also have the right to some meaningful and concrete information as to their role in meeting their child's special needs. So often the information given parents about the specific physical needs of their child and how they can meet these needs is so inadequate as to leave them feeling confused, frustrated and empty. In a most beautifully written book by Clara Clarborne Park called *The Siege* (1972), the author recounts the trials, tribulations, joys, and wonder of raising an autistic child. One of the matters of greatest frustration for Doctor and Mrs. Park was the lack of relevant information given them by professionals. Mrs. Park describes the many trips to offices of doctors and psychiatrists for what seemed like endless diagnostic workups. But no matter where she went, the information given her was always vague, often meaningless, always aggravating. In her own words, after hours and days of evaluations: "This is what they had to say about Elly. It is not a summary of what they said. It is *all* they said, although the psychiatrist, a hesitant, rather inarticulate elderly man, took more time to say it than it takes to write it here:

★ Elly needed psychotherapy.
★ She had performed above her age level on the part of the I.Q. test she could do, and it was their belief she had no mental deficiency.
★ She had many fears.

That is what they made of all that information," she continues, "we wanted information and techniques." She personalizes, "I need references. I need to find out about play therapy. I need to know all about children like Elly, because whoever else may or may not work with her, her main psychotherapist is me."

It is shocking to note how many parents come away from

conferences with no more additional information regarding their child than they had when they entered. If there is any new knowledge related, parents are seldom given the slightest notion of the practicality of such knowledge in terms of their complex and confusing role of caring for their child. Parents will make willing and able teachers if they are given the proper information and know-how. Not to use parents in the actual treatment of their child is to lose the most valuable resource. Who spends more time with, or cares more about the child? Parents might as well be taught the correct way of helping their child, for they will be doing something anyway and it might as well be the correct something!

Another very real concern of parents relates to available schooling for their child. Most parents are only vaguely aware that there are programs in their own communities for rehabilitation and education for the disabled.

A dramatic case in point was a family who had kept their blind child hidden for nine years, taking him outside only late at night, because they were fearful and under the misconception that all blind children had to be sent to state schools for the blind. They felt strongly that they did not want to part with their child, that they could take better care of him at home. They were surprised and relieved upon hearing that there were programs for the education of the blind in their own tax-supported public schools!

Almost all states in the United States have mandated programs for the education of exceptional children. These are often of high quality and standards, and staffed by competent, especially credentialed personnel. Many programs are now being organized for preschool children with disabilities. There are many parents who are not aware of these services.

This lack of information may also apply to local special agencies which specialize in specific disabling conditions such as Spastic Children's Foundations, The Kennedy Foundations, The Alexander Graham Bell Foundation, or the Braille Institute, as well as numerous mental health foundations. Many of these special community facilities, such as the John Tracy Clinic for the Deaf, offer much needed training for parents of preschool children.

There are also state and federal agencies such as the U.S. Office of Health, Education, and Welfare and the State Department of Rehabilitation which offer counseling, guidance, education, and even financial aid to parents and children who request it and qualify. (This will be more fully discussed later.) Parents have a right to know that there are such resources available to them.

Parents have a right to some form of reassurance and human consideration along the way. It is well-known that all individuals work best with good, positive reinforcement. So often the endless time adjustments and energies required of the family go unnoticed and are assumed by others to be the normal responsibility and function of the family.

In *The Siege*, Mrs. Park writes:

> We wanted sympathy—not the sloppy kind; we were grownup adults—but some evidence of fellow feeling which ordinary doctors give readily enough. And it was so unreasonable—we wanted a little reassurance, a little recognition, a little praise. It never occurred to us that these expectations were naive, that the gulf between parent and ministering institutions must deliberately be kept unbridgeable by any of the ordinary techniques of interpersonal relationships.

Certainly, it is not unreasonable that the family should be given this emotional support. The challenge of raising a disabled child is not all gloom, but it can be a difficult and special challenge.

In addition the family has a right to accessibility of information. There is a vast and in many cases excellent library available in the field of exceptionality. There are superb books on blindness, deafness, cerebral palsy, chronic medical problems and other disabilities. These books will often fill the emotional and intellectual gaps which professionals either intentionally or nonintentionally allow to occur between themselves, the disabled child and the family. (See the Bibliography in the appendix.)

The family has a right to interaction with other families who have children with disabilities, not to create a common bond in disability but to assure them that their problems are not unique and are shared by many. In this sharing, they may also learn of new ideas, new techniques, new procedures for being more efficient parents. They will be able to share, too, in emotional understanding and growth.

During the period when I was directing a program for exceptional children in a large California school district, I decided to inaugurate a program of parent education. We arranged six consecutive Tuesday seminars at the local college, and invited all the parents of disabled children in the community to enroll. Six hundred parents attended!

During the six sessions they were bombarded with the wisdom of neurologists, psychologists, psychiatrists, teachers, and every mentionable related discipline. They were blasted with lectures, movies, and slide demonstrations. Actual cases were brought in for illustrative purposes.

When the last seminar ended each parent was asked to evaluate the total program. One of the evaluation questions was "What *one* thing did you find *most valuable* in this experience?" I was certain it would be one of my unique pearls of wisdom, or that of one of my illustrious colleagues. Much to my surprise, over 85 percent of the responses suggested that the most valuable experience was learning that there were so many other parents who had children who were disabled like their own!

I am wiser for the experience, too!

Lastly, but perhaps most important of all, is the right a family has to know what its individual rights are. They must understand that the birth of a disabled child does not take from them their rights as people. They still have the right for recreation, for time alone, for time with each other, for time to read, paint, write poetry, visit with friends or what they will. It must not take away their right to complain, to bewail, to bemoan, or to cry. In other words, they still have a right to be the human being that they were before the child was born and to become the human being toward which they aspire.

There are those who will say that this final right is easier said than demanded. But *demanded* it must be! If there is no baby sitter available for mother then the other family members, father, brother, sister, must act as sitter while mother goes to art class or father goes golfing or daughter goes to the movies or son goes to his scout meeting. Things can be worked out if they are shared. If the mother assumes the total responsibility, she will find she has only two arms and legs and one body to handle the situation. If she can relinquish her uniquely assumed role of "responsibility for all family members" she will find that she has four arms or six arms or eight arms—certainly much more efficient than two! Things may not be done, of course, *exactly* as she would have it, but it will be done, and the important thing is that it will free her, and each family member, to individually continue growing as persons.

As has been indicated throughout this book so far, and will continue to be in future chapters, this is the singularly most vital realization: We will bring to our child only what we have. If we want to bring the best, we will have to be the best. That comes only when we assume the lifetime responsibility of growing to realize and actualize the unique, wondrous individuals that we are.

Families of the disabled have rights, too. Everyone would benefit greatly if each family member and each professional involved would honor and respect these rights.

Chapter 8: The Family As Counselor

Be proud of your child, accept him as he is and do not heed the words and stares of those who do not know better. The child has a meaning for you and for all children. You will find a joy you cannot now suspect in fulfilling his life for and with him. Lift up your head and go your appointed way.

PEARL S. BUCK
The Child That Never Grew

No matter how many professionals will work with persons who are disabled during their lifetimes, there will be none who will have a more poignant, influential, lasting and significant effect upon them than that of the family. The family members will be in constant contact with the individual. They will teach the child the mores and folkways of the culture and they will stipulate the rules for the game of life. They will, in a very real sense, guide the child in the struggle to be human. Their attitudes toward the child as a person will have great authority over the child's personal attitudes. Their feelings about the impairment will affect the child's feelings toward it. For better or for worse, the first and most influential counselor will always be the family.

If it were possible from the start for all family members to see the child who is disabled simply as another child in the family, there would be no reason for a book such as this at all. But the pressure of the many additional physical, social and psychological demands put upon each person in the family, due to the disability, is often so devastating as to make this immediate acceptance an almost impossible task. After all, it is a fact that the child with the disability brought the problem to the family, and it is, therefore, normal that the family should feel some resentment toward the impairment. But, it is also true that the child with a disability is simply another member of the family, and a child first. In the beginning it may be difficult to separate the child from the impairment, but if this distinction is not made, the resentment the family feels for the impairment may unconsciously become a rejection of the child. When this occurs, there can be no effective family counseling.

The family will find, most readily, that there are no formulas, no "how-to's," no special or right ways to achieve this subtle distinction. They will find it only by living through the day-by-day routines into new learning, self-discovery and insight. This will often be a slow, plodding process. Emotional strength, wisdom and flexibility come about gradually. *If their guide is always the well-being of the total family, not solely that of the special child, and if they are able to see, love and enjoy the child behind the disability, they may trust that their continual growth will lead them, and the child, eventually, into acceptance.* It is at this point where true counseling begins!

To be effective in counseling, there will be no special talents or qualities required of a healthy family with an exceptional child. They will simply be required to have a bit more patience, strength, persistence, knowledge and awareness. Their function will be that of any family. Their guidance goals will be essentially the same. Whatever unique knowledge, sensitivity and awareness is necessary will be directed toward any special problems dealing with disability-related aspects such as dependence and independence, unique feelings, special care requirements, motivation, grievances and gratifications, discipline and social attitudes leading to acceptance or rejection.

It is obvious, then, that to counsel creatively, as a family, regarding the many special problems that can arise for the disabled person will require that all family members bring to the total family their most outstanding abilities, their keenest knowledge, their greatest sensitivity. This implies that each person in the family must have equal and full standing as a contributing member of the family counseling team. Dealing with problems is always most effective when the process is made a total family function. Because of the intensity and particular nature of the many special problems, this becomes singularly true in the family of a person who is disabled.

DEALING WITH FEELINGS

The addition to the family of a disabled person will create many unique feelings for all the family members. Since there are no *right* feelings which *must* or *should* be felt in any situation, these feelings will be mostly individual and often unpredictable.

Clara Clarborne Park (1967), from whom I have quoted earlier, relates her confusion when told by several professionals how she *should* be feeling about her autistic child. She and her family, being sensitive, well-integrated and intelligent human beings, had their own feelings about the child, Elly. They felt neither guilt, shame, nor despair, feelings she was continually told they should feel. Rather, their feelings were mostly those of frustration, uncertainty, and inadequacy, because of a desperate need for information and professional guidance.

Each family member will have individual responses regarding the exceptional individual and the impairment according to how well integrated they each are as persons. No matter what the reaction, it is important that it be openly revealed and discussed. There is nothing shameful on the part of any family members who admit that the disability creates, for them, feelings of inadequacy, fear, or uncertainty. In the beginning, some family members may perceive these feelings as signs of personal weakness. They may find them too painful and not be willing to deal with them. Some will attempt to dismiss them altogether and treat them as if they were not there. Regretfully, they will soon find that strong feelings such as these are not easily ignored. Their feelings are real, and as such will result in responses and reactions whether they wish it or not. Any effort toward rejecting or dismissing them can create deeper and more disruptive feelings which may bring about negative responses and destructive behavior.

A vital aspect of the role of family as counselor will be in dealing openly with feelings. This is not always easy but it is often the case that, in so doing, family members may find that what they are feeling is not so evil or unique, but is also shared with others in the family. This knowledge can serve to alleviate much fear and guilt. It can serve to open the way to a more normal, refreshing and honest family interchange and bring about more constructive action. It will often unite the family and offer each the security which comes from group support. Group effort will offer more meaningful behavioral alternatives to those in the family who may have become trapped in a self-created, isolated, emotional dead end.

An honest look occasionally at what one really feels is always helpful. But this may only be done in a permissive, accepting atmosphere or it can be very damaging. I was told of a family who had inaugurated a special "sharing time" to help their exceptional child. During this period family members were asked to talk honestly regarding how they felt about their retarded brother. The youngest child said that he hated him because he took all of his parents' time and because the neighbor kids laughed at him and called him stupid. He was reprimanded by the other family members and told that it was wrong to hate his little brother, that his retardation was not his fault and that it was shameful not to love him! An interchange like this one is obviously not conducive to growth and may be extremely destructive.

Another family had a different approach to revealing their feelings. They never left the dinner table without sharing new things they had learned about each other that day. Not only did this afford them the opportunity to become observant of change, but it also gave each the opportunity to become more aware of the behavior of each family member, not solely that of the disabled child. One of the children after relating something about each person in the family said about his deaf sister, "She can eat an egg!" Certainly a positive start.

Feelings cannot be shared on command; they can only be freely related. There will be some persons in the family who will be less ready at different times to talk about what they are feeling. This lack of desire to relate must be respected. If the opportunity to share is always present, individuals will know when and to what extent they are ready.

If an opportunity for open, honest communication has never before been afforded the family, it is natural that the practice will appear awkward at first and may even seem foolish. But it will be found that the natural, honest flow of feelings in an accepting, creative atmosphere can be most stimulating, refreshing and even fun. It often affords the platform upon which the family as counselor may enact its most essential dramas.

DEALING WITH INORDINATE PHYSICAL DEMANDS

The disabled person will bring new demands to the family that will take their toll in time and expenditure of physical energy. Most families, especially mothers, find this a very real problem. The mother is forever having to bathe the child, conduct exercises, visit doctors for occupational and physical therapy or prepare special diets. That she should feel overwhelmed by these requirements is easy to understand. But, bringing up children, in all aspects, is a family role not uniquely that of the mother. Though, in the beginning, it may seem primarily the mother's responsibility, this belief must gradually be extinguished. All family members are responsible for *each* family member. The importance of this cannot be overstressed for if this is not the case the resultant family problems can be numerous. Husbands may begin to perceive themselves rejected and alone. The children may feel ignored and unloved. Mothers may unconsciously become so engrossed in their new role and responsibility as to lose touch with all of their feelings.

No matter what else she is, a mother is first and foremost a *woman*, and only secondly, a wife and mother. So much of how her family and her exceptional child adjust will depend on her continual personal growth, and the security and support which come to her through her relationship with her husband and children.

The status of a marital relationship is most significantly correlated with family adjustment to disability. An already poor relationship is responsible for more grief, pain and maladjustment than any of the problems created by the disability. The appearance on the scene of a child with a special impairment serves only to aggravate a tenuous situation. It makes it easier to ignore the real causes for the marital maladjustment. It offers each parent new rationalizations for the failure of the marriage and new ways to escape finding creative solutions. Often, the husband assumes the role of the unloved, neglected one. He now has good reason to retreat into himself, his work, or into extramarital activities. After all, his wife doesn't care about him anymore.

The wife, sensing herself alone and with the major responsibility for bringing up baby, often takes refuge in forming an unnatural, mutually dependent role with her disabled child. This frequently leads to an unconscious, dangerous holding back of the child, for she feels that her meaning as a woman and mother can now only be fulfilled through the child's continual dependence. In some cases, this evolves into a deep sense of martyrdom, her having given up even her marriage to do the best for her child. There are many variations upon this theme, but essentially the child and the disability are used as excuses for further unsatisfactory adjustments in an already disintegrating marital situation.

An inordinate amount of demands upon any family member may bring about resentment. The tragedy is that this resentment will have a powerful effect upon the special child. Fathers, brothers and sisters must become a part of the helping process. Often it is enough for the mother to express an honest need for help, for the family to respond. If a balance of responsibility is created from the start, the unified effort will profit each member in turn.

DEALING WITH DEPENDENCE AND INDEPENDENCE

It will always be difficult to ascertain the amount of independence required by persons with a disability. Each person will vacillate between dependence and independence. This is especially true since there can be no specific developmental guidelines for exceptional children. This will mean that families will have to be especially alert to conflicts the special children may be having in the area of these vital opposing tendencies. They will have to be alert to what the children can do for themselves, when to demand that they do for themselves, or when it will be necessary to do for them.

A good example may be taken from the area of feeding. Many parents feel that it is much easier to continue to feed children who are disabled than to deal with the subsequent mess. This deprives children of a most vital stimulus, the experience of doing for themselves in using utensils and knowing the pride in the independence they feel from this activity. These same parents are often those who bemoan the fact that their children are too dependent upon them.

Children begin to feel the need for some separation from others as early as the first year of life. If this opportunity for separation and independence is afforded, a sense of emergent personal identity will result. It is this sensed identity to which the family must become attuned, for upon this will depend the child's future emotional and intellectual well-being and independence. This self-identity will be, eventually, responsible for children trusting their own personal experience, asking questions, deciding upon their own limitations and forming their own concept and perceptions of the world.

The family's role becomes one of encouraging emerging individuality for special children, permitting them to make their own choices, to exert and express themselves. In order to do this, the family will have to rid themselves of their preconceived notions of the child's dependence, limited abilities, and inferior family status and allow the child to reveal his or her own needs and abilities.

DEALING WITH MOTIVATION

Probably the most often used word directed toward an impairedindividual is *can't*. As long as we are not locked into the concept of a *normal* way of doing things, the word has no place in the thoughts or vocabulary of the family of an exceptional child. The only real limitations the children have are those which are imposed upon themselves. As such, limitations are created by the family and society more than by the disability.

A well-known Vietnam veteran with no legs, only one arm and one eye, runs his own ranch, rides horses, tends animals and makes his own livelihood. He made the decision to do what he wanted, not what others told him he could do. But, in *his* way.

If impaired individuals are told they are limited, it is often easier for them to accept, believe, and behave as if this were reality, rather than to try to prove otherwise. Each person will have to learn if and when they can do for themselves. When one does not have all the physical or mental facilities this is not always an easy task. It will require time, persistence and determination. The physical therapist, the occupational therapist, teachers, psychologists and parents may help along the way, but in the long run, individuals will have to make the decision to discover for themselves what their real limitations are.

Pushing and nagging are negative forces to motivation. One cannot be forced to perform, forced to learn or forced to enjoy. One can only be encouraged, respected, and reinforced.

There will be times when realistic needs for help will present themselves and the family will have to assume the initiative and motivate in special ways. For instance, they may have to insist that the disabled person exercise properly, or follow prescribed therapies, even if the individual does not desire to do so. But even this can be done with loving concern. They can empathize with and understand the child's pain, but be firm in that it must be done. It was this caring but firm and persistent attitude on the part of Anne Sullivan which changed Helen Keller, both blind and deaf from infancy, from what she called a "no thing in a no world," to a contributing member of society. To find the balance between ineffective nagging and effective motivation will be a challenge to the family. The best motivation is always intrinsic.

DEALING WITH GRIEVANCES AND GRATIFICATIONS

Any impairment, no matter how minor, will create understandable grievances in the family. If the impairment is severe, obvious, and irreparable, the grief it will create can be great.

All too often, families do not, or cannot, seem to rise above the grievance. The disability looms up so strongly before them that it overshadows all other aspects of life. So obscured will be their perception that they may fail to observe when the individual's growth has brought about changes both in physique and personality. They may fail to sense that the child is maturing and in doing so, the physiological and psychological self are creating new possibilities, within and without. They become blind to new signs of motivation, new attitudes, new abilities.

An immersion in grief can also cause the family to neglect obvious sources of gratification. They ignore the many wonderful things children *can* do. True, they are unable to walk but they are able to talk, to smile, to joke, to use their hands, to propel themselves about with their arms and torso. A disability does not generalize to all situations. The child may be a failure in the fifty-yard dash, may be confined to a wheel chair, *but* he can win on the debate team or paint a beautiful picture or write a moving poem. Even though the child may have an impairment, it is not a *total* impairment.

At the beginning there may seem to be more grievances than gratifications, but it helps to be aware of the fact that even at the most difficult times the child can cry as loudly as any child, complain as bitterly, hurt as deeply. At the same time, the child can laugh as loudly, feel as lovingly, and give as completely as any other child. It is with this realization that acceptance as a total person can begin.

DEALING WITH BEHAVIOR AND DISCIPLINE

Another most difficult area with which the family will have to deal is that of the behavior and the proper methods of disciplining their exceptional child. This will demand no more understanding of the practical principles of child guidance than for any other child in the family. It will involve dealing with such issues as toilet training, eating habits, sleeping schedules, bed wetting, temper tantrums, sibling relations, sex education and training, developing growing pains, just as with all children. The difference lies only with the limitations imposed by the child's disability. Most parents of exceptional children will relate how difficult it is to discipline their blind child, for example, or scold their crippled child or reprimand their deaf child. Yet these children require the same learning and guidelines to adjustment as all children.

Siblings of impaired children will often tell of the unfair treatment given them as opposed to their disabled sister or brother. "They get to do all kinds of things and get away with murder. Whatever happens, we get blamed for it because we ought to know better." It is no wonder that sibling rivalry runs high in such homes. It becomes very difficult to love and accept someone who is always indirectly responsible for your pain and unhappiness.

The exceptional child needs limits, too. Though it may seem difficult to say "no," or to be decisive with these children, they need to learn that things are expected from them as they are from all family members. Permissiveness is a growth-producing phenomenon, but in extremes, it can create a permanent sense of confusion and disorientation in children. There will be times when they will need free run, but there will be other times when they will just as surely need to be curbed. The family rules which apply to all must also apply, when feasible, to the child with a disability. Emotional security comes from feeling a part of a group, through their mutual love, respect, interest and empathy. It also comes about through having the same rights and limits. Sufficient rights, so that they can grow in the freedom which will allow them to make their own choices, develop their own values and standards, and set their own goals; sufficient limits to help them to feel secure, gain some inner consistency and some knowledge that there are those who care about their well-being.

Discipline is not the process of shaping and molding children into what the family feels they should be (which in most cases is a carbon copy of them) but rather of helping them to become uniquely what they are. Much of the burden for accomplishing this task will actually fall to the individual. But the family may help, by being a guide and by each member's assuming the responsibility for his or her own self-actualization and, in this way, becoming models.

It is a fine line as to when and where families should permit or disallow. The key lies in remembering that the child is an individual and as such should be allowed to experience success as well as failure, joy as well as despair, accomplishment as well as frustration. The child cannot be protected from life nor can the family live life for any of its members. Its main function is to love them on to *themselves.*

DEALING WITH ACCEPTANCE AND REJECTION

As previously mentioned, the basic goal of counseling exceptional children and adults is eventual acceptance of all persons with all of their strengths and abilities but it also implies an acceptance of this person with all limitations. The acceptance of limitations, in this sense, does not mean to suggest a process of looking for compensations for limitations, or the process of rationalizing the supposed advantages of having them, or even worse, the implications of resignation to a sad fate, but rather recognizing that there will be limitations and that these limitations are acceptable.

This acceptance, like so many other things, begins at home. It will require that children with disabilities experience their own strengths and weaknesses, test their reality and set their limitations. They will have to experience their powerlessness, inadequacies and pain. Since children cannot totally comprehend the permanence of their disability or even the extent of it, they will often make their own ways through or around them to accomplish what they are truly motivated to do. Only they can determine what is impossible for them. Only they can finally accept the realities of what and who they are. It is often difficult for loving families to watch this, for at times it can be a very painful process, but any inordinate interference with the child's search may create unreal obstacles to acceptance.

The family can help in this process of positive acceptance by allowing and encouraging exceptional persons to work through some of the dynamic aspects of accepting reality limitations without debasing them as total persons. The family can, in many creative ways, help the children to discover and utilize their assets and abilities. They can convince them that it is not what they do *not* have that is important but the total utilization of what they *do* have. The children can be helped to see that their world is vast and varied, and goes beyond the family and the disability. They can be shown that there is a place and a need for everyone and there are many ways of getting there. They must learn firsthand that even with differences the same goals can sometimes be achieved.

If the individual's physique is severely damaged, the family's stress upon the worth of other human qualities such as sound personality traits will be of help. The social value of such non-physical traits as empathy, tenderness, understanding, kindness, and love can be reinforced. This will offer personality assets which may counterbalance the physical liabilities. We have all seen this effect in reality. One teenager who had volunteered to work with crippled children expressed this honestly when he said, "When I first saw the kids it really turned me off. I didn't think they were of much worth. They were in braces and drooling and all that! Then, I got into them. Their love, their joy, their happiness, really got to me. I forgot their appearance. When I left I only thought about them as beautiful kids!" When the beauty of the inner person emerges, one usually finds that the physical appearance becomes secondary.

Arthur Pinero, the fine English playwright, deals with this phenomenon in a lovely play, *The Enchanted Cottage.* He relates the story of a young man, severely disfigured in the war, who is put off by his wealthy family in a small country cottage so that he may escape the painful social contacts the city would inflict upon him. In order that he feel less stigmatized, they hire for him the singularly most unattractive housekeeper they can find. The close human understanding and interaction between the two soon create a very beautiful love relationship. Pinero illustrates this by erasing their disabilities for the second act and making the young housekeeper devastatingly beautiful and the boy equally handsome. As long as they love each other, they perceive one another in this idyllic manner. Tragedy strikes when they are visited by his parents who still see them both as hopeless, ugly and repulsive, and thus cause them again to perceive each other in this devastating, all but destructive, manner.

True acceptance comes when we stop generalizing the effects of disabilities and realize that disabilities are not *all* of the person, that all aspects of their lives will not be influenced by them and that they are more than the sum total of any of their parts. Acceptance comes with a realistic evaluation of the disability and the values which seem lost due to it. Acceptance also arises with the knowledge that there are vast areas of the self which are still very much intact, accessible and waiting to be utilized. These truths are always better experienced in action than formally taught.

The family, then, is the disabled person's major, day-to-day, counselor. Family members will best fulfill their vital role if they will remember the following:

★ Family feeling regarding each member will vary and can have a monumental effect upon the entire family. If these feelings are internalized they can lead to guilt, anxiety and impotence. On the other hand, if some kind of forum is created in the home for expressing feelings without fear of censure or rejection, it can result in new, creative relationships and more positive solutions for all.

★ Developing a well-integrated and functioning family is not exclusively the responsibility of any one person but the duty of each family member.

★ Maturity and independence for each person in the family will occur only if each is allowed to seek and discover his or her own person while being assured of the continual love and support of the entire family, no matter where the search may lead.

★ The family should strive to create the type of atmosphere where the only obstacles for growth are self-imposed and where the resultant joy and pain, success or failure, hope or despair can be shared with equal acceptance.

★ To grieve temporarily for something of value which is lost is a normal human response. To grieve forever for something which cannot be regained is emotional illness and can prevent the family from experiencing the many gratifications which living life in the "now" can afford.

★ To live together in peace, joy and love, each person in the family will need to have a mutual feeling of respect and regard. This recognition of others will require some limitations, some discipline, some giving and some taking, for the benefit of all. The rewards lay in a feeling of security, group support and a more vast repertoire of behavioral alternatives.

★ Acceptance of other family members is achieved only through allowing them the dignity of personal strengths and limitations, always recognizing the limitless potentials, not for being what we desire them to be, but for their being what they are.

Chapter 9: The Parents Speak

Among a hundred mirrors before yourself false . . . strangled in your own noose SELF knower! Self executioner! crammed between two nothings a question mark....

NIETZSCHE

BETTY LOU KRATOVILLE needs no introduction to anyone in special education. Her books, articles and active participation in the field of learning disabilities are well known, but there are those who do not know that she is also a parent of a disabled child. Her story is, perhaps, like many others; but her talent for communicating her mind, her heart, her deepest feelings, and her knowledge is more rare. As a close friend and coworker, I could not conceive of writing this book without requesting that she share her feelings and her story with all, as she has with me. We cannot help but be richer for it!

What parents feel

A chapter on the feelings of parents can, of course, be written only by a parent—hopefully, by one whose experiences are not only personal but whose life has been touched and enriched by many other parents and, it should be carefully noted, by a number of incomparable professionals as well.

Although the story of my son, Matthew, has been chronicled before, until the assignment for this chapter was tendered and accepted, I had never thought of it nor written of it purely in context of the counseling which we received over a period of years. In order to meet Dr. Buscaglia's charge that a contribution from a parent be one of *feeling*, and in order to live with an inner conviction that the target audience for this book deserved and would welcome relevance, it became necessary to search for attitudes long forgotten, for judgments long dismissed, for projections happily unfulfilled.

As a parent, my attitude toward all the professional men and women to whom I went in search of diagnosis and remediation for Matthew was one of absolute humility. In retrospect, my reverence may have, at times, been misplaced. I neglected to remember that counselors are, first and foremost, human beings. That they, too, laugh and cry and make mistakes and that they are not, really, larger than life. At the time they somehow seemed invincible, ten feet tall, with desks the size of battleships, their offices guarded by iron-spined sentinels who seemed always to be popping in with terse announcements, "Your next appointment is waiting." I, lily-livered and abject, would slink from the office, reeling under the impact of cool professionalism and a hundred unanswered questions.

Our first counseling session came when Matthew was two years old. We had spent several mornings with the counselor (social worker) who, bulwarked by an awesome stack of forms, had asked hundreds of questions about our family. Later we returned with Matthew for a 40-minute session in which he was tested and observed by the social worker, a clinical psychologist, and a psychiatrist. He performed typically—which means that he performed not at all well. He would not sit still and attend to tasks. He wiggled; he squirmed; he ran from wall to window to door to wall; he howled with frustration. We were then returned to the social worker's office and the verdict was delivered: immediate and permanent institutionalization. No preliminary, softening remarks cushioned this staggering blow. No alternatives were offered. *"Send him away. Now. Here is a list of private and state institutions."* The weeks that followed were so full of horror that they are difficult to recollect. The list was duly investigated—the facilities found to be so distressing that the decision was made to keep Matthew at home despite the constant care and attention that he required.

Several years later, when Matthew had begun to respond gloriously to various, intensive kinds of therapy, I found myself once again in a counseling situation. Matthew's visual function was obviously poor, and I made an appointment with a local ophthalmologist who had a reputation for treating "these kinds of children." We waited for hours, then Matthew responded with reasonable grace to charts and drops, and finally Dr. X and I confronted one another across the usual king-sized desk. She was very patient as I glowingly described Matthew's progress in recent months—his improved attention span, his decreased hyperactivity, his recently acquired skills of swimming and two-wheeled bicycle balance, his now quite fathomable speech. His functional vision, however, seemed to be markedly inadequate. What would she recommend? Her totally staggering reply: "Why don't you find a good residential school for this child?" I returned Matthew to nursery school and sobbed on the comforting shoulder of its director, "My God, isn't there anyone who will let me keep my child at home?"

Matthew "failed" public school kindergarten. Based on the years and the successes that have followed, it is now agreed that the fault was not his—but that is hindsight. At the end of his kindergarten year, I was counseled by the school principal: "There is an opening in one of the classes for the educable mentally retarded. We feel this would be a suitable fall placement." Perhaps this was progress. At least she was not suggesting that he be sent away. The offer was declined without thanks, and Matthew was accepted by a small church school with the provision that he be given extra tutoring in reading and math.

Six weeks later I was asked to withdraw him from the church school. He did not "fit into their program." At that time the tutor informed me that he was a sight reader, that phonics were beyond him, and that we must settle for this. Someone forgot to tell Matthew! Within months, using the texts and workbooks for which I had paid and which had been sent home with him from the church school, he was reading phonetically and well. It should be noted at this point that I had had no training as a teacher and that I elected to try a reading program with Matthew because I honestly didn't know where else to turn!

And then there was the counseling session with our family doctor. I had gone to him for help with a slight anemia. His counsel: *"Come in for iron shots twice a week and stop killing yourself over that child. He'll never be normal."* Why could he have not said, *"Slow down for a bit; take care of yourself; Matthew needs you; only you can be sure that he reaches the very top of his potential"?*

Fair is fair, so mention must be made of the clinical psychologist who said, *"It's hard to come up with a clear-cut I.Q. because of Matthew's poor speech. The score says 85 but I'm quite sure it is higher than that."* Or the head of a children's clinic who grinned, *"His progress is truly remarkable. You have brought him 95 percent of the way. Hang in there—I see no reason why you can't make the final 5 percent."* Dear friends, may your lives be long and lovely.

Matthew is now a fully operative seventh grader. He has not been in a special class situation for six years. He has friends, hobbies, interests, awareness—and a future. He came within a whisper of missing all of these things. I am still astounded and dismayed when I contemplate what might have happened to him, what probably has happened to countless other children whose parents were unwisely, ungently counseled. For that reason, the thoughts that follow may not claim complete objectivity but are offered with the deep-rooted hope that counselors will fully realize their life-and-death roles and will acquit themselves with the nobility that the responsibility of their profession demands.

* * * * *

Parents care about what counselors think of them. Yes, they do! A great deal of planning and preparation takes place before a counseling session. It has been talked about for days. The services of a baby sitter have had to be secured. Minute care has been taken in choosing the costumes and accessories. This day, this hour, may mean a new direction for the family—uphill or downhill—and there is nothing casual or perfunctory in the preparations. Ask any counselor. How often are parents late for such an appointment? The answer will be, "Never!" Ask any parent how often they are kept waiting in an outer office, under the cool eye of a receptionist, when every minute drags grudgingly into an hour. The answer will be, "Frequently!"

Most counseling settings seem to follow a typical pattern. The office is imposing—thick carpet, heavy drapes, impressive desk, leather swivel chair, two straight chairs for visitors, bookshelves lined with well-bound volumes. The atmosphere seems authoritative and, usually, expensive. Counselors are usually seated behind a desk, scanning a thick sheaf of papers. Parents, uncertain, tentative, are ushered in.

Counselor: *Please be seated.* (Couple sits rigidly in straight chairs.)

I have all of the test results here. Now let me tell you what is wrong with your child (or with you).

The dialogue does not improve as it continues. The counselor with that battery of test results (*"His performance is so much lower than his verbal"*) seems to grow taller. The parents seem to shrink, and by the time they are shown the door with the echo of *"Next"* ringing in their ears, their heads are reeling under the impact of a series of unfathomable statements. What, for goodness sake, is an "itpah" or a "whisk"? What is hyperkinetic behavior? What is sibling rivalry? What's a modality? What is "ead-i-o-logy?" And, most of all, what did she tell us to do?

Does a counselor ever wonder what happens to parents after a counseling session? They are all dressed up and no place to go! One case is on record of a mother who wandered aimlessly around a university parking lot for an hour trying to find her car. She said, "I think I'd be there yet but a nice campus policeman helped me." Usually, however, they drive away, mother weeping, father looking grim. They go home, take off their best clothes, and somehow come to grips with the business of the day. They go through the motions with minds far away, thoughts racing with what they have heard, what they have not heard, and with the decisions that lie ahead. And they regard with amazement the rest of the world which proceeds naturally and normally and merrily as if nothing were wrong!

Surely, some of the pain, some of the trauma endured by parents can be reduced, and just as surely it is the counselor who can reduce it if willingness exists to examine a few basic facts and alter a few long-standing attitudes.

No interview can have validity, relevance or meaningful substance unless the counselor is willing to accept one undeniable fact: these parents seated across that desk are not the same two human beings who glowingly anticipated a child, who heralded with pride the arrival of that child into the world, *their* world. At some point between birth and counseling, the first hint of exceptionality has occurred. Subsequent parental reactions have followed one or more of the traditional patterns:

Denial: "Nothing is wrong with my child." Counselors do not often see parents during this period. Usually, denial has more or less passed, and the parents are now reaching out for help. Occasionally, the father may have been dragged to the counseling session by the mother, still protesting that "there is nothing wrong with that kid." But the mere fact that the father is there indicates that he is on the brink of accepting the unacceptable.

Guilt: "What did I do to cause this?" This may be the common denominator of all parental reactions to an exceptionality. More destructive than guilt is the denial of guilt or the assignment of guilt to the other parent. Somehow parents must be helped to bring feelings of guilt to the surface, to identify them, and to deal with them as the unconstructive, although quite human, reactions that they are.

Confusion: "Where do we go for help?" Counselors can make their greatest contribution as they describe local facilities, current programs, present alternatives. Counselors must be willing to engage in an ongoing program of facility research and to stay aware at all times of community services.

Anger: "Why are there no remedial programs for my child?" Outrage at the lack of services or options can be a constructive emotion if channeled into action. Parents, singly and in groups, are traditionally the movers and the doers. "New" parents should be made aware of their power of advocacy in the schools and in the courts.

Despair: "Today I have no hope." In a time of enlightenment and awareness and change, parental despair can slowly be replaced by reasonable hope if the counselor is willing to take the time to describe the miracle of the past 20 years in terms of identification, remediation, services, programs, and medical progress.

But first counselors must be able to identify denial, guilt, frustration, anger, and despair, must be able to understand that these two people have searched, have wept, have pleaded, have been subjected to embarrassment, have received conflicting opinions about their child and demeaning judgments about themselves. They have changed—for better or for worse—as they have lived a day-to-day continuing confrontation with their exceptional child. They no longer are what they were, nor can they ever be again. How much better would they be served were the counselor to look at them, to really *see* them as they are at this moment in relation to what they have experienced and endured. Are they angry? Bewildered? Terrified? Belligerent? Helpless? No matter! They are the products of a total experience not to be envied, and they are dealing with that experience in the only way they know—in the way that has been found to be, if not comfortable, at least most reasonably tolerable.

How often have counselors (or, in the counseling role, teachers or social workers or psychologists or doctors) been heard to say, "That child's worst problem is his mother—or his father." How pat and how inaccurate! That mother's and/or father's problem is that kid, and she/he/they have been doing her/his/their utmost to resolve the problem long before landing in that particular counseling situation. Indeed, had their efforts been successful, they would not now be seated in those hard, uncomfortable chairs!

The heretical thought occurs that a prerequisite for counseling certification might be previous personal exposure to an exceptionality. How better to understand and to relate to the confusion of past experiences, the dilemma of present problems, the fading of hope for the future. Truly, in the light of the total experience, counselors might well be filled with admiration for the remarkable resilience which keeps parents searching for answers. A counselor truly interested in establishing a relationship of integrity might be moved to say with absolute honesty, "You know, *you* are the best thing your child has going for him. You are the only person who sees him as he truly is. Teachers and doctors and people like myself see him only in certain situations, under controlled conditions, in fragments, while you see him at his best and at his worst. You are the continuity of his life, and how marvelous that he has you."

And, indeed, it is marvelous! One wonders why more parents have not been moved to abandon the quest. People near and dear to them have suggested it. Respected professionals have strongly recommended it. Parents, themselves, have been on the brink more than once as they stagger through one disquieting, discouraging, humiliating, enervating, unexpected experience after another.

A mother of a retarded child wryly described one three-week period in which she did not leave the house, when she quite literally did not see an adult other than her husband:

> I don't know really how it happened. I certainly didn't set out to stay home for three solid weeks. First of all, it was January, the thermometer hovered around ten degrees, and all five kids were plagued with colds and sore throats. In those days we were operating out of a fully stocked freezer so, except for an occasional head of lettuce or sack of potatoes which my husband brought home, it was seldom necessary for me to shop.
>
> Sitters were hard to come by. Our retarded son was so difficult to handle, we no longer entertained; and invitations were few and far between. At any rate, one evening as I was washing the dinner dishes, I began to cry, and I simply couldn't stop. It seemed as if I hadn't seen anything but children and dishes and diapers since time began. I remember I just left the dishes in the sink, put on my coat and boots and scarf, grabbed the car keys, and left. When I was two blocks from home, I suddenly realized I didn't have any place to go! I drove around for a while, finally went to the library and picked out six mysteries, stopped in at the local sweet shop for a hot fudge sundae, and then went home. I hadn't been gone more than an hour and a half but I felt a lot better! Of course, the next morning the whole routine began again, but from then on I was careful to schedule an occasional outing, even if it was just to the post office.

This mother, a college graduate, had enjoyed a promising career as a designer of sportswear at which she had continued to work, at least part-time, until the birth of her fifth child. Then exceptionality loomed large, housekeepers could be found but not kept, and her days, weeks, and months—her life—fell into a set and unrelenting pattern of child care and housework. A warm, creative, loving person, she did not resent this turn of events, but she most assuredly did resent the counselor who said, "Mother, you cannot let this child upset your life." (*Note:* parents hate it when counselors call them "Mother.") "This child" and his special needs and special problems had already upset the rhythm of family life, and his mother was simply looking for ways to help the youngster and to lessen the family trauma. How helpful it would have been if the counselor had recognized the grief, the confusion, the despair of this parent, and, by the mere act of recognition, given comfort.

Another mother says, "I'll bet we're the only family ever to be thrown out of the Alamo!" Her five-year-old daughter, deaf from birth, had run from room to room, artifact to artifact, uttering the loud, guttural sounds which passed for speech. People stared, then moved away; guides froze; and it was gently suggested that the child be removed. The flaming-faced parent and her daughter departed to wander the San Antonio streets until the rest of the family had finished their tour of the honored historical site. "We can laugh about it now," she adds, "but at the time I was hurt and humiliated. A couple of weeks later a psychologist told me that I had to learn to accept my child, and I wondered how in the world he could expect *me* to do this when no one else in the world would."

Another parent tells of the time her son was scheduled for an electroencephalogram (EEG):

> I must have blocked it out in part because I can't remember which doctor suggested it or what we were trying to prove or disprove or learn. But, anyway, Billy had to have an EEG, and this meant he had to be taken off all medication for three days before the examination. At the time he was on Mellaril, had been for four years, and it was the only thing we had found that would make him tolerable—not a joy, mind you, but at least tolerable. So I battened down the hatches; the first day wasn't too bad, and the second day was worse, to be sure, but the end was coming into sight so we lived through it. The morning of the third day was pure murder, and I counted the minutes until our two o'clock appointment.
>
> Off we went to the hospital and were pointed in the direction of the EEG area which had its own waiting room. There I found, to my absolute horror, that they were running about two hours behind schedule, that the waiting room was so jammed there wasn't even a place for us to sit, and we were directed to wait in the huge, cavernous lobby outside. The first thing I did was to drag everything out of my purse that might amuse Billy—car keys, mirrors, pencils, and little scraps of shopping lists. That lasted about five minutes. Then we headed for the gift shop where I stocked up on coloring books and crayons, little plastic cards and other assorted items. That lasted about fifteen minutes. We then went through our repertoire of nursery rhymes, and patrolled the corridors, never going too far in case our name might be called.
>
> I literally did everything I could think of, and after about an

> hour, I just gave up. I sat back and pretended I didn't even know Billy and just let him run. And, heavens, did he run! Over to the huge plate glass windows to leave his fingerprints there and to tug on the elegant draperies. Up and over the furniture to do backflips. He never stopped, not for an instant, and I just sat there, getting a little smaller and a little smaller and a little smaller and trying to fade into the woodwork.
>
> Finally, one of those gentle little volunteers jogged over, and she wasn't smiling. "Mother," she said, "You are going to have to do something about that child." That's when the dam broke. I simply fell apart—you've never heard such blubbering! "We're supposed to have an EEG—and they're hours late—and he's a brain-injured child—and..." The poor dear was absolutely paralyzed, but just for a moment. The next thing I knew someone was handing me a damp cloth for my streaming eyes, someone else had popped Billy into a wheel chair and was taking him for a walk and he was loving it, and, best of all, within five minutes he was in the EEG room having sticky white paste applied to his noggin! It was then I decided that there was a time to be stalwart, and a time to weep.

These vignettes typify life with an exceptionality in which the most insignificant family plans can take on a dark cloak of dread. "What will he do next? How long may we have to wait in the dentist's office? Do we dare take her to the picnic? Why do people seem so uncomfortable when they are around our child? Will everyone stare and whisper at the shopping center? Will they even let us in? After all, last time he broke a plate glass window! There's always such a scene at the shoe store—could I guess at her shoe size and buy them without a fitting? We are the same as we always were—why does everyone treat us so differently? Why...? Why...? Why...?

And so parents protect themselves and react—and over-react—and are labeled for doing so. Labeling a parent can be no more constructive than labeling a child; counselors defeat the meaning and intent of their role when they do so. *"Mother is neurotic."* Is she really? Was she always so? *"Father denies the problem."* Father isn't denying anything. He knows. He knows. *"Parents are unrealistic."* Unrealistic? They have lived with the tragic reality of the situation for years. How unique would be a counselor who could completely ignore the label even of "parent," who could work with two human beings (mother and father) in their commitment to another human being (child). These two people, involved in parenting though they are, are so much more than that. They have their own special attributes, talents, beauty, which should be savored and enjoyed and relished and utilized in dealing with the problem at hand, undiminished by filtering through any kind of label.

Rather than labels, counselors are urged to think in terms of the current "stage" of the parents. Are they still in mourning over an irrevocable diagnosis? Are they still in the stage of denial? Are they inundated in guilt? Are they fighting mad? Steeped in resignation? Identification of these various stages which all parents of exceptional children work through is much more helpful in terms of advice and counsel than labels, and such an approach is infinitely kinder, gentler, more humane.

No matter what stage they are in, however, parents of exceptional children have a huge emotional investment in their children—they really love them! That may sometimes be difficult for a counselor to recognize or understand, for exceptional children are not all appealing on the surface. On the contrary, many may seem downright unattractive to the counselor in terms of behavior and appearance. But the parents have known their children in a variety of situations—warm and sweet-smelling after a bath, eyes alight over a birthday cake or the first snowfall, a small bundle of joy tumbling on the floor with a new puppy. They have beheld their children's beauty! True, they have been frustrated by behavior they could neither understand nor handle, have wept over the irrevocability of a diagnosis. Nevertheless, one constant factor remains, and that is their love, undeniable, unwavering, un-turn-offable.

How cruel, then, how unnecessary, for any professional, however well motivated, to "attack" children who are deeply loved by their parents and who also represent their love for one another. *"Your son's hopelessly retarded; put him in an institution."* What is the professional saying here? *"Throw him on the garbage heap. Dispose of him."* Parents cannot junk a child as casually as they might get rid of an unserviceable family car. In the rare cases when a child cannot be kept at home, it may require months, perhaps years, of the wisest, most gentle counseling to lead parents to the point that a valid decision can be made. But it must be *their* decision, no one else's. Only *they* know how much they can bear, what price they are willing to pay, either in keeping their children at home—or parting with them forever.

And so, bearing in mind the experiences and feelings that parents bring with them into the counseling session and the dilemma and confusion with which they depart the counseling scene, could we, perhaps, attempt to write a new script for the interplay between professional and parent? An honest human-to-human relationship must be sought, genuine concern must be evidenced, blame must not be affixed, one-upsmanship must be eliminated. How precious, how treasured, will be the counselor who can deal in what is now, what can be, and the worth and beauty which lies therein!

What parents need to hear

by Betty Lou Kratoville

What do parents *need* to hear from those in the role of counselor? Truly, nothing that differs greatly from what they *want* to hear! But, first and foremost, surely they need to hear the truth. The enormous responsibility of the counselor lies in the precarious fact that one must continually and steadfastly hold the deep conviction that the information being relayed to parents is, indeed, accurate. Since many exceptionalities are illusive, difficult to pinpoint, diagnose, or remediate, the matter of what is *true* and what is *not true* can often be cause for debate; and this has been attested to, over and over again, by the many instances in which one professional has diametrically disagreed with another. Further, no test has yet been devised which will precisely measure potential. No computer can accurately assess the divine spark we call motivation or the contribution to growth which parental love and determination can make. Therefore, counselors would be well advised to avoid making strong, implacable, unchallengeable statements. *"Your child is hopelessly retarded." "Your daughter will never go to college." "Your son will never relate to people." "There is no cure." "There is no hope."* Some comments are, at best, arrogant, and, at worst, morally reprehensible.

The issue is not the counselor's right to an opinion or a viewpoint which results, one would hope, from considerable training and experience. The opinion, the viewpoint, is there, and the counselor is stuck with it. The critical point is that the parents not be stuck with it, too. Admittedly, they have invested their time and their money and expect something in return. But how unjust if they must pay in terms of abandoned hope as well. When hope is gone, what is left? What can parents draw on in the weeks and months and years that lie ahead? Hope is sustenance; hope is a vital commodity; hope is the fluid of life itself.

Parents and children would be better served by counselors who search their hearts and their consciences for attitudes and comments that are descriptive, helpful, and realistic but which do not slam doors. *"The results show that John is presently functioning on a low level, and you were very right in deciding that tests should be run. You are really very perceptive."* (How often do counselors congratulate parents on their powers of observation?) *"You do understand, don't you, that test results do not always give us an absolutely accurate picture? They show only how John was functioning on a given day."*

Perhaps it is time that the entire procedure of interpreting test results to parents be closely scrutinized. As a rule, counselors tend to work with the same test or tests over and over again. Usually they have favorite testing instruments. Because the content of the test is so familiar to them and their colleagues, they are prone to develop a kind of casual vernacular which can be all but unintelligible to the layman. How kind it would be if a counselor would develop for parents a short, meaningful, written explanation of a specific test, setting forth aims and intent and including, if need be, a glossary. (*Note to teacher training institutions:* the development of a concise, easily read pamphlet on each of the various popular standard testing instruments would be a marvelous project of enormous worth for students!) The parents could be given the explanatory text to read while their child is in the testing room or could be allowed to take it home to study before the test results are discussed. (If such a tool already exists, I would surely like to hear of it!)

Since we have earlier established the fact that parents do care what counselors think of them, it may be easier to understand a parent's reluctance to interrupt a counselor's dissertation with comments such as, *"I don't understand that word—or that phrase—or that sentence. And it is critical that I do understand. Could you perhaps use simpler language?"* Mothers hate to admit this, and fathers certainly do! And so they sit and nod patiently as brain and eyeballs glaze. Surely it should be nonthreatening for a counselor to begin the test interpretation with a warm, prefatory statement. *"Please stop me any time I use a word or make a statement that is incomprehensible or confusing to you. Sometimes I get so caught up in what I am saying that I forget that you have no way of knowing all of our technical or educational or medical jargon. I'm really not trying to impress you with my brilliance. The important thing is that you take away from our meeting today as much solid information as possible."* And, of course, the follow-through on this humane approach would be a written report that is also drafted with clarity and simplicity.

It must be added, parenthetically, that the current, national debate over whether or not parents should be privy to information and records about their own child seems indefensible.

Parents are the continuum in the life of a child. Professionals of many disciplines enter and exit, each leaving an imprint or an opinion for others who follow. It is unrealistic, it is simply impossible, for parents to be expected to function as decision makers unless all facts are known to them. What they then do with such facts, be it wise or unwise, becomes a matter of individual decision. But how they are helped to deal with those facts can certainly be a commitment for counselors.

Surely somewhere in the educational background of a counselor exists a college course, a textbook, a chapter, a paragraph, at least a sentence, which advocates accentuating the positive! And yet it would seem that many counselors could use a refresher course in this important aspect of their mission. Surely no child exists about whom *no* positive statement can be made. His intelligence quotient is shatteringly low? How about the social quotient? *"How lucky you are that he relates so well to people."* How about a physical quotient? *"She is so well coordinated and gives off such a glow of good health, how proud you must be of the job you have done."* How about an emotional quotient? *"What a happy, intact kid! Your home must be a beautiful place."* Trivial? Not at all. Truthful? Absolutely! Humane? Without a doubt. Helpful? A lifesaver for parents to cling to as they navigate the storm-tossed seas of irrevocable diagnosis!

Counselors can be enormously helpful with perspective. Any exceptionality looms large in the family spectrum, especially at the onset of personal revelation or professional diagnosis, and this must be expected and sympathetically considered. Parents have had to adjust expectations and budgets and dreams for the future, and this huge, unforeseen mental calisthenic tends to make them view one another, the other children in the family, and the world through a veil of sorrow, bordering on despair. Let there be no mistake; the onslaught of an exceptionality can cast a heavy blanket of gloom over the healthiest, most solid family. We know, of course, that such a state of anguish cannot be allowed to continue in terms of mental health for mother and father and all of the children involved. Therefore, it is critical that counselors who recognize such a condition work toward alleviating it as gently and quickly as possible. *"Take care of your child with her very special needs, reach out for help and direction, but take care of yourself, too. Stay alert to the needs of your husband (wife) and the other youngsters in the family. More than anything else, your exceptional child will benefit from intactness within the family group.*

You have asked what you can do to help—well, this is one area in which you can do much. Indeed, only you can do it!"

In terms of perspective, parents must also be cautioned against hasty and inappropriate decisions and reactions. This can be implemented by a calculated approach of *"You might want to consider this possibility"* as opposed to *"Do this"* or *"Do that."* Counselors can urge parents to move with caution, to explore alternatives, to engage in a program of ongoing research in order to come up with answers which will fit the needs of the child and the family. *"The problem won't evaporate. It will still be there tomorrow after you have had time to digest all of this information. Let's move with resolution but with all of the caution and deliberation that the importance of the decision warrants."* Because parents are human, they want solutions, neatly packaged and promptly delivered, and so they must be counseled that no single approach or discipline or program or school or institution has all of the answers for all children; they must judiciously explore a number of possibilities, using all of the wit and wisdom at hand. Perhaps what is indicated here is an "extra" counseling session after a cooling-off period. *"Now I have given you the facts as I see them today. I think it might be wise if you were to go home and think about them for a week, and I'll think them through again, too. Then let's get together and explore what possibilities exist for your youngster."*

Parents need also to be cautioned at this critical time that all possible effort should be made not to dwell on the crisis confronting them to the exclusion of everything else. No easy task! At the moment it may be painful for them to see or to be with other people, but they can at least explore the possibility of getting away by themselves, of scheduling something very special, some activity that will renew and refresh—the theatre, a new restaurant, an art gallery. Or perhaps they can manage a diversion with or for the kids. *"We've been wanting a ping pong table for years—let's get one right now!" "Let's get the gang together and build an outdoor barbecue." "How about taking everyone out for breakfast and then to the skating rink?"* Perhaps parents can be challenged to see just how innovative and creative they can be during the preliminary dark days.

During this time of introspection, the counselor might wish to provide a list of reading materials that will shed light on the problem. Every exceptionality now has a plethora of books and pamphlets for parents which contain a wealth of descriptive, practical information. Such literature might also be helpful when the diagnosis or test results have to be explained—and re-explained—to friends, relatives, and other children in the family.

In summary, counselors are urged to scrutinize their own needs and their own personalities. Are they role playing behind that impressive desk? Are they acting as if exceptionalities are commonplace? Are they judging? Are they labeling? Are they looking at test results and statistics instead of human beings? Are they impatient when their pronouncements are not quickly and totally swallowed? Are they playing God?

Or, on the other hand, are they explaining carefully what parents may reasonably expect of them and what they expect of parents? Are they showing genuine concern, genuine warmth, genuine interest? Are they able to admit that they do not always have all the answers? Are they sending parents away with pragmatic suggestions for home management and with hope intact? Counselors encountered along the way will make the huge difference between despair and hope.

Finally, realistically, counselors are human beings, too, and must be allowed the privilege of shortcomings, bad days, errors in judgment. Perhaps what has been suggested here is that they do not get caught up in role playing, that they let their humanity shine through. And perhaps it is time that counselors feel sufficiently secure and comfortable in their job situations to be able to say, *"I am laying some heavy facts on you today, and I hate it! However, maybe it is good that I am the one to do it because I do care, and I do want to help. Feel free to cry or to get angry if that will help. At this moment it would be very easy for me to cry or get angry along with you. But, later, together, we will try to make some plans, some decisions, that will make sense. You are not alone; I am here. I care."*

Blessed would be the parents and child who fall under the guidance and gentle tutelage of such a counselor. And blessed would be the counselor who, with such an approach, rises to the summit of a demanding, enervating, but noble profession.

To be spoken sadly

I was thrust into a situation in which I had the opportunity to know and care for someone who was "different" from myself. In the process I found that many qualities unfolded within me which enabled me to grow as a person. Perhaps, as you read my story, you will recognize and identify with some of these qualities. I hope so. Then we will have communicated.

Picture this, if you will: you are a brand new mother. A strange doctor has just been in to your bedside to tell you—brutally and without preliminary—that your cherished new little son has a serious birth defect. You try to understand and hear what is said to you. At no time have you been aware of any problem, even slight, connected with your pregnancy and your child. Suddenly there is this. Where is the doctor who cared for you for nine months and a few moments ago delivered your baby? He's gone somewhere. You will never see him again. He left the telling of the news to a stranger. You can't believe what you've heard. Just a short time ago you and your husband were driving up the freeway to the hospital with highest hopes.

After two anxious days you are allowed a glimpse of your baby who is kept in isolation in a small room down the hall. You notice his bright blue eyes and he is lifting his head. You feel a little better. Still it is difficult to see all your roommates holding their babies while your arms are empty.

On the third day, after your husband has made frantic phone calls to all manner of experts for some counsel, you finally arrange to have the child transferred to a large medical center. One doctor has told your husband that it would be better to let the child die. Others charge exorbitant fees to examine and cluck over the problem. You still can't understand. Your heart is in your throat all the time; you feel so empty. Where is the promise of all those months? There is a sense of unreality about it all. Finally you check out of the hospital. Going down in the elevator, an unfamiliar nurse, perhaps trying to be reassuring, says to you (your precious child riding on your lap for a few special moments): "Don't blame yourself if his back ruptures and he dies." These are the only words you hear.

Riding down in the car to the medical center where the baby is to be cared for, you and your husband often glance lovingly down at the sweet little face, so serene. What will the next few days and months bring? You have no idea. Perhaps it is better that you don't. You check the baby into the hospital and head home for a little more rest. In days to come, you visit the hospital twice a day, pray for his safety as your baby undergoes major surgery at the grand age of ten days.

Now you are allowed to give him his bottle (breast feeding became out of the question right away) and, wearing gown and mask, to reach into his special bed to touch him a little. Sometimes you wonder if you ever had a baby; there is so little opportunity to get really close to him. Intellectually you know, of course, that he is yours but, emotionally, you feel remote from him. Nobody ever tells you that it is normal to feel that way; certainly you are not going to admit it to anyone. Oh no! Brave exterior—this you put up always—in public. A few tears fall privately but you have begun a long and intense period of grief which only eases somewhat in years to come. One can grieve over many things—not only death but also the intangibles. This particular grief has to do with the fact that this is your first child; his future is uncertain and unknown. Many times you come close to losing him. You are daily growing to love him more dearly and you are daily witnessing the fact that he is unable to move his legs and must lie on his tummy. What will his future be?

It is now that you learn to take one day at a time, to communicate as much love as you can to him through touch and support; you no longer try to live the next twenty years, projecting what will occur. In fact, you finally have to explain this to the pediatrician who seems to find it necessary to tell you of all the hardships and heartaches she feels will inevitably come. Why? Heaven knows. No doubt she feels this is a helpful approach. Alas, it isn't. At such a time, how very deeply parents need an understanding, genuine soul who would give encouragement, support, and a listening ear. The spiritual advisor you have sought tries to help but some comments carry an unspoken intimation that somewhere lurking in your mind and heart is sin which has not been conquered. This you cannot accept from any standpoint. It just isn't true. And, even if it were, what does it mean? What you most need is total acceptance. You need someone to tell you that it is all right to feel so devastated by the whole situation, that most people would feel that way, and that you will gradually find the strength to meet it. Yes, you will.

It is an intensely lonely time during which you and your husband are forced to make enormous adjustments emotionally and spiritually, to seek out answers for your own peace. You begin tentatively but instinctively to determine that you will do your very best for this new charge; you will leave no stone unturned in an attempt to see him grow and conquer. And this does bring some sense of peace. You love him, cherish him, support him, see that his care is the best available (you are guided to financial help to ease that burden) and then, having done all you know humanly to do, offer him to God's direction and love.

After a number of weeks during which further surgery takes place to offset the result of the first time, you are allowed to take him home. An exciting day! And you are, you realize, still a new mother, having to cope with diapers and bottles for the first time. Finally, you can introduce him to friends and relatives who have asked so anxiously about him. The biggest help they could offer would be support, spiritual and otherwise, not anxiety and a hovering-over sense. Friends can offer you an opportunity to share your shock and grief, in a nonjudgmental atmosphere. You need to know that people care.

How we all need to care more about each other; when we experience deep pain of an emotional nature, we need to be approached with great sensitivity; we need to be accepted in an upset state; we need to feel we can trust others enough to let down our guard, say what we choose and not be judged or criticized. In fact, the fewer the words, the better; the caring communicates itself without words if it is genuine.

There are several returns to the hospital during the first year to take care of complications. This is wearing and debilitating to all concerned. One day in the intensive care nursery, a volunteer, a warm older woman, makes a single comment to you. She tells you that children like yours have many opportunities ahead for near-normal living and can even participate in Boy Scout troops! For the first time, you think: "Why, of course, this boy will grow up." There *are* possibilities. In all the long, wearing weeks previously no one has approached you in that vein. You never have a chance to thank this unexpected friend but her words have given you some small measure of hope. All you have heard from the medical experts has been so detached and technical. No one has taken into account that this child is a person, despite all apparent physical limitations. You, too, are a person, and you and he will grow together. Who is to stop you? This child has gifts to give, contributions to make just as does everyone else. You begin to determine that you, for one, will strive very hard to see him as a whole being, concentrating on what he *can* do, what he *can* contribute and not on physical drawbacks.

At the advanced age of six months, the baby and you accompany Dad to another state for an eighteen months' stay, far from the established medical scene you have experienced before. It is not an easy period. There is constant worry over the baby. Will he be all right? How will you deal with an emergency? During that time a new baby arrives and you rejoice that all is well. Your son begins to scoot around the house over rugless floors on his bottom, sitting up. A marvelous adaptive mode of transportation. He learns to enjoy the bathtub. He is a bright, round, happy, little boy. At long last, except for periods of intense worry and yearning for a more normal life for him, your heart seems to settle down inside a little and life goes on. You are conscious of the unspoken questions in the eyes of some—the frank, upsetting stare of others—and you draw protectively around him. This is before you realize that most people are simply curious about anyone they see who happens to be a little different; most are compassionate; most would never wish to make your role harder. And this is before you learn that this child will make his own way in the world; you will need to give great amounts of support, physically and emotionally, but he is a person and he will be loved and appreciated for himself. In time you will see great, undeniable proof of this. It will help you to learn to appreciate yourself more, too, understanding that each of us is unique, valuable, special, despite any and all outward differences.

Back home once more, you arrange for nursery school experience for him as soon as possible. How did you know to do this? The only way was to have done a lot of inner listening, trusting for guidance. It became clear to you that it was the progressive thing for him to do. You were guided to the ideal place where every effort was made to incorporate him into all activities; he had a wonderful time, made friends, had some experiences apart from you and family, and began to live! And for you, it was such a lift to see this new little person developing. All during this entire time, with two other children to care for (yes, a third baby has arrived to complete the planned-for family) and the beginning of endless physical therapy sessions, more doctor appointments, you are sustained. First by trust in your concept of God and then by an encouraging family and by the deep, meaningful things you are making your own as you go. You have come to understand a basic concept which will grow steadily in time to come—that in such a situation you have two alternatives. You can rebel, resent, resist the situation, constantly question why it happened, play the martyr, mope, and be defeated. Or you can accept the challenge, take up the gauntlet and find the blessing and victory in it, building on and appreciating the positive points, looking for and appreciating the opportunities to grow in depth and sensitivity as a person, finding deep joy in all evidence of overcoming limitation, no matter how small. At low times you feel all the negativity implicit in the first alternative but basically you grow more and more into the second. And the victories, however small, are glorious.

Your son learns to talk nonstop after you silently agonized for months, fearing mental retardation, never being told that each child learns to talk at his own individual pace. You have read books wherein all these things are explained but so much has gone wrong that you are afraid. You are loath to voice your fears, feeling that it will be the ultimate blow if they are true. It would be good to unburden yourself of these worries with someone who understands.

Other signs of progress manifest themselves in his noticing the smallest detail of color and form in things around him, loving to ride in the car, sitting up more steadily, learning to use his arms to propel himself everywhere on a wheeled sled created by his father. Necessity is the mother of invention. It gives him such a sense of freedom to move on his own. In time you will learn to adapt many things to meet a particular need.

Things are beginning to fall into place. There is light at the end of the tunnel and you begin to relax a bit. Your son begins kindergarten in a specially adapted situation. And then it happens. He is hospitalized for surgery to correct a recurring problem. You are told surgery is a must—and you immediately comply. You are sitting by his bed after surgery, when a group of doctors come in making rounds. To your horror, they discuss the "case" as if you are invisible and you learn, by chance, that your son is blind. Something went wrong. He begins to stir and, wanting to dispel the horrid fear, you lean toward him. He cannot see you. It is true. Somehow you manage to telephone his father. Once again the old feelings of grief, anguish, hurt, shock, disbelief, helplessness, and frustration flood your mind and heart. How will you ever, ever cope with this? It was terrible enough for him to be paralyzed from the waist down but to lose his window on the world—it is a crushing blow. For long moments it seems like the end of all your hopes and cherished aims. Gradually you realize that, if you fall apart, you will be abandoning your son at a most crucial time. So, up goes the brave, stoic front once more. You don't expect any compassion or understanding from the staff at the hospital; they avert their eyes when you appear on the ward. There is no one to talk with who seems to sense even a bit of the anguish you feel. It would surely help to talk with someone. But that someone would have to be acutely sensitive to your needs at the moment and be prepared to listen.

You are allowed to take him home after the prescribed ten days' recovery period, and not a single suggestion is made to help you cope. You feel like railing out at everyone. What else can you do? Instinctively you carry on life as usual; he goes right back to school and begins in a few weeks to learn Braille. An enormous plus is the fact that care and consideration are given children with special needs in your school district so he *can* go right back to school.

Again your resolve to do your best for him takes over. A relative cries and pities him, painting graphic word pictures of how terrible it is that he cannot see the flowers. Impatiently you close your ears, knowing that once you allow yourself to go that path, it will be a long hard climb back up to a can-do outlook.

Once again you swing into the point of view: what *can* he do? You rent a wheelchair, and in a very short time he has learned his way gracefully through the house. He begins to read books in Braille, fingers flying over the pages. When you look at these accomplishments, in some ways, you feel they are small miracles. And that is the way to look at them. They are stepstones of progress away from limitation, toward freedom. The emphasis has to be placed continually on these small victories in order to keep a sense of proportion about the entire situation. You can certainly take a cold look at everything (and in your depressed moments you often will) and lament in lurid detail the injustice of it, the apparent burden, the frustration—you can just wallow in it! The result is that you feel devastated, beaten down and empty—very helpful! You cannot afford to wallow long, though. You need to get on with it. So you try consistently to convey to your son that what counts is the moving forward—the overcoming—the joy of getting over the hurdles. The more you can laugh together over things, the better. You convey to him that you and the rest of the family will stick by his side and cheer him on.

The moments before surgery or painful tests are always difficult. You ask yourself: is it the right thing to do? Do I have the right to put him through still another ordeal? As he grows older, he wonders, too. The moments after this particular surgery are some of the darkest you have ever known. Others occur when reports come home from school, stating that his academic achievement is fine but that he talks too loud (he doesn't know where people are anymore, not being able to see them); he gets upset easily (is this so hard to understand?). You are never allowed to relax your efforts. Each additional item seems to be another blow which causes your hard-won reserve of strength and resolve to tremble and threaten to seep away. You want so much for joy to be the quality most felt in his young life. You understand somewhat the enormous importance of the home-family atmosphere. It needs to be supportive and compassionate as well as normally demanding so that this child, as well as the other two, has his place and function in the family. You tend to overprotect him in some ways but, as a result of many contacts with wonderful, caring people, he gains a basic trust in people which enables him to meet new ones with ease and interest. He progresses from crying when you leave the room to going alone on a bus with a new driver and new companions to a new teacher.

As the years pass, your son has continued to mature in mind and heart. In yearning for a fuller, more nearly normal experience for him, you sometimes lose sight of some very special relationships he has shared. It has happened that individuals at various times have come forward and offered friendship—a most precious gift. When demands of time, work, family have made it difficult for one friend to continue, another has soon appeared to take his or her place. An abundance of love has poured forth. Your gratitude for these unselfish people is great. They assure you that it is a two-way street; they benefit, too. You come to see that your son has grown as well; he has developed a sense of humor, can carry on a good conversation, is interested in many things. You begin to understand that from friendships and sharings with others, each of us assimilate special things from one another and are the richer for the exchange. It is not the length of the relationship that matters so much as the quality of it. Like raindrops running down a window pane—sometimes merging, separating once more to go along their journey, each separate drop then fuller and more complete—sharing times enrich us as individuals. We can take the high moments, the closeness, the unique things learned from another and go on our way richer and fuller each time. These relationships outside the family circle help you and him to perceive what is meant by the family of man. You find a deep kinship with many others to whom, you discover, physical differences have no importance. Those individuals who reach out to your son and come into his life are giving him one of the most precious gifts of all—true kinship. They see the person, not the problem, and when they meet, it is on an equal basis; neither age nor background nor any other factor influences the relationship. The bond is one of true caring.

As a mother, you, too, are having to grow and stretch in many unaccustomed places. Most of the time you attend to diapers, physical upsets, the constant to-ing and fro-ing to doctors and therapists with some sense of equanimity. But sometimes the daily-ness of it gets you down. You soon learn that when you feel down, you really feel *down.* You have to work against feelings of fatigue, frustration, lethargy or else you tend to lose your coping ability. You find that what you really need is to find ways to promote your own individual growth so that you can continue to be a person, not an appendage to a needful child. This takes gumption, great desire, organization, and determination. And you have to rid yourself of guilt feelings—that you are being selfish, that you really have an inflated view of your self-importance to think that you dare even consider such a thing! Yet, it is essential that you do it. How else can you fulfill your own life's purpose if you are enveloped by circumstances beyond your control? You have to be the conqueror. For most of us, that isn't easy. On the other hand, how much more you will have to give and share with your family; how much better a mother you will be if you are your own person, seeking the depths of your own potential. If you grow into a fuller person, all around you will benefit from the added dimension you have. Best of all, you will feel greater content as you tend to the necessary chores because they are no longer the limit of your environment. You have some horizons to march over, too. You, too, have your victories to rejoice over and share. You, too, take each day as it comes and live it. So, it becomes a togetherness process composed of individuals moving forward, each at his own pace, but moving forward.

One of the things you can do to live your convictions and one you endeavor to teach to your children is to work for greater understanding of people for one another—in this case, greater appreciation of people for one another in the sense of looking beyond exterior appearances to the vital, valuable person always present behind the facade. You have witnessed scenes similar to the following many times over. In a hospital recreation room you sit reading to your son as he convalesces from surgery. A young child approaches. You smile and greet her. She stares at your son and then, in a loud voice declares over and over, "Ooooh, he makes me sick; he is so ugly. He makes me want to throw up." And then she makes loud retching sounds. Her mother stands impassively by. Your son has not seen the hostile expression on her face but he most certainly has heard the ugliness of the tone and the words. Could it be that if the mother drew her child gently aside and taught her a lesson in looking beyond the facade, looking with love and seeing a *person,* that the little girl might forever after have a more compassionate attitude toward those who happen to look or be "different"? Everyone is different in some respects from his fellows. The situation has hurt. But most of all you regret that such a shortsighted view has apparently been condoned. It need not be. In a moment's time, with a few appropriate words, it is possible the child could have learned one of the deepest lessons in life. It is possible that never again would she feel revulsion but instead kinship with all human beings. There are so many ways in which we are similar. Why can't the similarities be emphasized?

To you, the outlook is a larger part of learning to love, the real reason for being. You would like to share that outlook with others. How to do it? Perhaps the best way is without words but by example. You resolve in yourself to feel the caring and love you have for others and allow it to be felt, in turn, in any practical way you possibly can. When you see a person in a wheelchair struggling to get into a building through an unwieldy door, you move quietly to help. When you listen to one whose speech is halting and labored you wait patiently and supportively. When you see a person fighting to keep his composure over some ordeal, you try to feel with him, support him, let him know that you have felt the same many times yourself. Look for and encourage the bond of humanness you share and allow it to come to the fore. Put yourself in his place; what would help you? You are, in a sense, taking a risk in sharing yourself in this way, but if your desire is pure, surely it would be understood. The practical help you give will be understood without flowery speeches from you. Or worse—pity.

You know whereof you speak in this regard. In the orthodontist's office (one more place to go and be "worked on") your son has been poked and prodded until finally his mouth is bleeding. He has just undergone major surgery and is not fully recovered yet. Tears come to his eyes but he manfully chokes them down and endures. You help him out to the car. Instinctively you feel how tense he is, how full of unexpressed feelings. It isn't so much one short session in the dentist chair; it is the never-ending episodes of pain, fear, and upset which have occurred and built to a crescendo. Now that you are in the privacy of your car, you tell him quietly, "Cry, if you feel like it." You would feel the same. So for a few moments he gives in and cries deep wrenching sobs; you put your arms around him and just let him be. He knows you care. Quickly it is over; you head for home and he is his old bubbly, talkative self. But for that brief moment you really communicated heart to heart. He understood that you could be trusted with his private grief. You would not make fun of him or tell him to keep a stiff upper lip. You would feel with him and understand.

In situations such as this, you are convinced that the genuine thing to do is honestly to acknowledge your feelings, cry if you feel the need, know in yourself that it is a natural, normal reaction and that you are certainly not less a person to face it. It really matters not what other people think.

As time moves on it seems there is one challenge after another awaiting you and your charge. You manage to overcome one hurdle only to happen upon another. You realize that this is the human condition but sometimes you feel rebellion against the variety and number of hurdles. Couldn't they be fewer in number so you could have a couple of months' respite occasionally? And couldn't they be of a different kind? This or that one really doesn't appeal to you! Alas, you can't choose. During one eighteen-month period your son experiences daily fainting spells during which he becomes rigid and moans. It is a frightening scene, repeated over and over. You soon learn the practical aid; if he is immediately placed in a horizontal position the moment passes, and he is fine. However, things go from bad to worse. He has spells at school, at home, on trips, in Sunday School. You consult all the medical experts. No one understands the problem. Elaborate tests are negative. You feel defeated. He is scared. Finally the black day comes when you are told that he may have to have a home teacher indefinitely because of the problem. This would mean the curtailment of normal school activity which has meant so much growth for him and freedom for you to pursue your own life a bit. It appears to be the end of many hopes and dreams, for he is a good student and the development of his mental capacities has always been the primary consideration. Being taught at home would eliminate the social aspect of school, the broadening of his entire experience. One day you are thinking about it all, reaching out for an answer. You listen and you have an inspiration. You realize that when he sits on the family room couch he never has a fainting spell. You decide it must have something to do with the angle of the back which apparently supports him in a therapeutic manner. So you coerce your engineer husband to figure the angle. You drive madly to the appropriate store for a few pennies worth of foam rubber. Cutting the foam rubber to form a cushion which has the same angle as the couch back, you place it and your son in his wheel chair. And—another miracle has occurred, to the great joy of all. Never again does he faint or have any symptoms of that trouble. In a few weeks you receive a most welcome phone call announcing that it is now time to plan the junior high school schedule; there is no need to consider home teaching now. You learn still another lesson; follow your inspirations whether you feel they are the answer to prayer or they are the result of creative thinking. Answers are available; and the victory is so sweet!

You learn in the process to appreciate the small victories, too, many of which have meaning only to you and which you would hesitate to mention to others. For you, the victories may include changing a wet boy and bed in the wee hours with patience and gentleness rather than irritation and hurry (very often it must be done again in a short while), carrying out the umpteenth doctor's appointment, lifting boy and wheelchair out of the car many times with good humor and equanimity rather than resentment and frustration (so many times you have come away with no immediate solution to a difficult problem), nursing your child through protracted illness willingly and calmly rather than with a sense of martyrdom (often one episode ends only for another to begin). Sometimes you fail miserably in your resolve and feel angry and irritated. Other times you rise to the victory. You learn to understand yourself better and be forgiving; there is always a next time in which to claim the victory and you are mindful of always doing the best you can at the moment. When you have your victory you can have your own private moment of celebration. Cheers to me—I did it better that time! I was more the person I want to be. The victories will merge together into a patchwork of progress. You can remember and build on your peaks. Never mind the valleys!

Victories dot your son's career, too. Learning to read fast and well in Braille, grasping fractions without the crutch of seeing them, taking part in a recorder concert with the other sixth graders at the Christmas program (they watched the screen for the projected notes—he had the music by memory in his head), learning to type as well as use a Braille writer, writing contest-winning poetry, keeping up academically, learning grooming. These outward milestones are joy-producing. But perhaps even more meaningful are the unseen victories which occur such as developing a sense of humor which emerges even in the hardest moments, enduring pain without dwelling on it, going through many ups and downs with good cheer, persisting in learning when the concepts are so hard to grasp, feeling able to reach out to others with warmth, trusting for a return in kind, finding a basic goodness in people in life. It could be so different.

The addition of two other children to the family has been a steady blessing. You are thankful that you and your husband conquered your fear and proceeded with your long-ago wish to have three children. Since the first experience had been so difficult, it would have been easy (and actually was for a short time) to convince yourself that you couldn't handle anything more. It is not simple to balance the family in the sense of giving equal amounts of time and effort to each when one requires, of necessity, a lion's share. Yet if the household is geared solely to the demanding needs of one individual, the experience of each person in it will be warped. On the other hand, the experience can be an enriching one. The one child benefits in infinite ways from the relationship with his brother and sister, learns to give and take, share and think of others, be more adjustable. The others, you hope and expect, will grow into compassionate people who learn tolerance and understanding for individuals who are "different." A very precious insight. Parents learn to stretch, too, realizing that it is the *quality* of time spent with their children, not the quantity. You find the children all grow to understand each other's needs as you sincerely endeavor to treat them as your friends and helpers. If they sense that you see each as unique and special, the household can be normal and you will gain a sense of proportion about things. It can work.

You begin to see, too, as time goes on, that coping with this situation has given your life a depth you never knew was possible and you can actually feel thankful for all you have learned. You always did feel there was more to living than keeping the dandelions out of the lawn, having your floor shining bright, having the cleanest wash on the street! From long ago you yearned inwardly to live a life of growing in love, learning to share with others in depth, feeling a part of the larger family of humankind. Very idealistic! You've had some spectacular failures in human relationships as well as some very fine successes. You've had some terribly depressed times when you felt you could hardly lift your nose up off the floor as well as times of light and hope and deep joy. You realize that through it all runs a thread of richness. The richness comes from having experienced a great variety of situations which demanded your best efforts and left you little time to wonder how come and what to do. People have been ready with lots of advice, many suggestions, warnings, cajolings. But when it came right down to the wire, you had to act to the best of your own ability and never mind how strange the beat may have seemed to someone else. Remember the first day of school one of those years when your son's wheelchair got knocked over with him in it and you got the call from school? Picking him up in the doctor's office, head swathed in a bandage, you write *My Hero* in big black letters on the bandage, much to the amusement of everyone. Remember the time when a "friend," with all good intentions no doubt, read your son the riot act about his getting you up in the night for drinks of water, telling him to do without and be quiet? You had a lot to do to assure him that you understood his need and that you were willing. What was he to do—lie awake with parched throat, unable to get to water? Remember the day when he went into surgery in the early morning and you couldn't be there to see him off? You felt so bad at not being at his side then. Afterwards, when you asked how it went, *he* assured *you* that it was O.K., that he had remembered what you said about God's arms being around him and he had felt a "sense of peace." Remember the time after he had lost his sight, you took him to another doctor for something else and the man said, after observing a calm, cheerful little boy, "Well, I am amazed. I really thought this would throw him for a loop; I didn't think he could handle it." You recognized that your efforts to support the child and keep the sense of harshness about it all from enveloping the family had paid off in full. Remember the young director of a summer program geared for mobile blind youngsters but allowing your wheel-chaired son to join in, saying to you after the first day, "He's a joy to have." The very variety of the challenges presented to you and the resultant feelings and understanding have given you a basis on which to reach out to others as fellow members of a large family. In some situations a person might say to you, "You can't understand how I feel." And more often than not, you can say, "Ah, yes, but I do understand; I have been there, too."

You wake one day to realize that all the trials, the turmoil, the anxiety, the fear have given you a modicum of that which you sought—understanding. You find, somewhat to your surprise, that the lessons you have learned are priceless. Although you have sometimes rebelled against it all, questioned it, resented it, you would not relinquish these lessons. For you have begun to acquire that depth you have long sought. Your experiences have brought you into closer touch with others. Therein lies the victory for you. Therein lies your ability to appreciate your son. If he can understand that you have grown to this conviction, he will feel freer, not a burden to you or anyone, not a pulling-down element in your life but an uplifting one. If he can understand that, then he will know he has given you the opportunity to grow with him. And the growing process will continue onward. The possibilities are endless. Isn't that what it's all about?

O the people
who have chosen to know
only other people
who are like themselves.
O what they are missing
O missing without
even knowing what it is
that is being missed.

What lies in themselves
Waiting to be disclosed:
this they are missing—
the people who choose
to know only other people
who are like themselves.

DORIS PEEL
(printed in *The Christian Science Monitor*)

Section IV:

The Disabled Person Meets The Challenge

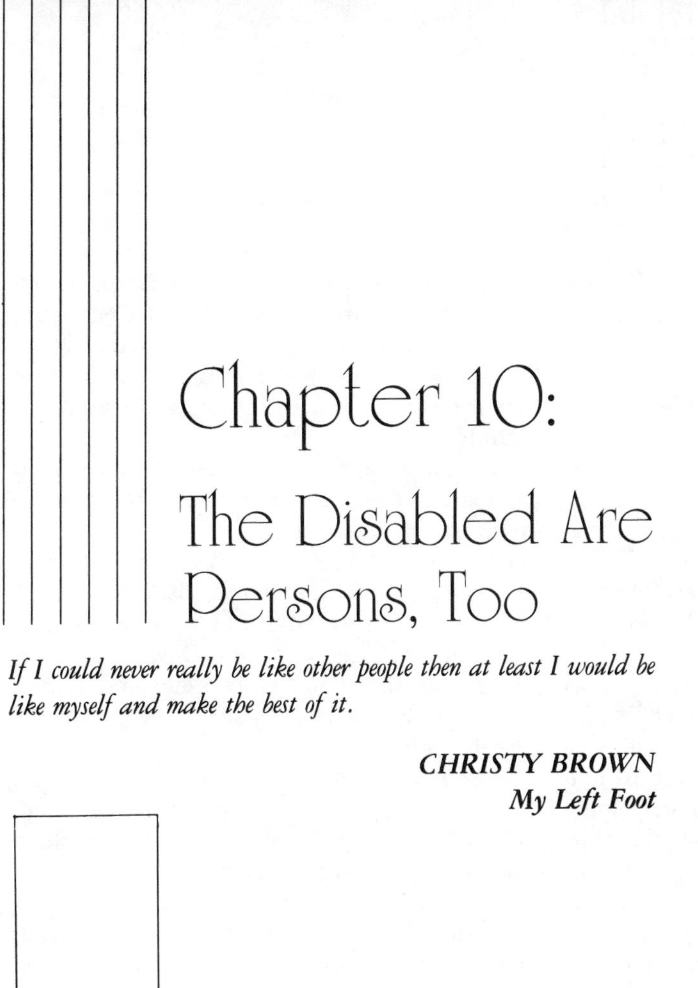

Chapter 10: The Disabled Are Persons, Too

If I could never really be like other people then at least I would be like myself and make the best of it.

CHRISTY BROWN
My Left Foot

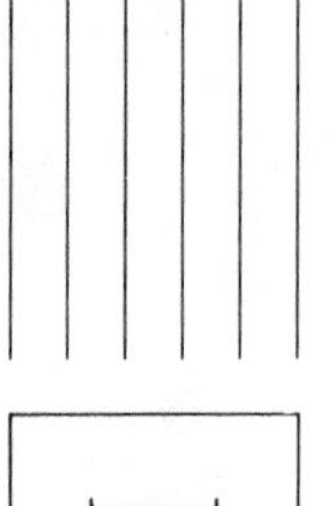

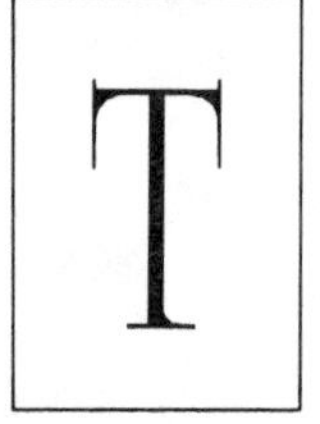

he Masai Indians murdered their disabled children; the Azand tribe loved and protected theirs.

The Chagga of East Africa used their disabled to ward off evil; the Jukun of the Sudan felt that they were the work of evil spirits and abandoned them to die.

The Sem Ang of Malaysia used their crippled as wise men to settle tribal disputes; the Balinese made them a societal "taboo."

The ancient Hebrews saw illness and physical defects as a mark of the sinner; the Nordics made them gods.

During the Middle Ages, the mentally and physically disabled were often seen as being possessed by the Devil, and thus, burned as witches; during the Renaissance many individuals with these same impairments were seen as unfortunate and were hospitalized and treated with care.

In our modern, enlightened society, two-thirds of the world have no special medical or educational facilities for the disabled; the other third of the world still labels them and segregates them physically, educationally and emotionally from the remainder of the population.

The history of the disabled has not ever been a smooth or secure one, and we still have a long way to go in our views, attitudes and treatment of them to make it so. Deviance of any kind has always seemed to be a threat to us. What was *different* upset us and we would not allow ourselves to rest until we had set it apart, and separated it from ourselves. We never failed, though, to be curious about these strange inexplicable things and they plagued us until we were able to find some explanation for them. Our explanations varied from the ordinary to the supernatural, from the mystical to the commonplace, as damned by Demons or blessed with God-given magical powers.

Studies of physical and mental differences were recorded as early as 384 B.C. when interpretations for deviance were sought by such an eminent scholar as Aristotle and later, Diogenes, Hippocrates and Galen. They wondered about epilepsy, dementia and imbecility. These and later studies of deviance have often been the basis for important discoveries about humans, their health, their future and their behavior. But, strangely enough, even with the coming of the scientific age, we have mysteriously clung to some of our old superstitions and attitudes. By many, exceptionality is still equated with ignorance, sin, and supernatural powers of good or evil. The different individual is still feared, looked upon with suspicion, and often responded to as inferior. These attitudes are carried, at times, to such an extreme, that people who have disabilities are often seen as nonhuman, objects, things apart from others, rather than people, and thus treated as such by their society. The original irrational, prejudicial attitudes are still among us.

We have continued to look for answers to our questions relating to *difference* by studying the animal world or primitive societies. We were certain that these studies would help us to discover satisfactory explanations which could be directly applied to the nature of humans. We have found little comfort and even less insight from our contradictory research. We have only learned that there were as many tribes who have ostracized their disabled as different as there were who accepted them; there were as many animals who destroyed their imperfect young or freely allowed them to perish as there were those who lovingly protected them for their lifetime.

It would seem plausible that attitudes toward the disabled would have changed radically in our humanistic, enlightened age, but far too often this has not been the case. Attitudes and behavior toward physical and mental differences have, to a large extent, persisted and been passed on from generation to generation.

It is possible that if we were to examine our own feelings regarding limitations such as blindness, deafness, cerebral palsy, epilepsy, crippling diseases, and others, we would find that we still believe, as did our ancestors, that their basic causes lie in the transgressions of parents, their lack of good judgment, or the punishment for their sins. We are certain that these conditions must be inherited and are even contagious. For those who believe these things, a reaction and response to disability of revulsion, avoidance and fear is understandable. Comprehensible, too, then, is our insistence that the different should be segregated in order that "decent society" may be protected from them.

Hebb (1946) and many others since who have become concerned with the psychology of perception, have expounded an interesting theory to explain the phenomena of avoidance and fear directed toward the disabled. They suggest a theory of expectation of perception. They explain that one tends to become frightened and uncomfortable when one perceives readily recognizable, familiar objects which, at the same time, have something radically missing. We perceive, at once, that the new perception of the object is not uniformly compatible with the known object. We are startled. We are made uncomfortable. We have been expecting the ordinary and are frightened to have to readjust our response to what has now become exceptional and strange. We see a person walking toward us and suddenly become aware that he has hooks for hands. Our shocked response is illustrative of the theory of expectation of perception.

It is not surprising that most persons, according to their own learning and expectations, experience differences in attitudes toward the disabled. There is no doubt that some individuals have fewer problems than others in this regard, but there are painfully too many people who have negative feelings, often covert, regarding them. They are prone to devaluate the disabled, avoid them, develop stereotypes about them, create a crippled world for them, put them into it and become most uncomfortable if the disabled do not accept it. The common stereotype often assigned to a person with a disability is that of one to whom we attribute great suffering, whose life is disturbed, distorted and forever damaged. We see this *poor* person as one who is permanently enmeshed in his problem and for whom any kind of real adjustment is impossible, or, at best, superficial.

One young lady, when asked to empathize with a deaf child who was brought into her class, stated that she was not able to do so without feeling totally appalled and devastated. It was impossible for her to imagine that there would be any joy in the child's life, any hope, any real meaning.

Often the stereotype we have created of the disabled, and their lives, manifests itself in allocating to them an inferior status in society. We see them as not really persons like us, not truly able to meet any of the *normal* standards of society or, at least, not as well as we are. We, therefore, do not expect as much from them as we would their nondisabled counterparts. We tend to pity them and try to help them when they do not want help.

In many depreciating ways we express to them their inferior positions.

If disabled persons do achieve, we tend to regard them as very unusual, lavishly praise them and often overvalue their achievement, simply because their behavior contrasts with our limited expectation of them. If, on the other hand, they exert their rights, demand or insist upon equal consideration, we respond to this negatively, suggesting that they do not know "their place," that they are being unrealistic or are lacking in gratitude for all we have already allowed them. Again we are imposing our own misdirected standards upon them. It is difficult for our attitudinal self to let them be.

There are those who believe they are making it easier for persons who are disabled if they avoid *seeing* their impairments. They act as if they do not realize the other person's *secret* and play the game of pretense. This attitude loudly proclaims the view of disability as stigma and usually results in causing both parties to feel uncomfortable to the extent that future normal interaction is avoided.

Important studies regarding attitudes toward impaired persons (Mussen and Baker 1944, Ray 1946, Strong 1931) have indicated that expressed attitudes toward the disabled are more often favorable when individuals are *overtly* questioned. In direct questioning they tend to explain that they have mostly positive feelings regarding their disabled brothers. They see them as *alert, friendly, self-reliant, persistent* and *brave*. All very affirmative traits, indeed. But in evaluations dealing with *covert* feelings, the results are more often negative in nature. In these tests we find that people pity the disabled, have fewer expectations of them, predict greater pain and have less hope for them than for the nondisabled. This was clearly revealed in studies where the same individuals were photographed in and out of wheelchairs or braces. The testees were asked to respond to their feelings regarding the same individuals in the different conditions. The response varied regarding the same people dependent upon the addition of the *handicapping* stimulus. In the wheelchair the individual was consistently seen as helpless, somewhat hopeless and of considerably less value than they were outside of the wheelchairs. So too, were they devalued in braces.

Attitudes toward persons who are limited are not always negative. It has been found that many persons attribute special qualities to them. They feel, for instance, that the deaf person has better visual acuity, that the blind person has greater auditory perception. They are certain, too, that since these people have suffered, they have a more *mystical* attitude toward life, a greater depth of understanding, and more patience and tolerance regarding life's tribulations. In essence, their *misfortunes* have brought them closer to adjustment. This may or may not be true but there is no objective evidence to prove the point one way or another. The blind have no better hearing than normal people; they simply use it more efficiently. The deaf have no keener eyesight; they simply, out of necessity, are more aware. Continued experienced pain and despair may indeed bring one closer to one's self, but the converse can also be true. For some disabled persons the experience of pain may be too tortuous, too incapacitating and may have permanent ill effects.

It is obvious, then, from this brief discussion that each of us has preconceived ideas about the person with a disability. To a large degree, these ideas are an accumulation of old wives' tales, superstition and misinformation, but, as for any notions, there will always be some truth as well as some untruth about them.

It is no wonder, then, that most people feel rather tense and uncomfortable when dealing with the disabled. Physical and mental deviations have very personal and social meanings for each of us which are often totally unrelated to the person with whom we are interacting. We may find ourselves vacillating between admiration and pity, between hope and despondency, between acceptance and rejection, between the individual's inferior status and superior status. Whatever we feel about the disabled person will arouse in us certain preconceived expectations of behavior. We will, to a large extent, determine what disabled persons will be permitted to be, and how they will be expected to behave, apart from the reality of the situation. Our limited attitude toward them may impose an ability limitation upon them even when their disability does not. In other words, because of the personal nature of our perception, we will tend to see what we want to see, hear what we desire to hear, and respond as we feel most comfortable responding. It is possible that our perception may have nothing, or little, to do with the reality of the disabled person before us.

The question often arises among educators and psychologists as to whether there is a typical "handicapped personality."

The research has consistently proved otherwise. There is serious doubt whether there is any direct relationship between variations in mental and physical abilities and emotional problems. In most cases where emotional pathology is present, a study of the specifics in each case seems to indicate that the body is the stimulus for, *not the cause of,* the emotional maladjustment.

A maladjustment is mostly brought about by the personality of the individual and subsequent societal variables. What often occurs, basically, is that disabled individuals find themselves lacking in some tool upon which society puts great importance. Society devalues them for this lack and they, in turn, end by devaluating themselves. This may be illustrated through the dynamic behavioral change which occurs when a child is told for the first time that he or she is blind. Up until that moment the blind child thought that all persons were so. All at once they learn that they are *handicapped.* Other people *see.* Equally traumatic, and far more common, is the person who goes through early life partially sighted with no experienced sight standards as guidelines. He thus believes that all the world sees in the same limited fashion. Often the difference is not discovered until the early grades in school when sight must be used for specific learning tasks. Finding out the problem and getting glasses which will correct the vision will, no doubt, bring a great sense of relief. "So this is what the world really looks like!" But it also brings knowledge that the individual is not *normal,* not like other people. If enough people view the thick-lensed glasses as a stigma and impose their prejudices upon the child by calling names such as "four eyes" or "cyclops," this otherwise simple, corrected disability may become a life-long feeling of inferiority, bewilderment and pain. The individual will allow the disability to become a handicap.

Therefore, though we know that as a group the mentally and physically disabled seem to have more adjustment problems and may be diagnosed as emotionally disturbed with more frequency than other groups, we cannot assume that it is innate in them, or in their disability to cause them to be so. If there is an emotional problem, the source of the problem is usually not within the individuals but rather inflicted upon them from without. The disabled infant is born into the world with the same possibilities for adjustment as anyone.

We then arrive at the same inference from which we started several chapters back, that first and foremost the disabled person is a person, too. In terms of the present facts accumulated by medicine, psychology and personality theorists, the only conclusion that can be drawn regarding people who are disabled, with any certitude, is that they are all unique human beings.

It is a fact that there are mental and physical disabilities which will realistically limit certain functions and experiences for the individual. Deaf persons will not be able to hear lectures. This will limit for them certain reality values to which they will have to adjust. They may need an interpreter to translate into sign language or finger spelling, in order to understand with their eyes as well as their neighbors did with their ears. Children who are blind may have to read books with their fingers, in Braille, before understanding as well as their seeing friends. But both, to some extent, because of the real limitations imposed by their impairment, will be somewhat dependent upon the normal. They will have to find ways to adjust to *normal* stimuli in the *normal* world.

We often hear talk about "the world of the handicapped," "the world of the scientist," "the world of the artist." No matter how hard these individuals try or will it, they will eventually be faced with the realization that there is only "one world" within which they must live; only in psychosis can they create their own world. Even then, not without a great price. They will, in the last analysis, have to accept one world, in which interaction is necessary to achieve full self-realization.

So, those with disabilities are simply people. The individuals become handicapped to the extent to which they internalize their limitations as debilitating and undesirable. Their attitudes will be largely determined by the labels imposed upon them, the society's reaction to these labels and the special treatment they receive. In addition, destructive, segregated environments and isolating behaviors which tend to remove them from the world will serve to convince them further of their handicaps. This is visibly enacted in many so-called "rehabilitation" programs whose main functions seem to be to define and label handicaps, select those who fit their labels, segregate these individuals and help them to conform to what the rehabilitators believe are the individual's limitations and potentials. This process can only be a ruinous one.

It is often assumed, too, that, because people having disabilities do not require the same access to experiences, information, and affect as do other individuals, they do not have dreams, desires and human needs. People seem to operate on the misguided assumption that the less the disabled are told about or allowed to experience in life, the less they will have to suffer from it. If anything, the converse is true. The disabled cannot afford to be naive about life, they must be sophisticated in meeting prejudice, conflict, confusion and even despair. They must be prepared, as are all people, to make decisions about themselves, their growing, changing attitudes and new insights.

The reader may be wondering why so much time has been taken with what they feel is the obvious. "Aren't these the opportunities afforded *all people?*" It is precisely because individuals who are disabled are not often perceived as *other people* that they are not afforded these same chances for self-realization as others are, that time has been taken to somehow "spell it out." If we agree that people who are disabled are persons, too, then we must allow them at least the same opportunities of all individuals, to realize the persons that they are.

In order to do this, they must be afforded the most dynamic education possible. It must be an education for life, not simply a fact-oriented education, segregated from life and meaning. They will need the most pertinent knowledge, the clearest insights, the most viable alternatives.

They must be schooled in the joy of life, the wonder of change, the special quality of life and the excitement it can offer. They must be instructed in the use of their nondisabled selves toward gaining a more accurate perception of reality by exploring the world in their way and by discovering for themselves. They must be told of their hidden gold mine of potential, not only to be what they are, but to continuously be searching for ways of going beyond their present selves.

They will have to know the invigorating feeling of achievement, the feeling of being able to do something and do it well. Surely the pattern for them cannot always be one of remediation! Like all people, they must be allowed to use their imagination toward building their powers of creativity. "To be is to do."

The affective needs of the disabled are even more ignored. They will need to learn to handle rejection, pain and loneliness. The attitude of most professionals implies that if they do not recognize these needs they will go away. The result of this attitude is that rather than helping the disabled to love themselves, they are, in many subtle ways, teaching them to depreciate themselves. Instead of teaching them to accept and use their uniqueness, they often suggest they hide it, disguise it and try to be normal. They teach the blatant lie that there is security in normalcy.

The disabled must be taught that only they are responsible for determining what they will be, what obstacles they will need to surmount, what they will become and how they will become it. They must be given the same love and respect afforded other people. Individuals are often so busy "doing for them" or "giving things to them" that they do not have time to see them or love them, let alone respect them. Love is a reciprocal process or it is not love. If they are done for, then they must do for. If they are given, then they must give, too.

They will need to discuss their feelings, to argue, to agree and disagree, to worry, to be praised, to be reprimanded and all of the other limitless things that go along with learning to be a loving human person. They will have a need for response, like all people, not only in terms of their differences, but in terms of their total selves.

They will have to learn a sense of *we* as well as a sense of *I*. They must learn that they are individuals of worth, that this becomes more meaningful as they share this worth with others, and that they need others, both disabled and nondisabled, in their lives in order to help them to discover their *I*.

They will have to be afforded the wondrous feelings of freedom: freedom to be, freedom to try, freedom to fail, freedom to grow, to succeed, to learn, to enjoy, to laugh and even to cry and suffer.

In spite of so many destructive attitudes and practices freely and openly practiced by society, psychologists, educators, and rehabilitation personnel, there are many disabled individuals who manage to survive the "system" and emerge as unique, proud human persons. Primarily they are those who are able to externalize their disability, and the attitudes toward it, as something put upon them which may cause certain limitations and with which they must contend. *But* they see this as only one aspect of themselves, representing only a small portion of what they really are—persons like all people and with all the wondrous possibilities of everyone else.

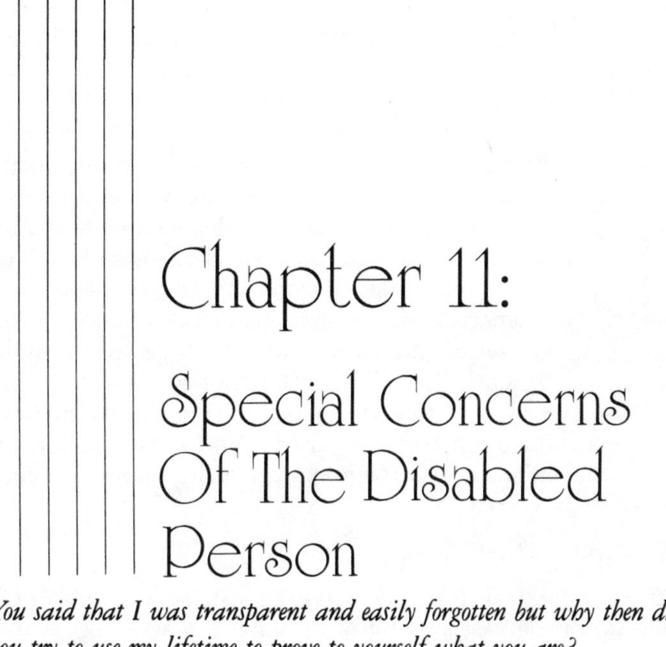

Chapter 11: Special Concerns Of The Disabled Person

You said that I was transparent and easily forgotten but why then did you try to use my lifetime to prove to yourself what you are?

MICHELLE
But I Am Present

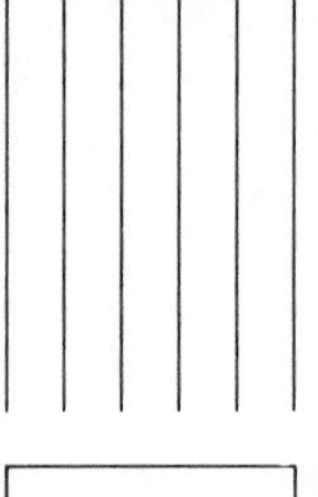

p until now this discussion has been primarily directed to the responses of others toward persons who are disabled. This chapter will deal with the special concerns, conflicts and feelings of the disabled persons and their possible influence upon their growing self-concepts.

It must be understood that the special problems discussed here are not common to all exceptional individuals and it would be a severe mistake to draw such generalities, but they appear enough in case studies, research and literature regarding exceptionality to warrant consideration and study.

THE DEVELOPING SELF

Every individual has a perception of self. This self picture is made up of the vast amount of personal characteristics which comprise the person's identity. This identity concerns notions one has about one's body, mind, abilities and disabilities, likes and dislikes, together with a limitless number of personality characteristics one has learned, such as being loving, demanding, accepting or rejecting. These qualities and notions are formed early in infancy and continue to develop throughout one's lifetime. One learns about and creates oneself during each moment of awareness. One learns who one is from individual firsthand experiences, from shared experiences with others, or through implied actions and covert feelings. One is continually amalgamating new learning with old knowledge and forever integrating it into an ever changing concept of self.

Once basically formed, this concept of self extends outward from ourselves and becomes mostly responsible for our perceptions or impressions of the world and others. Thus, the statement, we see what we are ready to see, hear what we are ready to hear, feel what we are ready to feel . . . we are continually creating a world in our own image. This *self* determines which individuals we will choose for friends, and in turn, which of these friends will have the greatest impact upon us. It becomes a reciprocal process. Others will affect our self-esteem and help us to form our achievements. For example, we may have a concept of self with which we feel comparatively comfortable. In the process of interaction with others we may encounter some resistance. Others whom we love or respect do not share our comfort with certain aspects of our present self and devalue them. If enough persons do this and if continued interaction with them is of sufficient import to us, we may be forced, or, indeed, be willing, to re-evaluate and to change our self. This process is one in which we act and are acted upon. As such, our image of self and the world we live in is continually changing and being formed.

The *self* of the disabled grows and develops in the same manner as that of the nondisabled. But many, and often stronger influences will work upon them. They will, in many cases, have to deal, from infancy, with negative, often degrading and personal devaluating experiences. They will grow with disability-related physical discomfort and suffering. They will find themselves, in many ways, realistically physically limited and encounter inordinate frustration. They will experience continual uncertainty as to their abilities and future independence. These concerns will greatly influence and have a lasting effect upon their developing, perhaps already unrealistically low, self-concept.

It is imperative, then, that the forces which most affect and influence the disabled person's self-concept be seriously considered. These major forces seem to relate mostly to interpersonal relationships, disability-related frustrations, social acceptance and rejection, limitations of experience, physical and emotional suffering, and inferiority and lowered status.

INTERPERSONAL RELATIONSHIPS

No matter how secure or tempting the thought for disabled persons, they will not and cannot exist alone. Their world is made up of people—family, friends and brief encounters with strangers. Interaction, as a phenomenon, implies that individuals responding to one another are doing so as differing objects of stimulation. No individuals in interactions can ever be certain of the other's feelings about or reaction to them. They may have some expectations of behavior based upon their past experiences which may determine, somewhat, how they will react in new situations. Though their expectations are often valid, they can never be sure. For example, if experience has told disabled individuals that upon meeting people they will usually be rejected, then they will come to expect rejection as a normal consequence of future encounters and thus, may avoid them altogether.

Many of their expectations will be realistic. (One learns very quickly to avoid painful situations, but there will always be a possibility that in some situations the anticipation of behavior will not be realized.) They may not have learned that mutual understanding and human communication can only be experienced when they allow each new situation to tell its own story. In other words, only when they are basing their responses upon valid information, the *specific* clues which are being sent out by the person during a *particular interaction,* and experiences what *actually* occurs, can they make valid interpersonal judgments. Each new interaction must chart its own course independently from what they have come to expect from previous experience.

Harold Russell (1949), well-known as the young man who lost both hands in World War II, found a solution to this problem. He stated, "The only way I could feel at ease with them other people was if they felt at ease with me, and the only way for them to feel that way was for me to feel at ease with myself."

It is often the case, too, that in order to avoid negative interpersonal experiences, disabled individuals will be tempted to hide their disability. Past encounters may have taught them that visibility focused attention on the problem and seemed to result in public rejection. It seems, therefore, of the utmost importance to them, especially initially in a relationship, to disguise or decrease the visibility of their impairment. They may feel that if they can hide their disability they can meet others on more equal ground.

Such a response to a disability more often has a negative effect in interaction than that which would have been created by the impairment itself. What is certain is that if a person, in an interaction, feels ashamed, the other person is likely to feel ashamed. If the individual feels guilt or embarrassment, so will others. Individuals are primarily responsible for setting their own *"interpersonal emotional tone."* If they will it to be one which is free, honest and aboveboard, then they will have to send off these clues and hope for the best.

FRUSTRATION

According to the research, though the disabled are more likely to encounter frustration due to their real physical and mental problems, there seems to be no correlation between the type of disability and the degree of frustration (Fitzgerald 1950, Shere 1954, Barker and H. Wright 1955). The blind, as a group, do not know more frustration than the deaf, nor do the deaf know more frustration in their life than do the physically impaired or any other group. As with other relationships between personality and disability, the degree of frustration suffered seems to be more directly related to each individual's personal adjustment. It is certainly true, though, that some disabled are faced with a greater number of frustrations with which they will have to cope than most other persons. For example, uncertainty regarding the degree and future prognosis relating to the disability can create a type of inescapable frustration. Those persons with disabilities will have more frustrations concerning physical management and the demand upon time and energies which this creates. Since many of these frustrations are reality-based and inescapable, they may have to face them squarely before they will be able to accept their permanent nature and deal with them realistically.

It is often the case that the disabled individual finds the means of using frustration as a positive force, for, indeed, it may be a source for discovery of new, creative solutions and gratifying alternatives. After all, no life is altogether free of frustration. If it were, it would deprive the individual of much source of motivation, challenge and stimulation.

Disabled individuals often discover a solution for dealing with frustration in making their goals and aspirations less rigid. This does not imply that they must give up their dreams, but rather they can find that the same or similar goals may be achieved through a simple modification in the manner of achieving them. There are many roads to Rome. Perhaps the most convenient may not be the easiest but another, perhaps longer road will bring them there as well.

REJECTION AND ACCEPTANCE

Disability is a social phenomenon as well as a mental and physical one. Differences, of any sort, do create social responses which can lead to discrimination, rejection and relegation to inferior social status. Since an irreparable, visible disability cannot be wished away, it must be accepted, at least initially, as a more or less negative social stimulus. Disguising the problem seems only to accentuate it and often serves to create more social discomfort, distancing and self-devaluation.

Most disabled persons will tell of their almost daily encounters with some form of overt or covert rejection. A college student confined to her wheelchair relates that each time she joins a group of girls actively engaged in *girl talk,* the conversation changes. "They stop talking about boys, dates and sex, their favorite subjects. They start talking about professors, school requirements and books. I know they feel they're protecting me from a potentially painful situation, but in a sense, they are creating a more painful one. They're assuming that I'm not interested in boys, dates and sex. They're, in their intended 'kindness,' rejecting me as a woman and relegating me to some sort of special world they've decided is more comfortable for me. I've tried to encourage the original conversations, but when I do, they become uncomfortable and find excuses to break up the group, rather than go on."

Rejection takes on many subtle forms.

The professor who *counsels* the disabled person out of his class because he feels that it will be *too demanding.*

The individual who *grabs* a blind person by the arm and, unsolicited, helps the person across the street, assuming that the poor person is lost and needs help.

The counselor who tells the disabled person that the goal of obtaining a Ph.D. is unrealistic, for, indeed, the counselor does not even have one.

The condescending attitude implied by the well-meaning teacher who excuses the disabled person from normal class requirements.

The policeman who, out of pity, doesn't give a citation to a lawbreaker who is disabled.

Persons with a disability find it difficult to escape rejection, even well-meaning rejection. It becomes necessary many times for them to find a means for instructing others, in often devious and subtle ways, that though they have a disability which may in some ways be unfortunate and inconvenient, it is not necessarily debasing. They must find a means for letting them know that they are more than a disability—a person with humor, knowledge and a unique contribution to make. They must teach them that they are not seeking their pity, charity, or sympathy but simply the dignity of being themselves. They will teach these things best in action, by engaging in mutually satisfying activities with them and being able and willing to reveal themselves as well as accepting the resultant responses. If they do this, of course, they will have to give up their expected roles which may have offered them a tempting refuge in the past, of the helpless but lovable, tragic figure.

When disabled persons are able to reveal themselves primarily as well-integrated, growing persons, in social situations they will be accepted as such. They will find, often, that what had seemed like a rejection of them by others, was more a rejection of their impairment, their differences, with which they had to deal, before they could deal with them. This will not be easy, but the only alternative is for them to retire into groups of similarly limited individuals. Only here will they be free of any possible social conflict, anxiety or frustration. Here, they will not be required to *educate* for they will have a common bond of *disability* and *experience.* (This, of course, is not all bad. There are times when they will need such acceptance and support.) But disabled persons will, at one time or another, be forced to deal with *normal* society. Success in this endeavor will come only through practice, growing strength and pride. It will take time, and it will be well to remember, along the way, that there can be no rejection or debasement for individuals who accept themselves.

LIMITATIONS OF EXPERIENCE

Impairments do limit. In fact, an impairment is only significant in terms of the extent to which it limits the individual toward realizing desired goals. Living life fully is mostly a process of eliminating confining barriers. This struggle begins in infancy and ends only with death. The early childhood efforts are described beautifully by Stone and Church (1973):

> This time of life is full of joy and abandon, of delightful discoveries and surprises, of wonder and amusement, but it is likewise full of dreads, terrors, anxieties, uncertainties, and worry. The child is touched with a sense of his essential human isolation in a vast, powerful, unpredictable and largely uncontrollable world. His childhood culture as expressed in shared group activity gives him the emotional strength to carry on. His culture as expressed in skills and rituals and collections gives him the magical dominion over an otherwise unmanageable reality. Without the devices of his culture the regressive components in his perpetual growth ambivalence might overwhelm him. But, as we have said, the culture of childhood is a crutch to help him through a stage of development, and if he does not gradually free himself of it, it becomes a millstone.

This is true, we might add, of all unconquered obstacles through all stages of life.

The restrictive nature of impairments such as blindness, crippling conditions, and amputations often makes it difficult for the disabled to fully explore and experience themselves in relation to their environment. So confined, they sense a deep feeling of isolation without the solace of a peer group to share it with. Without the crutch of mystical and real experiences offered by fully exploring each phase of their growing and developing being, they are often overwhelmed by the myriad of conflicts for which they have only limited experiences with which to form solutions. The impairment has too often caused them to be overprotected, isolated, segregated, pampered and pitied—a very inadequate psychological background upon which to build mature self-images.

It is vital that individuals who are physically and mentally limited throughout life, have every possible opportunity to experience the world—the objects that clutter it, the people who inhabit it, the beauty that enhances it, the wonder that gives it color and brings about change, the everyday happenings that offer security and the unexpected that brings with it the element of surprise. Why shouldn't the blind travel to Europe, ski, climb Mt. Everest? Why should the deaf not study music, sing, feel the sounds of the city? Why shouldn't individuals in wheelchairs play basketball, run relays, dance or make love?

Limitations may arise from disabilities, but this does not imply that the impaired individual must be a limited person.

SUFFERING

Physical and mental impairments will often create suffering of both a psychological and physical nature. The disabled will frequently have to contend with uncomfortable braces, painful muscles, excruciating headaches, varying degrees of digestive, cardiac or kidney discomfort. The pain is real. Drugs may be helpful to some extent, but the suffering will usually have to be endured. In addition, there may be a psychological suffering; the loneliness; the tears; the rejection; the many adjustments to an essentially nondisabled culture. Suffering of this type is never wished for. It is draining, debilitating and demanding. It may often prevent the individual from the physical and social experiences needed for selfhood. This is not imagined suffering. It is, in most cases, real suffering. Research has shown that so real and constant is the pain, that often persons with disabilities develop a much higher tolerance for physical anguish than the *normal* person. No individual should be asked to deal with unnecessary suffering for any reason. But, if suffering is unavoidable, it also may be used to advantage.

There is much research upon the positive aspects of suffering as it relates to keener self-knowledge, positive changes in behavior, and to the general phenomenon of a personal growth through "soul searching" (Rusk and Taylor 1946, Wright 1960, White 1948). Such persons as Helen Keller, Christy Brown, Harold Russell, Verda Heisler, Franklin Delano Roosevelt have all commented about the positive, as well as negative, effects of their suffering.

Dr. Heisler (1972), a clinical psychologist whose bout with polio left her physically disabled but brought about an interest in the psychology of impairment which produced a fine book, *The Handicapped Child In The Family*, puts it this way:

> When life brings suffering to us, we must choose between the alternatives of entering the experience head on and trying to know its deepest and fullest meaning, or of turning aside from our own feelings and emotions with a denial that they exist and a pretense that we are unaffected by the dark side of life."

She continues:

> My personal philosophy of life carries the conviction that the actualization of a person's potential must include his conscious experiencing of the dark side of life as well as the sunshine. Suffering comes to human beings in many, many different ways. Whenever I have met a person who has managed to live without establishing any conscious relationship to the experience of suffering, I have found that person to be vapid and superficial and limited by his inability to understand his own vague dissatisfaction with life. For life is full of paradoxes, and one of them is that the capacity for experiencing suffering and the capacity for experiencing joy are two sides of the same coin . . . It has been my experience that the degree of individuation I have achieved has come as much out of the valleys of the shadow as it has come from the sun shining on me near the peak of the mountain!

INFERIORITY AND LOWERED STATUS

Individuals learn that they are inferior, they are not born with feelings of lower status. They are taught this by their family, their friends, and their society. Once they have learned and accepted these feelings, they will often find confirmation for them in even the most insignificant occurrences. A friend may not call for a few days and they will interpret this as a personal rejection. A teacher may seat them at a certain desk in the classroom which they will equate with the teacher "not liking them." It is a simple matter for the disabled to interpret even the most casual actions as negative responses toward them.

It is somewhat natural for all of us to have an *ideal*. The disabled individual is often guilty of idealizing the nondisabled and holding up their *normal* performance as the goal for their idealized self. There are those for whom this normal performance is mentally or physically impossible, but they will continue to strive for its mastery. These individuals can only bring upon themselves undue suffering, depression and eventual loss of self-esteem. There are many instances of impaired individuals who have made remarkable adjustments to severe impairments. These are often seen as triumphs by the therapists, teachers and family. But the disabled person still perceives them as not meeting *normal* standards. Thus, even triumphs are relegated to defeat. This only further supports already strong feelings of unworthiness.

Though the reality of the disability and the responses of society are strong causal factors, disabled persons are largely responsible for determining their own status. If they are displeased with their position in society, there is a dual challenge in overcoming this. First, they must see themselves as they are, always more than their impairment. They must value themselves in a total sense, recognizing their abilities and strengths as well as accepting their real limits. Secondly, in order to effect countervailing changes in the attitudes they have regarding themselves, and those feelings which others have about them, they must learn to trust their own feelings, place more value upon their *own*, more personal self-assessment, and live in accordance with their felt needs and desires.

Persons who are disabled will have many unique concerns and conflicts as they create their personal selves. They will have a greater tendency to encounter problems in interpersonal relationships. They will possibly be faced with more and real frustrations, uncertainties, rejections, and suffering. They will experience devastating feelings of self-devaluation, insecurity, and real limitations to their experience. The temptation to succumb to these feelings and fall into self-depreciation and hopeless despair will frequently occur to them. The battle will be a difficult and continuing one, but if they are to realize themselves as total persons, the battle will be necessary. They will have to be strong. The battlefield for *self* survival for those who are different is no place for the meek. As Christy Brown puts it:

> I could now no longer run away from myself. I had grown too big for that. In a thousand ways, large and small, as each day went by, as the family grew up one by one and became—to me—strange self-supporting adults, I saw and felt the limitations, the boredom, the terrible narrowness of my own existence. All around me were signs of activity, effort, growth. Everyone had something to do, something to occupy them and keep their minds and their hands active. They had interests, activities, and aims to make their lives an integrated whole and give their energies a natural outlet and a natural medium of expression. I had only my left foot.
>
> My life seemed just like a dark, stuffy little corner in which I was thrust with my face turned towards the wall, hearing all the sound and motion of the big world outside, and yet unable to move, unable to go out and take my place in it like my brothers and sisters and everyone else that I knew. I wanted something to live for, and there was nothing. I wanted my life to have a purpose, a value, but there was none. It was hollow, meaningless. I felt flat, searching for something I couldn't find, reaching for something I couldn't grasp.
>
> I knew quite well that, no matter how I might appear, on the surface, no matter how I might pretend to others or how much I lied to myself, I would never be happy or at peace with myself as long as I was crippled like this. I remembered Lourdes and the people I had met on the way to the Grotto, and again I tried to be like them; patient, cheerful, resigned to their suffering, knowing the reward that awaited them in the next world. But it was no use. I was too human. There was too much of the man in me and not enough of the humble servant who submits willingly to his Master's will. I wanted to see and to know more of this world before I thought about the next. Despite the wonder and beauty of Lourdes I was still very much the boy who hadn't yet learned how to be meek.

Chapter 12:

The Rights Of The Disabled

I dreamed I had a child, and even in the dream I saw that it was my life, and it was an idiot, and I ran away. But it always crept into my lap again, clutched at my clothes. Until I thought, if I could kiss it, whatever in it was my own, perhaps I could sleep. And I bent over its broken face, and it was horrible...but I kissed it. I think that one must finally take one's life into one's arms....

ARTHUR MILLER
After The Fall

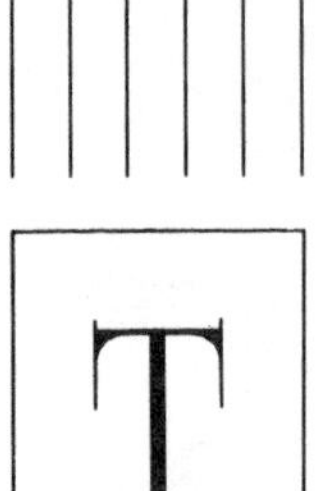

o say that the person with a disability has rights seems almost ridiculous at this point. But, indeed, the facts illustrate that this is not the case. It might, to the contrary, be stated that as a group they are one of the most discriminated against in our present society.

It was only recently that the disabled have banned together to any extent, mostly through their parents who have finally become vocal, and spoken out, however meekly, on their own behalf. They have not had public marches, become militant or made demands, but, as with any discriminated-against minority group, they would have equal reason to do so. In the past they have been content to remain silent, ashamed and apologetic for their difference, like lonely birds in winter, existing upon whatever kindness or handout *normal* people deigned to offer them.

Prejudice and discrimination toward the disabled is mostly based upon misconceptions, ignorance and fears which have been passed on through the culture. It is a case of misconstrued ideas regarding the causes of impairments, or ignorance and fears regarding the mysterious reactions they bring about. These attitudes have formed the basis for segregating the disabled into state institutions, hospitals or local public facilities, "where they belong." The inference being that they do not have a place in the *normal* world.

Illustrative of this are the numerous physical and structural restrictions imposed upon the disabled, even in public buildings. Schools, state and federal offices, public recreational facilities, grocery stores and department stores are often without ramps, elevators or the basic structural needs to enable the disabled to move about them, to pay their bills, shop and meet their day-to-day requirements for living.

This prejudice is also reflected in job discrimination. Not only is the job market limited for the disabled, but in many cases it is actually closed to them. Often job insurance is either not available or difficult to come by. Antiquated laws often make licensing of all sorts doubly difficult. Even where there are no such barriers, the attitudes of employers are such that their minds are all but closed to the possibility of hiring a *handicapped* person. There are occasions when an employer will hire a disabled person as a publicity "gimmick," a favor, or as a charitable gesture—not, of course, expecting that there is a chance that, as an employer, something may be gained by the employment.

For several years I served as a local chairman of the California Governors' Committee for Employment of the Handicapped. During this time I encountered situations and attitudes which, if related, would indeed shock one into disbelief. There were employers who could not be convinced that a paraplegic could still be a good telephone operator, a blind girl could make a great receptionist, a mildly retarded girl could work in a cafeteria line or bus tables. Especially frustrating were the many educators who preached equal opportunities as they educated the disabled in their own districts, only to turn about and refuse to hire their graduates as teachers or classroom aides, even when they were more than fully qualified. This attitude persists although there is living proof that hiring the disabled is a very profitable practice, that individuals who are blind, who are paralyzed, who are deaf, make outstanding, successful, skillful, reliable workers.

In fact, it was even difficult to convince some employers that there were disabilities which were advantageous in certain job situations. Deafness could be an asset in a noisy factory, blindness would offer little or no problem in a photographic dark room and retardation might be good in a job which required constant repetition of tasks which might bore the average worker into inefficiency.

Though perhaps not intentional, there is subtle discrimination even in housing. How many rental units or apartments make the necessary structural adjustments to facilitate mobility for the disabled?

There are institutions of higher learning which willingly admit the disabled, then offer required classes which call for someone in a wheelchair to climb three flights of stairs in order to attend.

The question is often asked, "Why should the necessary adjustments be made, the additional expense be incurred, for such a small percentage of our population?" The answer is simple, much of the key to the level of civilization a society has reached is to be found in how it treats its minorities, especially in a society based upon the principle of "equality and justice for all." It is a clear indication of the level of humanistic attitude people feel one for the other. Albert Schweitzer said that man was only truly human when he was able to see each man's suffering, each man's need, each man's despair, each man's pain, as his own.

Making adjustments for the disabled is also wise economically. Those who work become self-reliant, pay taxes, and support their society rather than become a drain upon it. Just a few years ago an eminent Scandinavian special educator visiting our state institutions for the retarded made the shocking statement that we treat our retarded as they treat their cattle! This may have been a bit of an overstatement but treatment of the disabled still has a long way to go to be considered truly human. It is sad that human rights must often be legislated. Regulations must be drafted to bring about what should be basic humanistic action and response. Laws must be created to keep men, women and children from being relegated to slave labor, secondary citizen status or despair even though it has often been argued that values and feelings can never be truly legislated.

Persons who are disabled have rights, too. These rights must be accepted as basic to their well-being and the eventual development of their potential as human beings. If they are afforded these rights they become, like all people, responsible forever for what they do for themselves. If they are denied these rights from the start *we* will become forever responsible for them.

Persons with disabilities have the same and equal rights as everyone else. They have the right to live their lives in the most comfortable, creative and fulfilling manner possible, in freedom, joy and continual growth. They have the right to work at a job of their choice according to their abilities. Whereas they do not expect special consideration, they should also not have to be superior, continually having to prove themselves, anymore than anyone else. They simply need equal treatment and equal opportunity, to live in equal dignity.

They have other more personal rights, too. In the beginning and all through their lives, for instance, disabled persons should be instructed about their impairments. They must know as much as possible about their physical or mental problems and what they are likely to mean to them in the future. It is not uncommon that children may grow into adulthood without ever having been "told" specifically what their problems are. They only know that they appear different and are treated differently from others in their environment. But they are not sure how, why, or the implications of their differences. This can even be true in schools, where children may be evaluated, diagnosed and placed in segregated classes without once being counseled as to why. Children will often discover from their classmates that they have been placed in the *dumb* class.

This secrecy was carried to such an extreme in one case, as to be laughable. A child had been going to a speech therapist for several months. Actually he loved this *special* activity. It was great fun. The shock came when he returned to his classroom after a therapy session and was questioned as to whether he had seen Mrs. X, his therapist. "Oh yes!" he answered. "I like Mrs. X, she plays neat games with me. But do you think she knows I stutter?"

Certainly we do not want to impose meaningless labels and technical jargon upon children, but before remediation of any sort can occur, the individual must know, at least, what is being remediated, how and why.

One special class teacher always made a practice of visiting with each child who entered her class for educable retarded children. Along with several happy and friendly revelations, she would explain that he or she was tested and found to be needing *special help* because, "at this time, you are not learning as you should." Her class, she explained, was a place where they could work together to see what could be done about it. Even such a simple and friendly interview as this can inform children of what is happening and set the atmosphere of cooperative learning so important to growth. But many teachers have new children thrust upon them by surprise in the middle of the day with no knowledge of them whatsoever, so there is no time for explanations. Others feel awkward about such explanations and do not feel a need to explain anything to them at all.

It is not unusual, too, that a child, once diagnosed, will be placed in a remedial program and forgotten. This phenomenon was illustrated in a recent Stanford University study of people who admitted themselves into mental institutions. They found it easy to get in but very difficult, indeed, to get out. This is often the case in large state hospitals for the disabled, where the very nature of the institution makes it extremely likely that one could get lost. But this can also occur in smaller public school programs.

Medical, educational and psychological re-evaluations must be made periodically to determine educational, physical and emotional changes which the individual may exhibit. This is especially true in the early years of development when radical changes can occur, but is equally important throughout the disabled person's life.

Persons who are disabled have the right to not only equal human status in society but equal familial status. It may often be the case that children are relegated to inferior positions by their families. This may be overtly or covertly done, but in either case it is destructive and inimical to the children's welfare. It may be covertly done through disguised familial attitudes toward the disability, in giving children the feeling of being real burdens upon the family. It may overtly be accomplished by family overprotection which serves to continuously point up to the children their inadequacies, and each family member taking over the responsibility *for* the child's life, needs and decisions.

One young blind girl related to me that everything she had accomplished (and it was a great deal) toward independence had been a battle. Not only had she been in constant combat with her mother and father who were more certain of her limitations than either her ophthalmologist, teacher, or herself, but she also had to battle her overprotective brother:

> He would always want to do for me. He never let up being the big brother. He never wanted me to go out alone. He wouldn't even allow me to go to the corner drug store without escorting me. If I would have allowed him to do so, I'm certain he would have fed me. You can imagine his horror when I told him and the family I was moving out and getting my own apartment!

Being independent often isn't easy for persons who are disabled but it can be made doubly difficult for them with the added burden of an overprotective family or society.

It is true that it is difficult for the family to know just how much to allow and when to disallow, for the child's welfare, but sensitivity to the individual is always the best guide. Parents must use the same judgment they do with all their children. How long does a mother escort her child to school? When does she know it is right to stop? In the growth process, when a specific level of development is reached it produces a certain behavior. This behavior leads to the next, more sophisticated behavior. There is a time to hold and a time to let go. It is only through this process that one can allow persons who are disabled to grow and determine their own degree of dependence and independence.

Disabled children have a right to voice opinions in family decisions and plans for the future. They also have an equal right to the same treatment and equal opportunity to experiment, to fail, to succeed, to become angry, to get dirty and to make stupid as well as successful decisions. They may be disabled but they still must learn that they are their own person. They do not belong to their parents, their family or society. They are part of all but still apart from all.

Persons who are disabled have the right to make the major decision regarding whether their disability will become a handicap or not. That is, no matter how strong the cultural and societal forces are regarding their being "less than a person," they will be the one to make the final decision regarding themselves.

Christy Brown relates to this in a most dramatic way when he writes that with only the support of his mother (family, physician, friends having abandoned him as a lost cause), *he* decided that *he* had to make *his* statement—even if he had to use his foot with which to do it. This same determination is shown by countless other disabled persons who at some point in their lives made the decision that it was their right and theirs alone, to decide to be, or to die.

Another important right for the disabled is the right to a superior education for life. Too often the educational opportunities for persons with disabilities are limited or inadequate. If they are in self-contained, segregated classrooms, they may find themselves in the identical physical space with the same teacher for most or all of their school experience. The teacher may be outstanding and well-prepared, as is usually the case, but cannot be all things to all subjects and all students. Nonetheless, the children will not have the possible advantage of many teachers, of many different educational opportunities and settings. There are some children who will be in segregated schools for their total education. This will offer them the security of a known environment and people who are sympathetic to their special needs but they will someday have to leave this unique environment. The question always arises as to how well they will be prepared to enter the real, not so sympathetic world.

There are many values in a Special Education if that education is for meeting the special needs of the child. But this may not be the case. Special needs are usually defined as the special *learning*, and special *physical adjustments* of the children. Do they need Braille, large print, speech reading, sign or finger spelling, special remedial classes in writing, reading, language, speech? In this restricted sense of education, most special schools and classes are very adequate, even superior. But in the larger sense of education for *life*, they often fall short. Vital problems, those that will occur to the person with a disability after schooling is completed such as job preparation, possible admission to college or university, and preparation for economic independence, are often not fully realized. Most disabled persons are ill prepared to face the world of work after school graduation. As a result, all too many spend their lives in some sheltered work environment, or much worse, in front of a television set to "pass the time away and forget the loneliness and pain."

An "education for life" must deal with the individual's adjustment to pain, fear, growth, loneliness, sexual needs, plans for marriage and a family. It is possible for individuals who are disabled to graduate from high school and even a university without realizing who they are, where they are, or how they got there. They do not realize that they have certain *human* rights and needs, too—such rights as satisfaction of sexual desires, needs for love and affection, needs for personal and emotional fulfillment and other such powerful human requirements. These are seldom, if ever, considered as a part of what is "special" about special education. Still, they are equally important, or perhaps more so, than other educational considerations.

A college student with cerebral palsy said to me:

> Until I read a book I found by accident in the library, on the sexual rights of handicapped persons, I didn't know that I could express this need in my lifetime, let alone fulfill it in my way. We all felt these needs in school and talked about them mostly in secret but no teacher or counselor ever discussed them with us. I remember a kid in a wheelchair who used to masturbate in class. We all knew what he was doing, even the teacher, but no one ever commented on it. The kids snickered but the teacher always pretended she didn't see it. We had girlfriends, too, but we were never alone with them too much. Sex was a big mystery for us all and we couldn't even imagine that we could really learn methods for sexual relations with the opposite sex, no matter what our impairment, let alone get married someday! Why the hell they don't tell us these things, I'll never know. They're certainly as important as spelling!

The right to an education for life is everyone's right. If the nondisabled do not receive this education in the family or school they have other means of acquiring it. For the disabled these are very real and frustrating problems which may never be solved.

The disabled must be afforded the right to act and react with nondisabled individuals. It is important that they come into contact with the majority. In doing this they will meet, head on, many frustrations and anxieties but only in this way will they ever learn how to realistically cope with and accept their differences. When I speak of contact, I do not mean artificially arranged social events like having a high school club organize a *mixed* dance as part of their *community service*. This type of socialization, so often experienced by the disabled, is demeaning. No one wants anyone to be with them as a *favor*. One disabled student put it this way:

> I hate those functions! It's often a process of their using *us* to make *them* feel better. What kind of an evening does that make for? And it's usually all so phony. When the night's over and they feel secure about the fact that they're superior and they've done their bit we go our own way and when we meet again someplace they don't even say 'hello.' Hell! I'd rather not even go.

It is true that, often, to make more normal contacts, persons who are disabled will have to be the aggressors, for most people will hesitate approaching them. They will find that church groups, political organizations, hobby groups, and other gatherings, where there is a common and strong *external* bond of belief and feeling, will open doors to a possibility for *internal* human bonds as well.

A blind girl in one of my classes, Susan, used to plan study groups at her home and invite several classmates to attend. She told me:

> A lot of them came, at first, just to be nice, but I'd try to make the groups as successful, natural and of real value as possible. Soon I found that I'd made some great friends, school work aside. I was going out more and being included in more stuff. It really broke the ice.

This, of course, does not mean that the disabled person should frantically be seeking contact with the nondisabled, throughout life. It means that an equal balance between disabled and nondisabled friends will offer more experience, more opportunities for growth and a keener knowledge of the world *outside*.

Helen Keller, though both deaf and blind, once having acquired language, never isolated herself. She was eternally going to receptions, meeting people, and totally emerging herself in the stream of life. She was not always accepted nor understood, but in this way, she said she remained forever refreshed and refreshing.

When one has acquired the social tools necessary for satisfactory interpersonal relationships one often finds that a disability becomes secondary. As mentioned earlier, part of the fear and rejection the nondisabled feel toward the disabled is caused by the inexperience, the newness they feel in the situation. Social tools will have much to do with the breakdown of the barriers imposed by these feelings. The disabled person has a right to know and acquire these learned tools.

One aspect of social acceptance is attractiveness. The disabled often have very attractive physical attributes which go unnoticed. This is sometimes true because they take little or no pains to accentuate them. The attitude may be one of, "Who looks at me anyway?" At best, a self-defeating idea! Perhaps more people would look if more effort was put into the accentuation of the positive. Watching weight and diet, the correct use of makeup, the choice of clothes, the care of hair and skin, and generally finding means to substitute for the cosmetic barrier which the disability may cause. These can be learned.

Another method for achieving the necessary skills for interaction is in learning the specific behaviors which bring about positive special responses in new situations and which permit interaction to continue. This entails the learning of problem-solving approaches to social interaction and a knowledge of the alternative routes by which positive goals may be achieved and negative experiences avoided. For example, such things may be considered as how to approach a stranger or a strange social situation. How to ask for help or politely refuse it. How to respond to overt and covert rejection and hostility. How to open a conversation and keep it going. These are all factors which make for more positive social interaction.

The disabled, as can be seen, have their rights, too. None are particularly unique or demanding. They are simply the rights of all humans. In essence, they are entitled to their right of self-actualization, and the knowledge, discovery and interaction by which it may be accomplished. This self-discovery must be an ongoing process that begins with birth and physically, at least, ends with death, but it will never be attained unless the person who is disabled is afforded equal rights to risk, to step out into the world and declare this worth as a human being.

Everyone, to some extent, is different. Some carry their badge of difference with pride, others with shame. Either way, the badge must be carried. One can spend his or her life hiding behind the impairment and thus become, not a person, but a symbol of disability. Or, one may carry it with acceptance. But carry it, one must. The choice is the individual's. One may as well carry it in joy as in despair! If one is not given rights freely, one must assume them, fight for them, demand them—not in the spirit of hate and violence, but in the spirit of love. For in a very real sense if rights are denied to one person, they are denied to all. No one was ever meant to reach the point of death without having known the greatest encounter—that of knowing themselves along the way. That is the right of all—disabled or not!

Chapter 13: Becoming Disabled Later In Life

The encouraging thing is that every time you meet a situation, though you may think at the time it is an impossibility and you go through tortures of the damned, once you have met it you find that forever after you are freer than you were before. If you can live through that you can live through anything. You gain strength, courage and confidence by every experience in which you really stop to look fear in the face.

ELEANOR ROOSEVELT
You Learn by Living

s it may appear from our discussion of disability so far, debilitating conditions are not solely the problem of children. All that has been discussed is equally applicable to those who become disabled later in life. No one is immune to a permanent disability. Thousands of debilitating accidents occur in our country each day. At one moment you are an expert athlete and in an instant you may suffer an accident which will make sports, as you have known them, a thing of the past. You may suffer a stroke which will leave you aphasic or permanently paralyzed. You may be taking a peaceful Sunday drive with your family and you are brought home from the hospital, several weeks later, forever mentally or physically damaged. This does not mean to suggest that one should live in constant fear and apprehension. If one is reasonably careful, the odds are still in favor of avoiding a major problem of this kind. It is a fact, though, that in any year, such as 1972, accidents caused 440,000 *permanent impairments* in the United States! One hundred and seventy thousand of these were due to automobile accidents, 90,000 were work-related accidents, 110,000 occurred in homes and 70,000 in public places.

Modern science has achieved wonders in reducing the death rate from accidents, but it is still a long way from learning how to deal with severed arms and legs, or the irreparableness of severe brain damage. It has extended life expectancy but it has still to find means of maintaining sensory functions which degenerate with age, such as hearing, vision, vascular and metabolic problems.

It seems safe to say that at some period in the lives of most of us we shall have to cope with a permanent physical or mental problem. A stroke, heart and kidney disorders, muscle and metabolic problems, an accident, are possibilities for all of us in our lifetime.

The reality of wars, too, has taken its toll upon young, healthy minds and bodies. The world appears to be a long way off from that "war to end all wars." It seems even nonsensical that we could still believe that we can end wars by means of war. It is like using hate to destroy hate. So wars go on, and physically perfect boys return crippled men.

Most often, impairments which occur later in life incur similar problems as those which happen at birth. They present, basically, only a difference in kind and value adjustment. With birth defects, children are born to blindness or deafness and form their own normal world, having no other standard to go by. Only gradually do they learn that they are disabled, that they are not like others. But, by this time their basic adjustment is made to the problem and they will not be required to change it too radically. In disabilities which occur later in life the main difference lies in the fact that they occur all at once, as a sudden, startling fact of life. Abruptly, with no previous warning, one's image of intactness is severely damaged, one's physical world is radically changed. One is forced to experience and deal with feelings of strangeness and unfamiliarity regarding a world in which one has previously felt secure and comfortable. One is faced with a major modification of the previous self, and is required to make an adjustment to a new, perhaps more limited, self.

Persons who, for one reason or another, had broken bones which required that their arms or legs be immobilized in rigid dressings of gauze-impregnated plaster of Paris have often experienced these same frustrations and adjustments for a period of several weeks. They were forced to move more slowly, readjust their time, find new ways of performing simple daily tasks like eating, showering, even sleeping. All at once they became clumsy, awkward, inefficient, dependent. They were required to curtail many of their activities and change plans which seemed no longer appropriate. The sense of relief when the cast was removed attested to the degree of frustration and major modification brought on by even a temporary impairment. What was once *normal* had, all at once, become *abnormal*.

Persons, born blind, often state that they feel no different from others. One girl informed us:

> It is as normal for me to be blind in the world, as it is for you to see. My lack of sight still creates some practical problems for me like mobility, and acceptance in social relationships. School is no problem since I learned Braille and typing. But I'm O.K., I have my world.

Essentially, she has stated the basic limitations of blindness from birth accurately. She will have to face social misunderstanding, continue her education by means other than visual and find new ways to achieve independent mobility. Aside from these, she says, she is "O.K.," her self is intact and the world she has created in her blindness from birth, remains the same.

On the other hand, it is very common, for instance, among young veterans who were blinded in Vietnam, to decry the fact that they will never again see a sunset, or the face of their children as they grow. They have severe problems with the esthetic loss their visual impairment has imposed upon them. No driving around to see the sights, no back-packing in the mountains alone, no stars, no birds in flight, no blossoms. With this, they are also faced with the threat and insecurity of occupational change. "I can't continue my job without my sight. I need my eyes!"

These are new problems for them, and very real. It is not easy to cope anew in the world which one has spent years mastering but which has suddenly become dark and full of dim, menacing sounds and images. Whereas the young girl, blind from birth, said she was intact and had her world in spite of her impairment, the Vietnam veteran felt that he was disintegrated and had lost *his*. This statement encompasses the basic adjustment differences for the person who is born disabled and the one who has acquired the disability later in life.

Many problems relating to adjustment in the adventitiously disabled have been studied. Factors such as the age at which the disability occurs, the sex of the person involved, the unique perception of the *body ideal* and the feeling one has regarding intactness, have all been researched for their relationship to adjustment. These studies have revealed no conclusive evidence that either age, sex, or perception played a consistently significant role in the adjustment processes of the adventitiously disabled.

Some findings did suggest that age of onset was less related to adjustment than the other factors such as the individual's previous concept of physique, concern over physical intactness and society's prejudices regarding these. When athletes lose their limbs it is a devastating experience for them. Their values regarding their physical self are extremely high. The investment they have made in their body and its development is great. The association they have made between body and self-worth is strong. On the other hand, the nonathletic, more esthetic type students may have only minor adjustments relating to how their impaired body will adjust to physical activities but their problems will become greater as they limit scholarly or artistic pursuits. Individuals who are very beauty conscious will have a greater problem of adjustment to facial deformities than less concerned women or men. Often, though, due to society's attitudes relating to physical beauty, the problem will probably be a difficult one for all of them. The cogent factor of the individual's attitude toward physique will not always determine adjustment, but it cannot be minimized.

The degree, or extent of the impairment does not seem to have a predictable value in adjustment, either, nor does physical intactness. Catherine T. lost a finger on her right hand in a household accident. She related the following revealing statement:

> Don't minimize the trauma one feels upon losing even a single finger. It affects your entire sense of wholeness. When I left the hospital, and for several weeks later, I could hardly think about anything but methods of hiding my impairment. Actually it wasn't much of a problem at all. I was able to function as usual. It was more of a social stigma. I tried to hide it even from me. Every time I washed my hands, set the table or cooked a meal I saw the missing finger and was almost totally devastated. Each such experience left me ashamed, sick and revolted. My missing finger had become the center of my self. My whole existence. I couldn't see that there was more to me than my finger. It took me a long time before I could accept it. As I accepted it, others did. As I forgot about it, others seemed to. At any rate, the greater me took over again, at long last, and now I'm as vain as ever.

Verda Heisler (1972) was severely crippled from polio when she was eight years old. All at once she was transformed from an energetic, active child to one whose entire body was paralyzed from the neck down.

She says:

> From the perspective of my present age and state of union with life, I look back upon *all* the experiences of my life with deep appreciation for their value in the process of my own development as a person. Who I am as a person—what sort of person I am—has always been of utmost importance to me. When I was a little girl approaching adolescence, I felt painful envy of the beauty, grace and physical agility of my older sister, but even then I knew with complete certainty that I would never want to have been able to change places with her. I did not want to be anyone but myself, despite the terrible, unalterable impairment of my physical structure.

Dr. Heisler, unlike Catherine, was almost totally impaired, being unable to use her body from her neck to her toes. Catherine experienced her loss of a single finger to be as monumental as Dr. Heisler's paralysis. They both felt similar pain and the equal loss of beauty and grace, with uniform intensity. Their final adjustments to life and their impairments, even with the vast difference in kind and degree, were equally as demanding, and the processes involved were analogous. It seems that it is not the degree of loss or the feelings regarding intactness that the adventitiously disabled experience that becomes most significant in adjustment, but rather their basic attitude regarding themselves as total persons. The adjustment process seems to commence, in most cases, when disabled persons are again able to see and respect themselves as individuals capable of change and readjustment, even to the most singular challenge. This knowledge leads to the process of relinquishing the old concept of the intact, physically perfect self, an acceptance of what is left, and a start toward a new, more realistic concept of self.

This, then, brings us back to the person. The major influence toward any future adjustment in life, at all times, will always lie in the individual's present adjustment. Age, perception of the ideal body, sex, may or may not be variables in disability, but, in the final analysis, it is what persons already *are* that will determine whether they will have the courage and strength to accept what they have become. Depending upon their present integration, they have several alternatives to adjustments from which to choose. They may, in essence, withdraw from their past world and enter into the more segregated, safe and protected world of disability. Or, they may try to assume their old life style and try to behave and appear as normal as before. They may also choose to accept their impairment and its limitations and strive to regain a new self-image as much as possible, accepting their new self, with limitations, but without devaluating themselves for the limitations.

The major factors which will influence the readjustment of the adventitiously disabled are many. For simplification, these may be grouped under a few main headings:

Changes in intention of others; Changes in value system; Changes in expectations of self; Changes in perception; Changes in occupation.

CHANGES IN INTENTION OF OTHERS

With congenital impairments, individual choices of adjustment will depend largely upon the reaction of the *others* in the person's life. These others will include a wife, or husband, children, the extended family, their intimate friends and the rehabilitation team, as well as the society in which they move.

So often persons who have become disabled will find that how others behave toward them may well become their major adjustment problem. One such person, Loretta E., expressed it well when she said:

> The worst problem for me was how my family and friends treated me after I lost my sight. They were oversolicitous and always trying to help. They moved over me like vultures, like they were waiting for me to fall to pieces, so they could descend. Their messages, verbal and nonverbal, all seemed to say, 'You're blind so how are you going to get a job?' 'You're blind so your life is over.' It almost drove me crazy! Every time I'd have a positive feeling or take a step forward, they were there to remind me through help or tears or advice, that it was no use. It was as if I not only had the job of getting myself together, but was responsible for helping them to get together, too! My adjustment was made doubly difficult.

Such attitudes toward disability, limitation and handicaps can be very stigmatizing. When internalized, individuals may begin to accept these limiting attitudes as reality. They may come to assume that they are truly unable to do for themselves, to become independent again, to continue to grow as human persons. These self-devaluations may prevent them from seeing themselves as total persons and thus create for them the self-image of disabled persons, precluding change and growth.

CHANGES IN VALUE SYSTEM

Today you believe you have the world by the tail, tomorrow it slaps you across the face. Today you are a functioning, well-integrated person, tomorrow you fall into conflict and confusion. You may believe that many of the things you prize and appreciate and which are deeply ingrained in your value system are dependent upon your being a *whole* physical person. A disability which causes you to lose a valued part, produces great anguish. In developing your value system you never stopped to consider that what was truly essential about you was often not measurable in terms of the parts which made you up, or the objects you valued in your life space. You were not aware that the true values existed independently of your physical self or things outside of you. In his classic, *Anatomy of Melancholy* (1627), Robert Burton makes the point well.

> Deformities and imperfections of our bodies, such as lameness, crookedness, deafness, blindness, be they innate or accidental, torture many men: Yet this may comfort them that those imperfections of the body do not a whit blemish their soul, or hinder the operations of it, but rather help and much increase it.

The literature is replete with examples of people who only *found* themselves when they were required to re-assess their values. Often they discovered that their values were not really theirs but those which had been imposed upon them by their families or society.

This insight comes, often, as a result of a period of pain or confusion, of loss, of missing something of value which requires search through the morass of accumulated feelings, beliefs and ideas which had seemed essential up until this point and were simply accepted without question. This, then, leads to a revaluing of what is still present and possible, and results in a drastic change in our essential value systems. This process may be quick for some or it may take months or even years for others, but the major discovery is that of the changing nature and frailty of our value system and the danger of becoming so locked into it as to be inflexible and unable to free ourselves even after we find that it is serving only to imprison us!

A very active woman friend of mine in the San Francisco Bay Area was stricken with a stroke at the height of her professional career which has left her paralyzed and bedridden, in a more or less physically dependent state, for the remainder of her life. She said:

> It was terrible, at first; it seemed like the end of the world. I felt that all of life had been taken from me. I was valueless. What good was one who could not even move from a bed, who had to be waited upon for even the most simple need? What reason was there for me? What meaning? Then, all at once, the old pioneer feeling welled up in me and I discovered that I was still alive and that there were plenty of ways of doing what I had to do, of being what I had to be. It just meant a change—not in the essence of me, so much, as in the manner in which I would have to do them. I assessed myself. I was still intelligent. My speech was intact. I could still be as 'crazy' as I ever was. I got a trusty tape recorder and I soon found that I could do as much or more from my bed as I could from my desk. I could still, with some

> mechanical adjustments, read, take phone calls, and if I willed it, my life could go on as usual. Not life as I physically knew it before my paralysis but rather life, in the essential sense as I knew it. My spirit wasn't disabled. It was as ornery and determined as ever.

She had used the strength of her old value system to create the base for a new self which did not require her previous physical abilities. She had discovered her worth and in doing so, what was essential about herself. She had found that what was truly essential about a human being was not arms, legs, eyes, ears or hands, or for that matter, any physical part. These were aids but not ends. (It is well-known that many people are physically intact but use their physical and mental faculties so seldom as to cause them to atrophy.) She found that what was essential about one was to be discovered in that "ol' pioneer spirit" toward life, which was invisible to the eye.

It sometimes takes a long time for adventitiously disabled persons to learn this simple fact, but when they do, they find that they have become truly free.

CHANGES IN PHYSICAL EXPECTATION

Often adventitiously disabled persons will feel that their newly-acquired disabilities have imprisoned them. They see the impairment as setting up great barriers, separating them from others with *normal abilities.* "I can't be with other people. I can't hear anymore." "What good is there in going on a vacation? I can't see anything." "My wheelchair can't make it up the ladders to the Indian pueblos, so why go?" These obstacles are often not reality-based but self-created. If we will to do something, experience has shown that we will find the way. No disability is a deterrent; only we deter.

Lucillia Moore, a teacher of the deaf who became deaf herself, so loved the company of others that she made herself so proficient at lip reading that she could have passengers in the back seat of the car and follow their conversation perfectly through her rear view mirror. Scores of sightless individuals leave daily on trips to Europe, on treks to conquer Everest, on winter skiing expeditions. Maria French, one of the contributors to this book, left her wheelchair and found her own means for seeing the Indian pueblos.

Certainly there may be real limitations but they will only limit in certain aspects of one's life. The effect of a limitation in one aspect of self need not spread to engulf the total self. Disabled persons may have to give up basketball as they know it if they have no limbs, or find ways of getting similar experiences from a wheelchair. One may find that hands, still intact, offer a different range of recreational possibilities—table tennis, chess, writing, planting flowers, throwing pots or painting pictures.

It is vital that the adventitiously disabled assess not only what activities are lost due to an impairment but which are left, and as yet undiscovered.

CHANGES IN PERCEPTION

Most all of us, disabled or not, use only a small insignificant amount of our potential for perception. In fact, Orenstein (1971) has indicated that most people never got beyond using sense modalities, sight, hearing, smelling, touching, except as delimitors of experience, to screen out environmental stimuli. It never occurs to us that there is a vast world beyond our present perceptual abilities which, because of our ignorance or apathy, does not exist for us. This world is often discovered by those who lose a sense modality later in life. Those who become blind, for instance, often comment upon their keener awareness of sounds in the environment, sounds of which they were never before cognizant even though they were surely present. Until blindness necessitated more perceptive hearing, their ears were mainly used to delimit stimuli. Their eyes had given them the necessary clues they needed to function and had, in a sense, deprived them of the development of their other senses. Everyone has a greater potential to see, hear, taste, smell, or to touch than they are aware of or use. It simply must be consciously worked for.

By losing a modality, a person may learn that all is not lost. Blind persons, for instance, may find that there are many more sensory experiences available through those senses still intact. They may discover the joy of attending lectures or *hearing* the wonder of music for the first time. So few of us have truly heard music—we have simply listened to it. They may never have heard the beauty of nature, nor the wonder of a human voice.

Changes in perception are often forced upon us with the occurrence of a disability but included with this may come the challenge to develop the limitless sensorial capacities still available to each of us.

I had a blind friend once ask me, "Have you ever heard a sunrise?" When I answered, "No," he said, "Pity!"

CHANGES IN OCCUPATION

One of the most difficult areas of adjustment for the adventitiously disabled is in that of work, for in this area, indeed, often lies social and economic security. With the advent of an impairment which will affect occupational status they immediately see themselves as helpless, lost and charity cases. Often heard are such statements as, "I don't know anything else but auto repair. How will I make a living?" Or, "I've been a painter all my life, what will I do now? I'll have to go on welfare."

Of course, persons who become disabled later in life, are not aware of what is available to them vocationally. They will need help in order to discover the many opportunities which are open to them. They will be amazed at how many jobs there are which still fit their talents and interests. Furthermore, individuals find themselves in occupational ruts into which they remain tied for security reasons or because they have no knowledge that there are other things they could be doing with even greater pleasure and success, or because they fear the risk involved in vocational change. It would be interesting to find how many workers truly gain satisfaction from the work which they are performing. It would be surprising if there were many people who were. Still, it is known that the relationship of "joy in work" to "joy in life" is very close. Persons with acquired disabilities often find that losing their jobs is not the end of their occupational opportunities. It might, indeed, be the beginning of new-found, more satisfying positions.

This discussion has suggested that adjusting to any acquired permanent disability at any age, will most always require some new modifications of self which will often be a difficult task. It will require also that each person re-examine and change an already integrated self-image functioning in a familiar comfortable environment. This may affect the individual's self-esteem and can arouse undue anxieties. But the process is not an impossible one. Some form of a more or less satisfactory adjustment can be expected by most adventitiously disabled persons if they are given time, respect and some alternatives and knowledge.

Harold Russell (1949), previously referred to, made this statement after a difficult period of adjustment to hooks for hands:

> People like to feel sorry for me. I suppose that's only natural, too. Once it used to bother me but it doesn't anymore. It isn't important now what or how anyone feels about my being without hands. The only thing that matters is that I've learned to live

> without them and that I have mastered my handicap, instead of letting it master me.

The major responsibility for success in adjustment to physical impairment will always be that of each unique person. What a person is before an impairment will be an important determining factor in what they will become if impaired. Self-concept, attitudes, values and flexibility will also contribute to the ability to continue to grow no matter what confrontations are ahead. No one is immune to a permanent disability. What immunity there is lies only in a continually growing, well-integrated personality.

Chapter 14: Disabled Persons As Their Own Counselors

...for to be a man does not mean merely to be a creature forgotten by living-dying life, cast into it and beaten about, and put in high spirits and low spirits by it; it means to be a being that looks its own and mankind's fate in the face, a being that is steadfast, i.e., one taking its own stance, or one standing on its own feet...The fact that our lives are determined by the forces of life, is only one side of the truth; the other is that we determine these forces as our fate.

LUDWIG BINSWANGER
Sigmund Freud: Reminiscences of a Friendship

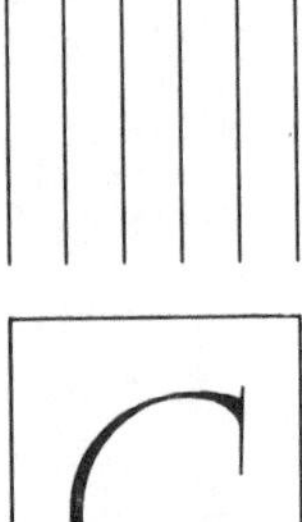

Counseling, for a person who is disabled in the broadest sense, becomes a lifetime process. This is true for several reasons. The very nature of the altering physical condition itself, brought on by the individual's growth and development, will require constant adjustment. The changing social stimulus which the disability creates and the new conditions it may bring throughout the individual's life may demand total vicissitude. Differing stepping stones will line the path as the person moves from childhood to adolescence, from adolescence to adulthood, from adulthood to old age. There will be continual adjusting, readjusting, accepting and rejecting, relinquishing and acquiring.

There will be many people throughout the lives of disabled individuals who will try to influence their behavior, even attempt to make their decisions for them, but only they will be their own best counselor. Only they know themselves. Only they know their real limitations and abilities, what gives them joy or despair, what creates in them a feeling of selfness as opposed to a feeling of selflessness. It is true that they will always want and need others in their life to offer them alternatives, reinforcement or help along the way—but whoever these people are, they will never be more than coworkers in the counseling task—the disabled will always be their principal counselor.

Wright (1960) states this beautifully when she writes,

> After all, who works at the job of coming to grips with the patient's problems, of trying to understand them? Who lies awake at night thinking of the "ups and downs," the "ins and outs" and where it all will lead? The specialists may, at times, but we can be sure that the patient does so far more persistently. We must not forget that insight is built up by the person himself with the help of outsiders if he is fortunate but only with their help. The process goes on within the client, but without his active participation, it becomes dissipated for lack of stimulation.

Disabled individuals more than anyone else will know their desires, their needs and their problems, their strengths and their weaknesses. This will be true whether the adjustment is physical, emotional, educational or vocational in nature. They will have to make their own plans, their own decisions about where they are going or how they are going to get there. They will be the ones who are required to learn, to change and to act. They cannot be continuously passively accepting answers. Their part must be rather that of alert questioners. They must not allow themselves to be simply made *case histories*. They must be active in evaluating this history and making decisions for the future based upon it. They must not only have the power to vote but also the right to veto, for no one can suffer their pains or know their tears, or experience their *self* as they do. They must, in other words, pilot their own ship, understanding full well that they will need auxiliary personnel to keep the ship on its course in top functioning condition, but that the sole responsibility for its direction must be theirs. It is understandable that there will be times when individuals, impaired or not, will feel inadequate and lost at sea but they must accept the fact that their answers are already within them. They must, therefore, develop the inner strength to suffer, if necessary, their way to their discovery.

To do this, they will need a stout will. Will, in this sense, is the acceptance of the fact that there are powerful external forces working upon them, over which they have little or no control, but that they also have inner resources which have at least an equally powerful effect upon them as well as upon these external factors.

Arnold Toynbee, the great historian, has often written about the wide gulf between the inner powers and external forces of humans which have caused them so much confusion and despair. Some gulf between internal and external forces will always exist but it can be bridged through individual recognition and development of their own inner strength. Only in this way can they maintain a sense of control. Only then will they be able to realize that as *willing* individuals they are capable of exerting some power over what is to be done and how it is to be accomplished. This knowledge will afford them the strength to face whatever obstacles and difficulties may lie in the way. They are not only ships at the mercy of the storm, they are the master seamen who, through skill with their instruments, knowledge of their vessels and understanding of the ways of the sea, can safely "see out" the storm.

Roberto Assagioli, in his book, *The Act of Will* (1973), proposes that the will can be trained. He sees the training of will as a three-fold process: 1) Recognition that the will exists; 2) The realization that *you* have a will; and 3) That beyond having a will, you *are* a will. By the latter point, Dr. Assagioli suggests that our will can become our "I," our very "self."

His theories are too vast and complicated to discuss freely here, but form the basis of a new psychology called "Psychosynetics." It is possible to note here what he considers to be the qualities of will. These qualities, he says, are basically those of energy, discipline, attention, resoluteness, patience, courage and integration. The very words suggest the process.

Will suggests a matter of inner strength, the energy to develop it, the attention and discipline to observe it, the patience and resoluteness to study it, the courage to practice it and the facility to make it an integral part of the self. With will, persons who are disabled are ready to risk, discover and find. Without will, they are forced to accept the alternative of being constantly at the mercy of other, seemingly more powerful forces than themselves—doctors, parents, therapists, teachers and the hundreds of others who will come into their life. This attitude can only lead to a feeling of total impotence and inactivity.

The acceptance of the power of will within humans puts the responsibility for their very existence upon themselves. Nikos Kazantzakis (1960), the eminent Greek philosopher and writer, puts it this way: "You have your brush and colors—you paint paradise—and in you go." We may accept the challenge or reject it. Of course, we also have a choice of painting our *hell*. It's up to us. But if we prefer to paint *paradise,* we will be responsible for the type of brushes we choose, the colors we select, and the final picture we paint. From that point on, we can no longer put the blame upon paints, family, society or God. The responsibility for our life picture belongs to us.

This does not imply that the disabled should ignore all guidance from others. They will always need the reflection of perception and alternatives offered by others. Doctors may offer alternative treatments, surgical methods, types of prostheses, hearing aids or eye glasses. Rehabilitation counselors may be in a better position to suggest possible available occupations. Psychologists may offer a greater repertoire of behavioral possibilities. Occupational and physical therapists may be better able to assess physical abilities and how best to utilize them and educators may be able to meet remedial or special educational needs in superior ways. They are all experts and the disabled will need to trust in their abilities. The important element of understanding is that they must decide, at least on an equal basis according to their *own real experience* what is best for them. They will be their planner, their *key* decision maker, though others may offer them new doors of possibilities.

Assuming the responsibility for their own counseling will also require that they have some understanding of the personal dynamics of adjustment. Such aspects as dissatisfaction with self, self-defeating ideas, hope, forgiveness, the processes involved in the study of self, trying out new behavior, the integrating of new learning with self, will all play a part in the process of their adjustment.

Most sociologists and psychologists who have investigated the phenomena of change have agreed that the initial motivational force to change is always dissatisfaction—dissatisfaction with self, with objects, with conditions, or with others. This dissatisfaction must be of such an intensity that it will shake individuals from their previous state of comfort to a desire to make things better. It should be noted that the key word here is *make* things better, not simply *wish* things better. Most of us are dissatisfied with our political leaders and wish they could be more honest, more concerned and more carefully selected, but few take the time to help in campaigns or even to vote. Most of us are appalled by hunger and poverty and suffering, but seldom move to do anything about it. Dissatisfaction alone is simply anxiety-provoking or irritating and serves no real purpose unless it moves one to change.

Charles B., a young man who lost a leg and an arm in the Vietnam war, was constantly complaining and bemoaning the fact that no one ever asked him out, that he had not gone out of his house since his release from the veteran's hospital. It had never occurred to him that if he wanted to go out then it was he who had to take the necessary steps to do so. He had to inform people that he was ready, take the initiative for asking others or go alone to places where he might meet interesting people. Dissatisfaction is the first impetus toward change; action, the second.

Hope, too, is an essential ingredient of change. I speak of hope, not in the idle sense of wishing things to be different, or dreaming that they will be, but in the sense of knowing that all things are possible, if one is willing to exert the energies to realize them. Hope, in this sense, is a new start. It may not seem rational or reasonable, at the time. Others may perceive it as lacking even basic logic. But hope offers an enlarged sense of possibilities and uncharted new directions which go beyond logic. People's hopes have, throughout history, proven the inadequacy of theories of what is possible. A sense of hope is a sense of life; without hope one is truly hope-less.

Forgiveness is a human quality too long ignored in the dynamics of change. In their book, *Man, The Choicemaker* (1973), Howes and Moon state:

> Forgiveness is the rescuing "through something in us," events and acts in the past that have hurt our neighbor, or self, and above all, kept us from hearing God in us. Wounds received and wounds given lead to repressions, deep fears, hostilities and to a host of lesser demons armed against wholeness. We hate ourselves. We hate those who have hurt us so that we hate ourselves. Through our self-hate, we are destroying our most valuable possession, our own selves.

It takes great strength to *forgive* but the only alternative to forgiveness is more hate. Hate is perhaps the most destructive of all human emotions for in its darkness it finds no place for the light of hope or understanding. Hate begets hate. It is only through forgiveness that there is any hope of rescue. I am not suggesting that we spend years seeking to discover our hurt and those who hurt us. Often, this simply leads us to becoming possessed by self-pity or wallowing in pain. I am suggesting that we recognize the pain, hold it gently and learn from it, then let it go. Forgive the inflictors. Forgive those people in your life, parents, who themselves are merely human beings trying so hard to be perfect for your sake, brothers and sisters who have their own hurt, and the people who move about you, often locked into their own hate, confusions and fears. See them for what they are, and forgive them. Most of all, forgive yourself for hurting and hating. Forgive yourself for being less than what you want to be. Realize that it is only through the process of forgiving and reconciliation with yourself and others that you have any possibility of truly realizing yourself and your potential.

Howes and Moon (1973) sum this up well in the following statement:

> To see where we have been hurt, and then recognize where, because we have been wounded, we have inflicted pain on others, and finally to realize that this endless wheel of being hurt and hurting can be stopped through our willingness to assume responsibility (not guilt) for both sides. This is forgiveness in a man for himself and others.

Forgiveness, in a sense, is to wash the slate clean and to start anew. This factor is often ignored in counseling which seems to suggest that to dig up the hurt and to deal with it is enough in itself. As one's own counselor one must forgive as well. Forgiveness of oneself and others sets the scene for action which is free of the deadly incapacitating albatross of hate and guilt. One is only guilty of being human. One is only hating another like oneself who is guilty of the same thing.

Counseling, in a very real sense, is a study of behavior. It is teaching us to become aware of the conscious and unconscious forces which cause us to behave as we do. Life and behavior can become so routine, so taken for granted, that we feel we no longer need to observe it in action. We experience and continue to respond to the experience in precisely the same way, month after month, year after year, for a lifetime. It usually takes a great trauma to again awaken us to behavior, for us to begin to *study life* again. When certain problems arise with consistency, and we tend to respond to them in a similar fashion, it is well to study them as precisely as we would any scientific phenomenon we need to comprehend. For certainly human behavior is as complicated as any scientific phenomenon. Only through a conscious study of our behavior can we discover our responses, the sources of our responses, the effects of these responses upon others and the manner in which we deal with the effects.

Disabled persons may find that each time they are scorned in public their reaction is self-pity. The self-pity turns to hate of other people, whom they may perceive as stupid and cruel. This self-pity and hate, this stupidity and cruelty consistently have the effect of causing the disabled to retreat further from society. In studying this behavior, these dynamics become clear to them. They must, then, ask themselves if retreating from the society is the only viable alternative? Perhaps it is, but if the result is loneliness and isolation, and if this is more painful, then they may be required to seek other possibilities for responses or change their behavior.

The next step in the process of change will require the greatest creativity. At this point, the disabled must discover as many alternatives to action as possible. As mentioned before, they may have to use the creative powers or "know how" of experts in the behavioral fields, psychologists, counselors, educators, sociologists, etc. Or they may find the behavioral alternatives within themselves. Whichever, they are now armed with new possibilities for response. When they are confronted with the old stimulus situation they need not react in the same negative, anxiety-producing manner. They may try out new, more successful alternatives.

Harold Russell (1949) illustrates the dynamics of change in two different reactions he experienced to a similar situation. When he first left the hospital, after losing his hands, he met a man in a bar whose awkward response to him caused him great pain. His first immediate reaction was one of anger. The experience ended with his shouting at the man, "Scram!" Shaking his hooks at him, he added, "Before I give you these!" After several months of reflecting upon his response, Mr. Russell encountered a similar situation. This time he was approached by a gentleman who said, "I couldn't help noticing how skillful you are with them" (referring to Mr. Russell's hooks). "You can just about do everything with them, can't you, Sergeant?" "Everything," was Mr. Russell's grinning *new* response, "except pick up a dinner check."

Mr. Russell found the second alternative response to curiosity brought a laugh and relaxation to all present, a far more satisfactory solution for all rather than violence and anger. For behavioral change to occur, it must be tried out in action. If the new behavior is a source of more satisfaction to you and others than was the previous behavior then this new solution must be integrated with, and become a part of, your response repertoire. Thus, the process of change.

A most vital aspect in the process of observation of oneself is to become cognizant of the self-defeating ideas that people attempt to impose upon others. These impositions will often be well-intended but they can have a subtle negative effect upon behavior. Soon one may find that these self-defeating ideas have internalized and been accepted as reality.

There are few persons with a disability who have not heard or spoken such self-defeating statements as:

"I can't. My problem is different."

"I tried that before and it didn't work."

"I don't have the time."

"I don't have enough help."

"I've always done it this way."

"It's not practical."

"I'm not ready for that."

"You can't teach an old dog new tricks."

"It sounds good, but it's not that easy."

"It's a good idea but..."

"It's too complicated."

"I don't care."

"It doesn't make sense."

"It will be too much trouble to make a change."

"It's not my problem."

"Let's be realistic."

"They'll laugh at me if I do that."

"They'll think I'm crazy."

"I've done all right without it."

"It's impossible."

"But what if I fail?"

"Why change?"

"Nobody cares."

"Nothing can be done."

"I won't!"

"I can't."

These self-defeating ideas should be studied by every individual with a disability, at regular intervals, if one is going to assume the responsibility of being one's own counselor. Self-defeating ideas can become addictive; they can freeze one into inaction. Once internalized, they will prevent any new input into awareness without its being sifted through these narrowing, limiting, self-defeating concepts. By the time this psychological sifting is completed and the new possibilities reappear, they are no longer that they might have been but have become as they were. One has managed, through preconceived linguistic limitations, to destroy any future possibilities.

Before one can "see" clearly, one must rid oneself of self-defeating concepts. Paul Reps makes the wondrous statement, "How do you wholify? Stop againsting." It seems strange that we should actually be working against our own personal growth—but such is often the case if we do not rid ourselves of our self-defeating ideas.

Hope, will, forgiveness, dissatisfaction, observation of behavior, discovering new alternatives for behavior and the integrating of these new learnings will bring one in touch again with *self*. It is from this reunion that adjustment starts.

In the beginning disabled persons may tend to see more about themselves that they do not like, than that they like. When asked to evaluate their positive and negative qualities, in most cases, people have a far longer negative list than positive list. The reason for this is often confusing but becomes more understandable when we realize how much more often we tend to accentuate the negative. "Good" things are relegated to Pollyanna status and are often assumed or implied, rather than stated.

A review of medical, psychological and educational case histories and workups will reveal how often the negative aspects of an individual are detailed compared to strengths. Evaluation is often relegated to a description of deficits. Even the word *criticism,* which actually means good and bad qualities, has come to assume a mostly negative connotation.

It would be well if we could make a list of our positive qualities and strengths. Though it is often considered egocentric to describe ourselves in positive terms, it is essential to do so. So seldom are good qualities accentuated that it has become difficult to accept even simple compliments without either embarrassment or denial. A woman may be complimented on her attractively set hair only to respond, although she has just spent hours at the hairdresser, "Oh, it's a mess!" Another person may only recently have bought a new suit with great care and at great expense. Someone compliments her and she will blushingly reply, "Oh, it's just an old rag." How healthy it would be if she could answer, "Hell, it should look nice! I spent a fortune on it!"

It is essential that we not only see and accept our strengths but also that we develop them. It is well to be secure in the knowledge that there are many things about us which are superior and upon which we can rely before we begin to deal with those things which need to be improved. If we build our strengths first, then we will more readily study, accept, and deal with our weaknesses.

Persons with disabilities will find that assuming the major role for being their own counselor will be their greatest challenge. Change and growth will not be easy. It may, at times, be painful. At the beginning they may often have to ask for help or spend time floundering in confusion. I am not implying that creativity and self-actualization will always result in want and suffering. I am implying that they can occur together. But the process is mostly exciting, always stimulating and can be very self-satisfying and self-fulfilling, as well.

It is a rare individual, indeed, who has not become a more sensitive, aware and accepting person through self-knowledge. Often a disability which requires self-study gives rise to latent creative expression and produces a unique social contribution. Robert Louis Stevenson, Charles Darwin, Friedrich Nietzsche, Wolfgang Goethe all suffered from severe chronic medical disorders. Aristotle and Demosthenes had physical defects. Byron had a club foot. Franklin Roosevelt was paralyzed. Julius Caesar and Hannibal were epileptics. It is not to say that these people became great men *because* of their impairments but rather *with* their impairments. All of them admitted that their disabilities were always harassingly present while they lived, created, developed, and shared their uniqueness with all of mankind. Still, they lived, loved, and gave of themselves intensely. With a disability, they found joy, their own unique perception of wonder, and beauty, which gave their lives a personal meaning and, when shared, helped us all to become more aware and sensitive.

Kasten Ohustad (1942) relates his mixed feelings of irritation and elation in having to use a cane in his blindness:

> The cane was a nuisance, clattering against everything and catching in my trouser cuffs as I twirled it idly about like a baton; but at street corners it proved its worth. Car drivers saw it and stopped. I held it out before me and walked across the pavement with an assurance that I had never felt before. I was a worker of miracles. I was the Moses of the metropolis. I held out my staff over that roaring, honking sea, and lo, the traffic parted, and I stepped up on the opposite curb sound as a dollar.

Not everyone is able to be the "Moses of the Metropolis" but persons who assume the responsibility for their own selves may also find their own wonder.

Chapter 15: The Disabled Speak

I always feel somewhat inadequate when I discuss MARIA FRENCH. *Her own words speak far more eloquently than any I could use to describe her. I first met her several years ago when, as an undergraduate, she wheeled herself into my classroom and parked herself in the front row. Since then, our relationship has changed many times, each time bringing us closer. I am grateful to Maria for teaching me so much, for being so honest, and for allowing me to become her friend and teacher.*

Stepping stones

It is hard to introduce who I am and what I am like, when I am all that has happened to me and more. I can only give highlights of the life experiences, ideas, and feelings that have gone into shaping the whole of my being.

Part of what I believe is that I am not handicapped in any way. To me, cerebral palsy is not my handicap. The problem does not lie entirely with me, but also with you. The sight of someone who is physically twisted, in a wheelchair, or who has the gait of a drunk, exhibiting contortions and poor balance might elicit in you fears, feelings of inadequacy. It might bring out your protective father or mother instinct. It is sometimes hard to conceive that someone who is really screwed-up physically, with the speech of a drunk, or no speech at all, has *the same human needs as you,* and perhaps, in some cases, a higher intelligence than yourself. This is where the problem lies, and this is mainly why I agreed to do this chapter for Dr. Buscaglia. I am not doing it to gain pity. *Pity is the last thing that I, or individuals like myself, need.* I am doing it to make you *aware* that disabilities are but a fraction as disabilitating as attitudes, attitudes that attempt to define, limit and compare. They are what comprise a handicap.

With regard to individuals with cerebral palsy or other disabilities, I will not use the term *handicapped,* because I believe it to be a limiting term and meaningless in its own generalities. The responsibility for what will be said—or omitted—is mine. It is based upon my experiences and constitutes my attitudes.

DIFFERENCES

I imagine that if asked what this book was about, your answer might be: the counseling of exceptional persons; persons who are mentally retarded; blind; epileptics; or emotionally disturbed—counseling those with *differences.* These are all physical or mental impediments which constitute physical or mental limitations. To a large extent your answer would be right.

I was different, but I was lucky. My parents gave me the basis for becoming my unique self when as a child they told me I could be anything I wanted to be. To me, this came to mean that the decision was up to me, and the capacity to progress was inside me. My parents dealt with me as if I were normal. When they decided to change their minds, it was too late; I had already bought what they had been trying to sell themselves (or me). They had already set the foundations for who I was and am: an individual, someone unique—a person. My strength came and still comes from the idea that I, and only I, have the potential of becoming me—a complete me. I may have involuntary movements, talk strangely, and push my wheelchair to get around, but once I set my mind to do something, though I may not do it in the established "normal" ways, *I do it.*

I was born in a Latin American country where there were no facilities for treatment. My mother made two trips to Texas for diagnosis, my braces, and to learn the exercises that were required for my physical growth and progress. She had luck in finding therapists who were understanding and very patient and so she became a speech, physical, and occupational therapist, along with being my mother. We started with a body that could not hold its head up, much less sit up. We could only progress. With each success I was reinforced to believe in myself. With the help of my mother and father, I learned how to sit, talk, walk, read and write Spanish (though no one could decipher my writing and the letters were half my size).

Later on, when we moved to Los Angeles, I was put in one of the elementary schools belonging to the special school system. I did not know any English. I was very quiet and subdued. I think I was put into a class for the retarded, but my eyes must have been too bright or something, because they gave me away to the teacher who immediately put me in a classroom for the orthopaedically disabled at the second grade level. At that time, I could walk and talk, but because they did not know too much about me in school, I used a wheelchair and was given speech therapy at least twice a week. In about two or three months, I had learned enough English to get along. To them it was a miracle. *They* had taught me how to talk in three months! My mother's reaction was to wonder how they had managed to keep me quiet for such a long time when at home I talked like a parrot. The only thing wrong with the parrot was that it spoke only Spanish. Now it was bilingual. The speech classes resulted in my losing my Spanish accent and gaining speech that, while being slow, improved to the point of being quite intelligible.

I CANNOT, NOR COULD I EVER, BE NORMAL

As I grew older, a paradox emerged in attitudes toward me. While everyone encouraged me on the one hand, they also said

I was a dreamer and should not believe in miracles, and, later, that I should not try to do the impossible. For example, as a five-, six-, and seven-year-old, I wanted to do little things for my grandmother (who was blind) and others, including myself, but I was promptly told or reminded, "Thank you, but it is too hard for you"; "Call someone else"; "You can't do it!" or "It takes you too long; let me do it." My answer to these attitudes was a line from a poem I had read when I was four: *"Querer es poder"* ("To *want* is to be able to do.") And so, I *did*. I crawled under the bed, getting hair snarled in the springs, but got my grandmother's shoes. This was one of the subtle modes with which people, through their concern, began to define my capabilities as *they* saw them. They ignored the necessity for me to have the freedom to fail. (My hair is still getting snarled—not on bed springs, but on things I am still trying to do and do.)

The years nine through twelve were carefree and wonderful. I was now running and wearing out shoes. I took up the entire width of the hallways with my wide gait and swinging arms. While walking (especially if there has ever been a time when you were unable to) there is a strange freedom in the ability to get from one place to another. I extended that freedom by running, climbing monkey bars, falling down and picking myself up again. Knowing what it used to be like sitting and watching kids play, nothing was going to stop me from enjoying my ability to walk. But others were not pleased with my new-found freedom. They were not satisfied with the way I walked, talked, and fed myself. I was left-handed, talked too slow, walked like a drunk, and ate with my elbows on the table. (If I did not put my elbow on the table, there was a lot of food on me and the table, but very little in my mouth.) So when that certain relative came to lunch while my parents were not home, I went on a temporary diet. I was told that if I kept eating my way, my parents would not take me out to eat. They would be ashamed of me. People would stare.

Everyone, guided by social norms, put pressures on me. They would tell me to stop drooling, for only people who did not have all their senses drooled; to slow down and walk with my arms by my side (I guess my way of balancing was not proper because I was not a bird, though it was better than making more hard landings on the cement than I already was making); to behave properly....

They did not seem to understand that I cannot, nor could I ever be normal. Brain damage is brain damage. Brain cells do not regenerate; therefore there will always be the resultant symptoms. This does not mean that I could not or should not try to improve. But why the hell did professionals and society have to constantly dangle the most unrealistic goal before me, that of having to be normal! Is anyone really normal, or are they feeding their own egos by classifying? The classification served only to indicate to me where the boundaries for normalcy were drawn. If I assumed this image of normalcy as my goal, it only brought me frustration—need for withdrawal, and an inferiority complex.

People who work with the physically or mentally limited have to understand and accept their own fears, prejudices, and attitudes before they can work with the disabled and their parents or they run the risk of laying their own standards on them. I am not saying that educators, physical therapists, occupational therapists, and doctors do not or should not try to help, but rather that they should be careful and that in trying to aid the person, they do not allow their own prejudices and preconceptions to interfere with the uniqueness of the individual. This is especially true in the case of someone having cerebral palsy; physically the problems may be overwhelming while mentally there may be average or above normal intelligence.

In the eighth grade I fell and broke my hip. I lost the ability to walk. All at once, I seemingly had lost all the progress I had made. I was suddenly cast on the sidelines. Even my parents, after so much work and so many acts of unselfishness, could not accept this setback. My father, in a type of desperation, tried to motivate me to walk again (going on the assumption that I possessed the ability within me but was too lazy to use it) by reminding me that boys would not like to take to a dance a girl who could not walk. He insisted that life would pass me by if I stayed in a wheelchair, not to mention the hardship this would make for my mother who would have to take care of me again after going through it all once before, when she was younger. This was the hardest period of my life. Like most setbacks in my life, this did not last too long. This time I was helped by a teacher I fortunately had. He was the first person to see hope for me beyond the wheelchair, as more than a project that had suffered a setback. He treated me like an intelligent human being, and I started on my way back to *me*.

This wonderful teacher also presented me with new alternatives. Alternatives I had never considered. For instance, one day he casually mentioned college programs for people in wheelchairs. He asked me which one I would be going into. The idea blew my mind! College? I was ashamed to have never thought about higher education seriously. This was the impetus I needed. Again I started to fight. I picked up my old spirit, and started on the long road of ignoring my old goals and accepting myself as a new individual, one who was always going to vary from the norm. No matter what my physical condition, I had a brain to put to use. The difficult process of deprogramming old ideas was to be mine, to be faced alone. There were no counselors to guide me.

The suggestions and confidence my teacher offered helped me to accept my new self and to finally accept the challenge of higher education. He had unknowingly implanted a seed that gave me a new direction—I was to become independent through education. When the project started with the announcement that I must learn to type, my mother thought I had gone mad! How could I learn how to type when I could not write intelligibly or command my own fingers? Obviously they had never heard of the cat that got skinned in more than one way. A story they were going to have to start accepting.

I embarked on a whole new "insane" way of thinking. My mom told me that I should face reality or I would end up with a handful of broken dreams. And besides, how the heck was I to transport myself to school? Well, the answer to that question was a very simple and logical one: I would learn how to drive. At that, she could no longer keep a serious attitude toward my "impossible" dreams. They became a joke to everyone but me. I entered high school and did well scholastically. When the time came for driver training, my parents were asked to sign the driver training permit. This they signed in good humor and disbelief.

When I broke my hip I had fallen to rockbottom. I became a social outcast. After all, as my father had so bluntly pointed out, who would want to hang around with someone in a wheelchair—especially since my coordination at that time was such that I could only maneuver my chair at the pace of a turtle. My speech was bad; my typing was slow. What could be concluded from those facts? Only that my dream of a higher education was unrealistic. I knew that if I wanted to make it, I had to do it myself with what I had. So, I became a diligent student; I developed social assets; I made friends. (The boys liked me mainly because I could help them with their homework. Those who didn't need help enjoyed me because I could carry on a good conversation.) Those qualities, along with my persistence and sense of humor, helped me to be admitted to all the clubs and work my way to the top of the social hierarchy. I was up again.

UNDERSTANDING WHAT IS GOING ON DOES NOT MAKE THE PAIN OR FEELINGS DISAPPEAR!

My studies provided a vicarious new atmosphere where I could live, escaping the harshness of my physical reality. I discovered poetry and history and difficult algebraic worlds into which I could escape. As the eldest of three daughters, I should have been responsible for at least half of the chores, but my second sister (younger by two years) was required to do what would have been my duties. This offered me more time to study but created almost daily conflicts between my sister and myself. What I remember most about this period were my feelings of uselessness and the resultant depressions. It was a period when professional guidance would have helped, not only for me and my parents, but also for my sisters.

This was a time when I wanted the companionship of boys, like other girls my age. It was a time when we were looking for who we were, sometimes compromising ourselves for an identity that would fit what someone else wanted. I was unwilling, even then, to compromise. In any other role but mine, I felt uncomfortable. I was unsure of myself, my self-image was weak; but I was still unwilling to compromise who I was, even for a boyfriend.

Others, not as strong and willful as myself, found other means to acceptance. If they encountered trouble in being accepted, there was always alcohol and drugs, or pregnancy. These problems are prevalent in special schools and to not have any program for education for these problems indicates serious naivete on the part of educators, parents and general public. Drugs, alcohol, and being an unwed mother just aggravate the existing problems of brain damage and emotional problems already present.

I did well in high school. I felt secure. The thought of graduating was terrifyingly exciting. The school counselor did not think that on the basis of the SAT I had it in me to go to UCLA, much less USC. This was the least of my troubles. How would

I get to college? Where would I get the money? Would I make it?

The Department of Rehabilitation gave me a battery of tests and were somehow convinced that I had the brains to make it. But helping me would only be feasible if I agreed to become a translator or a librarian. Neither of their alternatives was appealing. My interest lay in teaching in a special school or in becoming a writer. Nor was I happy about going to UCLA. My dream was to go to USC. With the help of my college counselor I took classes to meet those requirements of Rehab and mine as well. I prepared in the fields of teaching as well as library work and the role of translator.

Since I had been so isolated during my schooling to this point, I think I was frightened of college more than anything else. I felt as if I had been in a closet for twelve years. It seemed that I had been allowed only to listen to or catch glimpses of the outside world through cracks, but never really being allowed to come out—segregated to imagined freedoms, apprehensive of rejection from the unknown. But the door was opening. People were still trying to pigeonhole me into what *they* thought I could and could not do, measuring me to the norm, assessing what *they* thought was worthwhile in me. I was being suffocated. I wanted to find myself in my own capabilities and failures. To follow others' dictates was a form of still being in the closet. It was with this attitude that I enrolled in East Los Angeles College.

The people at East Los Angeles College were all I could ask for. I was delighted that they did not have any "special" program for the disabled. I did not want another crutch. Professors saw me as just another student, and I had to compete with others and prove myself. Vocational Rehabilitation Services provided me with an attendant who drove me to and from school and helped me out with typing my assignments. Although my mom still laughed, and initially opposed many of my crazy ventures, once I got them under way, she was always behind me. I could never have gotten through math without her hands writing all the unusual mathematical signs. And she spent hours acting as tutor and quizzing me, since I did not have anyone with whom to study.

Even though I had an attendant to drive me around and push me to classes, I still had problems with the "closet effect" mentioned earlier. There were conflicts within me. My self-image was practically nonexistent. The only sure thing I was certain of was my will and strength. In the beginning if I dropped a pencil I would debate with myself as to whether or not I should ask the guy sitting next to me to pick it up for me. (After all, I was brought up with the idea that only my family cared enough about me to help me.) Was this idea applicable in this instance? Would it be an imposition on him? Another problem was whether I should risk and assert myself. Should I raise my hand to answer or ask a question? Surely someone else could answer in faster speech. But it was hard for me to be silent, when I had an opposite or original point of view.

Having an attendant around taught me humility. It was like having a mother hen over me at all times. It impeded any socialization; it made me feel inadequate. My spirit was much too independent to stay with that arrangement. (And besides, I never was one for humility. Once you learn it, if you have an impairment, you can be lost.) I started to break away from her whenever I could. I put my books and tape recorder in the wheelchair and pushed (walking behind it, not riding in it) to all my classes. In the bungalows where I had to tackle steps, I found that most guys were only too glad to lend an arm. Soon, in classes I was verbalizing ideas, giving answers, asking questions, and making mistakes. In some classes it was easier to be me than in others. The Spanish professor, for instance, was kind, intelligent, strict, and demanding. I sat at the end of the first row in the electric wheelchair the rehabilitation counselor had gotten me. The professor did not want to embarrass me by asking me to recite like the others. He would go down the row, get to me, and switch to the back row. It was necessary for me to educate him out of this attitude. I studied my lessons super hard and when questions were asked, my hand was always raised. Finally, there came the time when it was the only hand raised. He was caught. He had to call on me. This experience helped him to learn that I knew my subject and could hold my own. (I learned to regret this for from that time on, when no one volunteered to answer a question, he simply asked me.) Most of the time these experiments caused me to feel ill at ease. I had more than my share of spasms, but I was learning to smile and greet strangers—to be myself. By the end of two years, everyone knew me by sight. Every professor and student I met at East Los Angeles College provided me with opportunities to prove myself and compete. I finally experienced a major triumph. I received a scholarship to the University of Southern California.

The graduation ceremony is one event never to be forgotten. I was talked into taking part in it. I never dreamed it would be as it turned out. We were called in alphabetical order. Each person walked on stage, got his diploma, and walked off stage. One of my instructors had the bright idea of having me walk up to the stage to accept the diploma with him as my escort. He assured me I had nothing to worry about. I knew this was physically true as he was a well-built, tall, physical education instructor. So I agreed. Everything went as it should have until I got my hands on the diploma and shook hands with the president; then everyone started clapping. I kept walking straight to the other side of the stage, but my escort gave me a firm pull to face the audience and acknowledge their tribute. What beautiful people to have given me the chance! The Associate of Arts Degree was nothing compared to the doors of possibilities it had opened for me as a person. It was mine through my efforts but made possible by others' acceptance.

For a year I had been driving to school with my mother as a backseat driver (after discharging my attendant, I learned to drive), a condition that had been a compromise reached the weekend before the start of the fall semester at East Los Angeles College. It was that summer when I got an old beat-up car, had my father take out the back seat, tied a wooden block on the gas pedal, raising it to the height of the brake, and my driving instructor put a six-inch-diameter steering wheel in the car. I drove around and even taught my sister how to drive (my father's nerves were not up to it). All this went on that summer only to find out that my mother wanted my sister (the one I had just taught to drive) to go with me in the morning, then drive *my car* to her high school and drive back, so I could drive home with her. Boy, was I angry! After all I had gone through, they did not believe enough in me! At that point I did not care that what they were doing was out of love; all I could feel was that in their eyes I was not enough. My sister was better than I was, not because she drove any better (which she did not) but because she was "normal." In my book they were all crazy if they thought I would go along with this. I would move out rather than give in. It was then that the compromise was reached. My mother, who was too nervous to learn to drive at first, accompanied me to school. To keep busy, she took classes of her own. It wasn't until a year later that, with the help of my youngest sister, I started driving all by myself. We would tell my parents that I was taking her to her friend's house and I would drive off by myself. When the summer ended, I had the confidence that I should have developed long ago, and told my parents there would be no more backseat drivers. To USC, my drives would be done in solo.

ALL IN ALL, IT IS IN THE CAREFREE AUDACITY TO TRY IT, TO PUT A STRAW IN A WINE GOBLET, AND SMILE

All during these years, while appearing cool, defiant and sure about all my undertakings, inside there was a real discrepancy. The discrepancy between the me who wanted to try—the dreamer with no limits—and my true physical limitations created a split personality. One part of me was very frightened and weak, not wanting to try new things, but the other believed in going to the university, speaking out in classes, driving, and doing everything it knew I dreamed of. The positive side was the stronger, even though I always did (and often do) question my own perception and sanity. I had graduated with honors. Now, to enter USC, I had to convince the university doctor to give me a chance to prove I could make it on campus. The Associate Dean of Admissions had admitted me on the same basis as other students, my emotional stamina, a good grade point average, superior recommendations, and his own willingness to want me to succeed. Everyone helped, from students, secretaries, parking lot attendants, and financial aid counselors, to the Associate Dean of Admissions. They all worked as a team to make it easier for me to surmount whatever barriers there were in my way. There were no full-time students at USC who were as physically involved in their disability as I was. In this sense, not only were they taking a chance with me, but they were also experimenting with their architectural boundaries, limits, and attitudes.

My mode of approaching the University of Southern California was the same one I had used before. I wanted to compete with the other students with no special privileges. I used a tape recorder to take notes. If the exam was an essay type, I would work things out with the professor, at times using an emanuest or a tape recorder.

It was Dr. Buscaglia's class which I took in my senior year that pushed me off the edge. What sanity I still had was now totally gone. He was the first physically normal person who talked with the insight of knowing that people, regardless of whether physically, mentally, or/and emotionally limited, had the same needs for love, belongingness, sex, etc. I knew all these things, but to hear someone verbalize it in ways that made me laugh, instead of cry, was freeing for me. Part of what he said was that one had to express their feelings and not second-guess people by thinking that they already knew how one felt. He taught me not to assume that others would react adversely to me but that if one expressed one's positive feelings, if one told others who one was, they would respond to one as a person. The resultant effects on me were those of more experimentation. I began to accept invitations to coffee, lunch, dinners, and picnics. And that summer and the following one, I went camping and to San Francisco with a girlfriend, Jan. We even took along a mutual friend on one trip, a crazy guy named Dave.

These trips were more than trips. They were adventures into myself, nature and other people. Before, I had had a lot of trouble accepting invitations to eat out. I would come down with the fastest loss of hunger, homework-overload, stomach-ache, or any excuse my mind could latch on to. I did this, feeling it would embarrass anyone in my company to have to eat with me, to have to ask them for help in cutting my food, or submitting them to elbows on the table. All at once, this didn't really matter. On our trip to San Francisco we did some really wild things. I learned to trust the better nature in people. I learned that by being who I was, people were willing to accept me and even help. In restaurants we got the best tables and service. Eating never was a problem and even wine can be drunk with a straw!

A book could be written about our camping experiences. From getting rescued by eight or nine Girl Scouts who helped dig our car out of the sand just before the tide came in, to being awakened in the dead of the night in an old abandoned fairground by the local Flagstaff sheriff who was checking to see if we had stolen the car we were sleeping in, and, when realizing we were harmless, warned us about local Indians who frequently got loaded and enjoyed playing tom-toms on parked cars in the path of their pow-wow. I became an adventurer, not only geographically, but in a human way as well. The wheelchair went and went, and where it was not able to go, there was my friend's arm, or the arm of a stranger, offering help. People never turned up their nose at me, even in my grubby jeans. They offered salutations, smiles, and aid.

The "split" me was beginning to come together through real experience and the knowledge that I was a real person and as such that not everyone was going to like me or accept me. Dr. Buscaglia's class helped me to realize this at last. I could say the heck with it to some people, instead of trying to please all of them by trying to be something I was not. I no longer had to feel guilty for not being whom they wanted, or measuring up to their expectations.

WHERE TO NOW?...AND SOME LEFTOVERS

After several classes in psychology and special education, I changed majors in my senior year and received a B.S. in abnormal psychology. I applied and was accepted into the Rehabilitation Counseling Program, where I began working for an M.S. My first year has been completed on a thousand-dollar grant from the School of Education and two thousand dollars in loans, with another chance to prove who I am and what I can do. I have continued to meet wonderful people, open and receptive to giving me suggestions and help when needed. The program has challenged me scholastically and caused me to revel in personal introspect, to change. It taught me new ways of interacting with people and with myself.

I still have concerns, fears, doubts. I am still somewhat of a social klutz. But I do not want to play games anymore, in that the only person I know how to be is myself. This is hard at times. It takes psychological strength, audacity, and a very strong love for life and belief in people.

Aloneness is something I am beginning to feel comfortable with; I do not seek to avoid it through the frantic forming of casual friendships. I am realizing that, in the end, everyone is alone. As a woman, my education completed, I see myself finding an apartment, furnishing it, experimenting in the kitchen, entertaining, and having fun. I want to travel. (All these, of course, after I pay my loans and find a job.) I want a career. I want to be a total woman. If I reach the point where I want to have children, I will adopt them, if I must. Marriage and children are unplanned alternatives. Who knows, maybe I will become a writer, lecturer or world traveler! The unpredictability of life, in my eyes, is to be enjoyed and not questioned.

As far as my personal desires and goals go, they are open to the future. I have learned the hard way. I shall never have a specific image of what I should be. I shall never leave myself with only one alternative. What I have done up until now has depended to a great extent upon my openness to tomorrow. I see my life as a gift from God, and what I do with it is my gift to Him and myself. Miracles, for me, are something I create through dreams, hopes, and work.

In closing, I would like to say that I am not a martyr, a saint, an example to others, or a Helen Keller. I do not want to be an example for others because I think they should develop and find who they are, for themselves. I do not blame anyone for what I have come through. I shall continue to try to make people aware of some of the difficulties one encounters by being different so that others who may not be as hard-headed and stubborn as I have been can have a chance.

All in all, it is summed up as my accepting me with a smile. It is like the carefree audacity to try, to put a straw in a wine goblet and smile!

For my parents and for you, the reader, I leave you with this…

My obstacles have not been obstacles…
Maybe tripping stones, at times,
But you can recover from a fall,
And make it into a stepping stone.
Anyone can do this if they survive
And are able to build resistance and emotional strength,
Coming through the bruises of the first few falls.

There have been some worse than others,
In the sense that it took longer to get up again.
The important thing is that they are part of life,
I can swear, if they hurt, therefore,
Treating them as such — LIFE.

CYNTHIA DICKINSON *may have little "sight" but she is rich in insight. I do not know her well but each time I have met her I have been impressed with her deep desire to realize herself, to accept no limits which will keep her from attaining this goal. Her strength, her perseverance, and her will combine to form a very rare human person. She has much to share.*

To learn, to do, to experience, to enjoy

No children are born with the awareness that they are blind. I was not. I knew and played with other children my own age who, I suppose, knew that I was blind. (I remember one playmate who handed me an oak leaf and suggested I eat it!) But I had enough vision to work rather haphazardly in coloring books and to draw pictures, and I could tell dark colors from light colors although I couldn't distinguish among them.

My father was enrolled at the University of Texas working on his master's degree, and I recall how I looked forward to being old enough to go to school, too. The time finally arrived, and my first teacher set to work to teach me to read Braille. I found the process mystifying, and I wondered when she was going to get around to teaching me to read Dad's typewritten pages because I had always been so eager to know what he had to say.

The realization that I was not quite like everyone else came gradually and was not fully absorbed until I was, perhaps, about thirteen. For those who are totally blind, I should imagine that the realization that they are different from other members of the family comes at quite an early age. Partially sighted people generally realize this much later. One of my partially sighted friends says that she is still in the process of learning about her limitations—in the two years she has been in the university, she has changed her major half a dozen times! At one time she wanted desperately to become a physical therapist, but the department head said he did not know how she would be able to tell when a patient was rolling off the bed. So far I have found that blindness has not gotten in the way of anything that I have wanted to do. (Of course, at times I have had to change my opinion of what I wanted to do!)

Blindness in itself does not pose insurmountable limitations although, to me, one of the saddest things is that people tend to think of you as blind before they think of you as much of anything else. If you have a parent who is willing to look beyond that blindness and to make a huge investment—in terms of time, not money—then you can get some perfectly fabulous results! I am so glad that my parents refused to coop me up in a playpen, feeling that the dangers involved in my roaming around the house were greatly outweighed by the deprivation of my not being free to learn through trial and error. My bumps and bruises were not greater than those of my brother and sisters. And it is true that a sighted child can absorb much from the vantage point of a playpen or crib which a blind child cannot.

And so experiences, as many as possible, are invaluable for a blind child. I remember so well a dollhouse which helped my sense of touch—and Mother reading books over and over again until I knew them by heart—and toy dishes and stove and refrigerator—and a favorite car which they told me was blue—and puzzles with large pieces—and sets of stringing beads and Tinker Toys. Perhaps you can tell how much I treasure these pre-school memories.

My father also saw to it that there were adventures out of the home—the beach with shell collecting, mountain climbing in Texas, a journey to Carlsbad Caverns. (I think it would be wonderful to be a cavern guide in that lovely, cool, dark place.)

School opened many new doors. It was then that Mother began to do the reading which is not available in Braille, a pattern that has continued through the years, while Dad has been a great help in math. And there were field trips. I remember one special day when we went to a "touch me" exhibit at the art museum where each piece of art had its label written in Braille. I suspect there were many places we visited which had signs saying *Do not touch* but that, happily, is one of the advantages of being blind!

My parents have been fine in providing not only experiences for learning but the instruments as well. I could not function without my Brailler (typewriter) or my standard typewriter or my tape recorder or my stylus for note-taking in class. These instruments are my means of communicating, not only with myself but with the world.

Another indispensable "instrument" is my cane. I initially fought the idea of a cane, feeling that I was giving up dignity and individuality. However, one of my instructors at a summer training course was gently insistent, pointing out the hazards of cracks and bumps and curbs and assuring me that my speed of getting from one place to another would be greatly increased. He was right! I now use my cane for the great out-of-doors but generally can manage indoors without it. I always carry it in line at the university cafeteria because then the servers are quick to tell me the special of the day! I have a blind friend who would benefit from the use of a cane. He has devised a system of claps as a means of getting through large buildings, using the echo to warn him of obstacles. I know this because I heard his clap just before he plowed into me one day. But blind people approach the problem of mobility in different ways. Some like exploring. I do! I usually avoid going into a totally strange area without a definite purpose because if I get into difficulty and someone wishing to help me asks where I am going, I feel very silly if I don't have an answer! If I get absolutely lost (which doesn't happen very often) I usually don't mind asking someone where I am, although, if it has been a particularly frustrating day, I may cry (which also doesn't happen very often). And although to me independence means proving to myself that I can do it alone, at the university I am quite willing to walk with someone if I am sure they are going my way. I really don't want anyone to go out of their way for me but I do like to meet new people, and I think they can learn from me. It is terribly important, for example, that people not feel that I regard my handicap as a tragedy, and it is always nice when someone other than close friends can accept one's blindness and accept it lightly.

Grooming is a problem which blind people cannot always do a great deal about. I remember reading a book about a woman who became blind quite late in her life. She went to a party and wore one black shoe and one white shoe, and no one told her about it. I can identify with her huge embarrassment. It is so much better to know what is the matter than to find out about it later and wonder in anguish, "Why didn't anyone tell me?" This can be true of stains and spots and holes and rips, although I sometimes think that people really don't look at one another anyway! Yet I do want people to tell me if my hair ribbons don't match or if my lipstick is smeared all over my mouth! At the present, my mother and sister help me select my clothes which has solved that problem to date although it is pure murder when those two don't agree. One of my favorite cartoons shows a merchant who calls his brother and says, "I finally sold that iridescent orange suit." His brother replies, "Great. I'll be right over." When he arrives, he finds the merchant in dreadful shape—battered and bruised and his clothes ripped to shreds. "What in the world happened?" he asks. "Oh," replies the merchant painfully, "His Seeing Eye dog didn't like the suit."

In most respects, a blind person can keep house as well as anyone else. My goodness, dust is very apparent to the touch! I must admit that my life has been so full of other things that I haven't yet tried my hand too much at cooking, although I do remember one day when my partner and I got the baking soda and baking powder confused, and our banana bread wound up being quite flat!

Some of my blind friends think I am stuffy but I do not particularly admire people who use blindness to get out of things they do not want to do. For example, I have always hated physical education classes but I suffered through three semesters of it at college. In retrospect, I remember getting lost on the way to P.E. class several times, and I wonder if my subconscious had taken over. Because I have a great interest in foreign language (German and Russian), I have a great impatience with people who use blindness as an excuse for avoiding this fascinating field. Blindness does not lower one's aptitude for language—quite the opposite. With the awareness which blind people instinctively cultivate for listening and for hearing the way in which the spoken word is used, it can be an asset. Frankly, I sometimes think my unsighted friends who have taken the easy way and avoided the foreign language department are simply lazy!

I must also mention another pet peeve if not a downright vendetta! I am really angry at modern architects. If wishes could kill, they would become immediately extinct! Sublime examples of modern architecture abound on every university campus designed by unthinking men with two good legs and two good eyes who have never had to consider the mechanics of getting themselves from one place to another. I wish that every architect who has ever designed a round building would have to try to navigate in it blindfolded. It's no fun. Modern acoustics seem similarly baffling. I have sat in the middle of huge rooms and could not tell from the sound in which direction was the stage.

Individuality is very important to me although I have come to realize that I live in and must function in a world that is basically a sighted one. However, I know that the opinion the world holds of me as an individual will undoubtedly be transferred to the entire blind community for whom I feel a very real responsibility. If I have, indeed, limitations, then I must learn them through experience. No one must presume to tell me what I can or cannot do. If there are limitations, then I will learn to live at peace with them. Feeling sorry for oneself doesn't accomplish a thing. I consider it a waste of time when there is so much in the world to learn and to experience and to do and to enjoy.

I first came to know JENNIE PARKER *through a letter which she wrote to me several years ago after she had heard me address a Texas conference. Her letter was full of confusion, pain and bewilderment. Running through the letter was a sense of lack of direction. She had no idea where to "go from here." I answered her letter at once. I suggested among other things that she might start by helping others who had similar problems to her own, for certainly she had a deep and meaningful knowledge of their needs, their problems, and their frustrations. This resulted in her volunteering to work with children who had learning disabilities.*

Years later, upon my return to Texas, I finally met Jennie. She was now a young adult, beautiful, sensitive, and becoming. There were no preliminaries necessary. We were instantly "one," for in so many ways we had helped each other to grow.

I have asked her to write her story in the hope that it will help you as much as it did me.

To understand

There are many obstacles disabled persons must face. They must learn how to cope with problems, people, and life like others who want to make a good future for themselves. For the impaired, coping, or adjusting, is much harder, and can be very frustrating. I, like many other disabled people, know the feelings of frustration, rejection, and the struggle that one must go through to overcome one's disability to any degree.

At the age of six I was diagnosed as having psychomotor seizures caused by encephalitis. The initial insult to the brain was at the age of eleven months when I had two convulsions that lasted one and a half hours each. I had had a throat infection that reached the brain, and caused a permanent scar. So, when electrical charges or impulses became very active around the scar, a seizure was triggered.

I am now twenty-one and in my junior year of college. For fifteen years I have had epilepsy. Many people think of epilepsy as very frightening, mostly because they do not understand what epilepsy is all about. To have heard of epilepsy does not necessarily mean to understand it. This is what I have been faced with every day of my life. It is necessary for people to understand that there are many different types of epileptic seizures. Those who have not lived with epilepsy may not be aware of this. So much emphasis has been placed upon "grand mal seizures" through books, television, and by other means, that many people go through life unaware that there *are* other forms of epileptic seizures. Mine is a case in point. I have psychomotor seizures in which I become unconscious, "blank out" for only a minute or two. I have no warning as to when I am going to have a seizure, as many do who have other types of seizures. My seizures occur irregularly. I never know when, or if, I am going to have a seizure. I experience an aura. This produces a momentary state of confusion. Everything becomes blurred and dark. I may want to speak, but I can't. People and things seem far away. This condition lasts for a few minutes, and then I am "conscious," aware again. After I have regained consciousness there is a strong desire to sleep. This presents a problem, of course, for a seizure may occur anywhere, at a party, in a class, or while conversing with others. Sleep is impossible. I have had to develop a way of keeping awake. I shake my head, slap my legs, and try to concentrate again on what is being said or what I am doing. This is not easy to do, and sometimes it doesn't work. It hasn't been easy.

During psychomotor seizures, I also have acute auditory perception, and a keen sense of smell. At times I hear "funny" words or sounds. I may be looking straight at a person I am talking to, and all of a sudden I hear a jumbled language. I cannot tell what is being said. This often proves to be very embarrassing and very frustrating. When I first began to experience these conditions I wondered if I was becoming "nutty." I found out from my neurologist that this was a complaint he often heard from his patients, and that it was due to my specific type of brain disturbance; since there is nothing that can be done about it, I have had to learn to accept it, to laugh about it, and to not let it bother me.

I used to listen to a popular radio station all the time. One advertisement often repeated on the station went as follows: "KILT...610 in Hous...ton." It had a catchy sound that "stuck" in my mind. At odd moments the sound would without warning repeat itself, loud and clear, in my head. I could be talking to my mother in the kitchen but I'd keep hearing the tune. You can imagine how difficult it is to think, to talk, and to hear others answer, with a tune bugging you. This, too, is due to my type of epilepsy. I have tried to solve this problem by telling the person I am talking to exactly what is happening. I have learned to sense if people will be understanding, or if they will reject me. This knowledge has come about through many humiliating experiences. I know now that there are some people whom I cannot tell, for they will reject me. I know, intellectually, that it is not always *me* they reject, but rather my problem which they fear and misunderstand. I can understand it. I know they are concerned with questions such as: *"What can I do if she has a seizure?" "What will she do?" "What does she mean by psychomotor seizure?" "Is there a danger that it will kill her?"* It is no wonder they fear me or reject me. But their avoidance doesn't help me feel any better.

There are times, too, when my acute sense of smell plays games with me. I have often walked into my house, and remarked to my mother, "What's the strange odor I smell?" "I don't smell anything," she would reply. I was convinced that I had smelled a special odor. After a few minutes of retracing my steps, it became evident that the odor was no longer there, but to me it definitely had been there. This odd phenomenon may occur at any time or place. It really drives me up the wall. Sometimes my close friends will remark, "Jennie, you and your mysterious tunes and strange smells. Both are just plain loco!" I can laugh at that now, but as I grew up I couldn't. It hurt. It made me feel different.

Besides having acute auditory perception and an acute sense of smell, there is my problem with body movement. With psychomotor seizures there is always some part of the body moving. For example, many times in the classroom I come out of a seizure, and find that I have scribbled all over my notes. During a seizure I grab at my clothes, or other objects that are within reach, and seem to play with them. Once I had been visiting a friend in Kentucky, and was returning home on a plane. We had landed at the Houston Intercontinental Airport, and as I was waiting in the aisle to get off I dropped my purse. At that moment I had evidently gone into a seizure, and was trying to grab my purse which was on the floor in front of me. When I "came to," I found myself kneeling on the floor still reaching for my purse. I thought to myself, "What in the world am I doing on the floor?" I had had no recollection of kneeling on the floor. Then I saw my purse, and only then did I realize that I had had a seizure. I was quite embarrassed. A man standing in front of me was asking me what was wrong. What do you do or say in a situation like this? I could not speak, because I was still in a state of confusion. I felt lost, scared, and helpless! I finally managed to gather up my purse as if I *had* just dropped it, and was just trying to pick it up. You see, I could not say, "Well, Mister, I have psychomotor seizures, and you're a lucky man for you just witnessed one."

In so many situations I must play the role of actor and think fast on the spot! If the seizure is obvious and noticeable I make up excuses such as, "That was clumsy of me!" or "I'm always dropping things," and just give the person a smile. It seems to work!

I also mumble during a seizure. This does not occur frequently but when it does my speech is so jumbled that no one can understand what I am saying. Since I have never heard myself, of course, I cannot give an accurate description. The only reason that I know this occurs is because people ask me, "What were you trying to say?" If the people know that I have seizures they will say, "You had a seizure. I could tell because you didn't hear me. You spoke strangely." Once I was talking to a friend of mine on the phone, and had such a seizure. I immediately hung up the receiver. When my seizure was over I called her back.

She told me that I had said the word, "alligator," before I hung up. She thought "Boy, that girl is insane!" Our conversation certainly had nothing to do with alligators. I had told her about my seizures before but she had never been around me when I had had one. Later, we almost died laughing about the whole thing. Now, when I am faced with people who experience one of my seizures, I just sit down with them and tell them very frankly that I am an epileptic. Usually, when they first hear the word, "epileptic," I pick up all kinds of different vibrations from them. Sometimes those vibrations are loving, sympathetic, and understanding. Other times they are fearful, curious and rejecting. (I might do the same if I were in their shoes.) I have learned to try to explain my seizures in a joking way. This is easier, because things are easier when they can be laughed about. I tell of some of the funny things that my seizures have caused me to do. I tell them of the time I ate my dog's Ken'l-Ration when I was getting ready to feed the dog. Oh, it was gross! Anyway, this way it seems to make the other person more relaxed, and not so afraid. This is hard to do because I must smile, laugh, and talk gaily, and epilepsy, to me, is *not* a laughing matter. I have had to laugh because I know that tears or feeling sorry for myself only make people turn away from me. This, I think, applies to most everybody. I have learned this from the experiences. I have learned the hard way.

One very important aspect of my problems which I have had to overcome is that of dependence. I grew up learning to feel dependent on my mother, teachers, close friends, anyone who wanted to help. When I was four, I never wanted to be alone. I was very afraid of the dark, and I would not walk down the hall in my house without my mother or father. I believe that at that time I was having seizures and brief black-outs of which I was unaware. I could not understand why things seemed at times so dark, and scary. When I'd "come to," there was a feeling that I sometimes experience even now. I felt lost, and I was afraid of something I didn't understand. It was all so strange. I'd get a hot, tingling sensation starting from my head and moving to my toes. I actually felt this sensation move throughout my body. People's voices faded. These strange happenings and the feeling of being alone were incredible to me. To help overcome this I would find someone, or call somebody on the phone to talk to until the fear went away. I was constantly depending on others.

Although I am unable to remember other things in my first years in grammar school, I do recall clearly that many times I was corrected for "misbehavior" by my teachers. Once, in nursery school, I was seated with my friends on our little rugs. My teacher was reading aloud to all of us when all of a sudden I found myself feeling bewildered, afraid, and terribly scared. "Jennie, Jennie! Quit that right now" roared this large, tall, and powerful-looking lady.

I thought to myself, "Why is she yelling at me?" Frightened, I turned to my best friend, Cathy, and asked, "What did I do? What *did* I do?" Cathy could not tell me because the teacher frightened her, too. Cathy (one year older than I) had always been my "security blanket," and I had always leaned on her for help, or guidance when I needed it. I grabbed her hand and held it tightly for fear that I had done something *really* bad. Cathy whispered, "Jennie, you shouldn't play with the air conditioner. That's bad!" I had evidently gone into a seizure, and had reached up to the control panel of the air conditioner! I was bewildered. I grew to become very fearful of teachers. I became dependent on my close friends to help me. I thought that by being as *perfect* as I could be I would make my teachers happy. This took great effort, of course, but I seemed to have succeeded. For example, my mother recalls the time when my kindergarten teacher had told her that "Jennie wants to be perfect, and right ALL the time." My parents rejoiced when I finally did something bad. When I was in the third grade a boyfriend dared me to jump out a window onto the wet grass which was not a far jump. So, while our teacher was out of the room at break I did it and—what do you know—I got caught. My teacher called my mother that evening to tell her the good news!

About this time my parents put me in a private school where I could get some special attention. The doctor advised my parents to tell *all* my teachers that I had a problem so that if I had a seizure the teachers would understand. This presented another problem, though. Well-meaning teachers became anxious and oversolicitous, which called attention to my problem and gave dependence free reign. Some of my classmates resented this, and sensed the favoritism toward me. This made it hard for me to make friends. I became extremely dependent on my teachers.

I was not as tough as the girls I was competing with. I was always slow in developing socially. Most of the girls seemed more sophisticated, sharper, and wittier than I. I always felt left out. I was so sheltered that I did not understand what the other girls talked about at times. It was the little things that bothered me, such as not knowing the meaning of a four-letter word. It's funny to think about that now, but then it was not funny at all. I began to feel different from the other girls. I could not stand criticism. It was one thing to feel that I was different because I was an epileptic but, in addition, the feeling that I was not capable of keeping up with the other girls made me feel inadequate as well. Children all around me were learning to become social, independent beings. I was not.

I was advised as a child not to tell others about my seizures. But I soon learned that it would be impossible. My girlfriends would watch me take out my medicine at lunch time, and would always ask me what it was for. I'd just tell them shyly that it was for an allergy. This worked out fine until another girl recognized the medicine, and said, "I take that, too, but it's not for allergy." So, I felt that I had to explain that I had black-outs. This satisfied them, though they did not really understand. Through those years from the first grade to the fifth grade I became very, very sensitive. I was extremely insecure. I knew that *I was different!* The kids sensed this, and teased me. I had only one friend who I felt accepted me. She became another "security blanket" for me during those five years. When she left school at the sixth grade I was miserable. I had depended on her so much, I had made only a few other friends. I began to withdraw from others. Everyone seemed so different, so much happier than I. As I withdrew I was more rejected, more isolated, and more dependent upon the few people who accepted me.

I finally went to a public junior high school. There I began to make more friends than I had made before. But there seemed to be many disadvantages for me in going to public school. I did not have the "extra attention" that I had been used to. I told most all of my teachers that I was an epileptic so that they would not think that I was misbehaving if I had a seizure in the class. But there were still many very real problems. Many teachers did not understand my type of disability. I would often come out of a seizure with the teacher fussing over me for tapping my pencil loudly on my desk, scolding me for talking out in class without permission, or reprimanding me for daydreaming and not paying attention. I would often not try to explain my behavior. It was too embarrassing. Now that I am in college I have learned that they must know, that they need to be educated, they need to understand.

Another experience that happened at that time stands out in my mind. I was new in school and felt uneasy around the strange new environment. I had come two weeks late to class because I had been sick with a bad ear infection. I was so excited to be at a different school and I hoped that the new students would accept me. I was relieved when I saw an old friend in gym class that I had met at my previous school. I walked up to her, and asked her if she remembered me. I hoped that she did. I almost died when all she answered was, "Yeah, aren't you that epileptic?" I just knew that all the girls around us had heard it, and I could hardly speak. I was humiliated, but said, "Yes." There are still times when I encounter similar situations.

In high school I met many new people in a mixed chorus I joined. Though I was happy, the seizures became more severe and got to be too much for me to handle. In the tenth and eleventh grades I was so worried, and anxious about myself, I'd have several seizures each day. I was afraid of what my friends or classmates thought of me. Every time I had a seizure I would get the feeling that everyone was aware, laughing at me, or avoiding me. When my seizures began to occur as many as three or four times a day in school I began to feel desperate. The more seizures I had the more depressed I became, and the more fearful and withdrawn I was. I tried to work these feelings out by talking to my parents, but they could not seem to help me enough. The final straw that broke the camel's back came when I was told that I could not sing in the mixed chorus which I so loved. I was blamed for ruining a performance. It seems I had been singing, had a seizure and meaninglessly turned in a circle where I was standing. One person remarked that I had looked "drunk." I loved being able to sing in this select group, but I could not because *I had seizures*. This was too much for me to take and I finally had a nervous breakdown. I just could not stand the pressures anymore!

I dropped out of school. I needed psychiatric help to build up my confidence, and learn to cope with my problem and other people. It took a long time. Finally, when I was physically strong enough, I went to work with my mother at a private school for children with learning disabilities. I played the guitar, and sang for the kids, because at the time they had no music class. I grew to love, and care so much for these children. I felt so needed by them. They seemed to understand me. After all, they too, had been rejected by friends and teachers. How wonderful it was to have children running up to you asking for *your* help, love, sympathy, and understanding. I knew I had it to give. I was inspired by the dedicated help their teachers were giving each child. The atmosphere which surrounded me was full of love. I knew, then, that this was where I belonged. This was where I wanted to be. The more I believed this, the harder I tried to get well as fast as I could. I refused to give up. Even my seizures seemed to occur less frequently.

Finally, I was strong enough to go back to school. I repeated the eleventh grade, and finished high school. College was now my dream. My eventual goal was to get a degree in Special Education so that I could do what I love best, work with and help others with disabilities.

From all of my past experiences I have gained a deep understanding of life. Sometimes I am even glad that I have had epilepsy. If I hadn't I might not have acquired the deep feelings and understandings I have for special children and for individual differences. Epilepsy has been a tool to help me and to help others. My disability could have become a great burden for me for the rest of my life. But all along I have tried not to give up. I have learned to let things happen, and make the best of everything, no matter what. I hope that those who are disabled will be inspired, as I was, to take up this attitude! There is a place for all of us if we will only open our eyes, and look hard and share. We must make the most of what we already are and finally be able to say with pride, "It doesn't matter about my disability, I'm still glad I'm me!"

Section V:

The Counselor Meets The Challenge

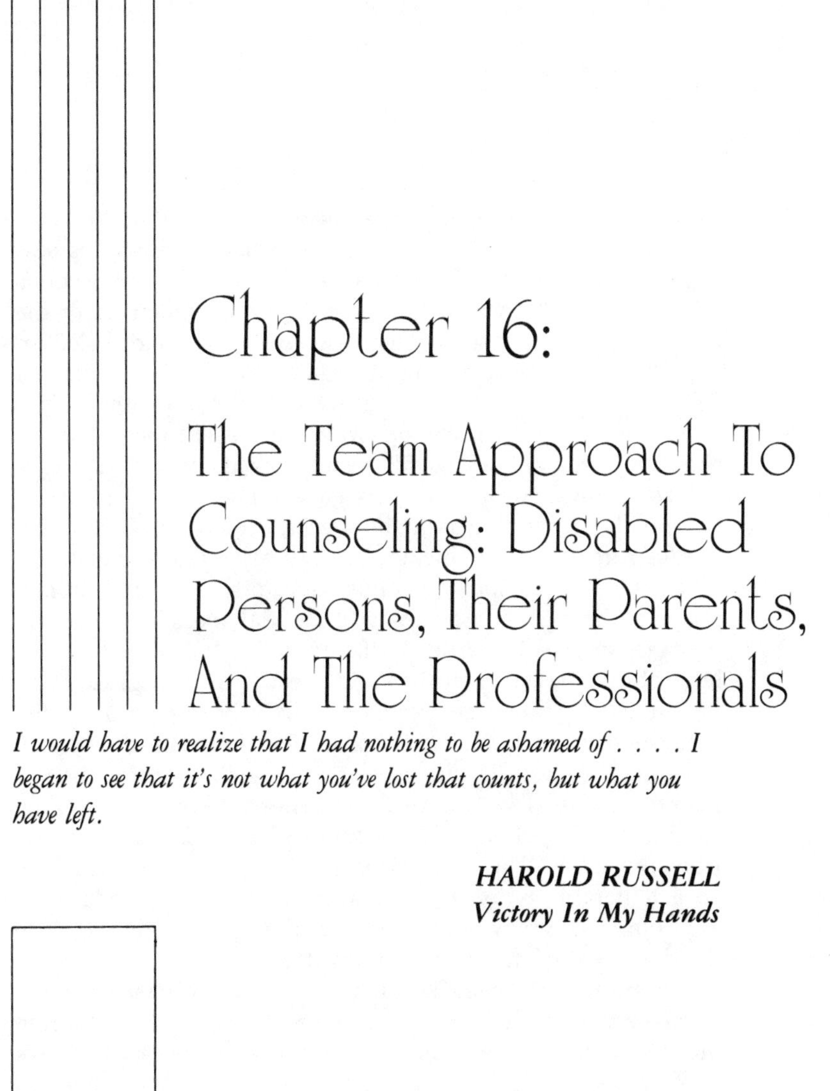

Chapter 16:

The Team Approach To Counseling: Disabled Persons, Their Parents, And The Professionals

I would have to realize that I had nothing to be ashamed of . . . . I began to see that it's not what you've lost that counts, but what you have left.

HAROLD RUSSELL
Victory In My Hands

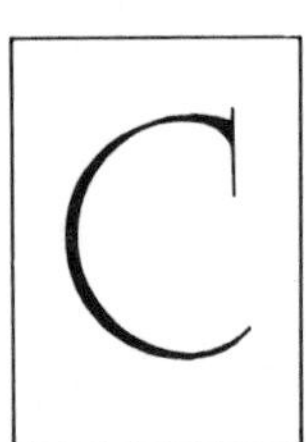

ounseling of the disabled will require the interaction of many individuals, professionals and nonprofessionals. As already stated in Sections I and III, the most important members of the counseling team will always be the disabled individuals and their families. But, they will need the active participation of many other disciplines, without which full realization of the disabled person's potentials will go unrealized. At first the team will be mainly made up of a physician and medical social worker. Eventually, depending upon the specific needs of the individual, the team may grow to include a physical and an occupational therapist, a psychologist, various educators, a speech and language pathologist and a variety of medical specialists. The significance attached to any specific discipline will vary with the kind of exceptionality. If the child is exceptional because of an amputated leg, then greater stress might be placed upon the medical, psychological, and social needs rather than educational.

The best way to facilitate positive rehabilitation for the impaired individual is to have these various disciplines working as a team. Too often professionals will work in isolation one from the other. The medical doctor may not know what the speech therapist is doing, who may not know what the educators are doing, who may not know what the family is doing, all to the detriment of the disabled individual.

It is understandable that attaining this close cooperation is often very difficult. Time, priority, and availability will often interfere with the intercommunication process; but, if the child's welfare is at stake, then some alternative means must be found for the sharing of knowledge and treatment if maximal meaningful benefit is to be attained.

Before any plans can be made for the disabled person, medical diagnostic work-ups, full treatment histories and psychoeducational studies must be available. Only with this material can a meaningful staffing be carried out and a plan made for the child's future.

There are often many difficulties incurred in any attempt to examine the person with a disability. It will require more than raw data obtained from tests. More often than not, these tests have had to be adapted to the needs and abilities of exceptional individuals. In themselves, then, they have very little meaning. For this reason, it is only through a group sharing that a clear diagnostic picture can emerge. The final remedial program will result from a pooling of data based upon the physical area, the area of intelligence, the area of education, achievement, social and personality adjustments. It will be much like a patchwork quilt—simply a group of well-defined patterns but not a quilt at all until it is synthesized, stitched together.

It is necessary for the group to see the disabled individual in the capacity of various components, so that each discipline will know its specific and well-defined role in remediation; but it is also important (though too often ignored) to see the individual as a whole, fully, at the moment. There is an inherent danger when the doctor sees the patient as a limb, the physical therapist sees the patient as a muscle, the occupational therapist sees the patient as a task, the psychologist sees the patient as a place on a normative scale, the educator sees the student as a deficit and the parent sees the child as an insolvable mystery. It is not uncommon, at times, for each discipline to see their unique *patch* as the most important on the quilt. It is only through an equal sharing that the team can aspire to objectivity and be certain that the person does not become lost in the maze of the parts.

The evaluation and staffing of disabled persons is, by the very nature of the exceptionality, a frustrating but subtle task. It will require highly skilled and trained persons who are able to translate and interrelate their disciplines both as exact sciences and as an art. This takes on great import when one considers that the results of their finding will continually play the most significant part in the educational and physical planning for individuals throughout their lifetimes.

The key professional on the team will change according to the specific purpose of the staffing. If the group has been brought together to discuss educational progress and placement, then the strategic member will be the educator. If the physical therapist needs to know more about the physical nature and the relationship of physique to the child's specific educational needs, that professional may become the center of the team. In spite of the changing nature of the key professional on the team, the central persons in the interdisciplinary group will always be the disabled individual and the parents. The lack of realization of this fact is one of the most serious problems in the rehabilitation process. Parents are often not even included as a member of the rehabilitation team, or they may be asked to play a very minor role.

When parents bring their child for an evaluation, it is not uncommon that they are asked to wait outside. If they request information on the child, they are put off or embarrassingly talked down to. Someone may be used as an intermediary between the professional staffing group and the family, the inference being that information on their own child is guarded and private even from them; that they could not understand even if it were all explained; or that there would be no reason to explain, for what would they do with the information even if they had it?

This lack of participation has the effect of isolating the child and the family and offering them little or no ideas of what the speech therapist, the physical therapist, the occupational therapist, the psychologist and even the educators are doing with and for them. Keeping the family from participating as full contributing members of the staffing group is to lose the singularly most valuable resource available.

The parents and their disabled child must be the center of the team for, in the first place, no matter how wise, observant and able the professionals are, they will never be as familiar with the child as is the family. It is the parents who will be able to recall and relate the child's first signs of deviation, the months of pain, the growth and development pattern. They will know the child's present performance better than anyone; eating, sleeping and playing habits. They will be able to tell what the child can and cannot do and what the child seems to do. Of course, some parents will not know all they are "expected to know," but nevertheless, they will know more than anyone else. For who, other than they, has spent years in sensitive 24-hour contact?

Parents have also seen the individual's behavior close at hand. They will sense emotional strengths and weaknesses, they will watch their child reach out or internalize. They will know when the child is comfortable or uncomfortable, fully functioning or withholding. They will have a thousand clues which will help the professional better reach and evaluate their exceptional child.

If made an equal part of the evaluative and remedial team,

parents will make willing and capable therapists and they will carry out their charge, in most cases, with the tender loving care that many professionals do not have the time for. The logic lies in the fact that since they will be doing for their child anyway, would it not be advantageous, for all, to teach them the *right* way? What is so mysterious or guarded about what a physical therapist does with a muscle? What is so secret about what goes on in a speech therapist's office? What happens in a classroom that demands closed doors? Studies which have been concerned with parent involvement have revealed the great value of the well-informed parent as part of the rehabilitation team. But parents will only be of value if they are treated with the same dignity, respect and regard as any other team member would expect. They must never be talked down to or made to appear inferior because of their lack of *technical* knowledge.

I have known many parents who, in a matter of weeks, have learned the technical jargon, special techniques and gained specific abilities as effectively and efficiently as their teachers.

One mother expressed this feeling strongly:

> No one would show me what to do. Finally, in desperation, I had to go back to school and get training so that I could help my child. Now that I am credentialed, I am still the same person I was before, a little less richer monetarily, but with the addition of a bit more knowledge and a few more techniques. Any trained, caring person could have given me what I learned in a matter of weeks!

This may be an overstatement but there is indeed some truth in it.

The disabled person must also be part of the staffing team. This has been accomplished in many ways. In one school for exceptional children the parent, as the center of the diagnostic team, was asked to sit in with the child at all the testing and evaluating sessions. The parent, usually the mother, was made the active explainer of the work-up process at that time.

After the formal staffing, she and the psychologist would be responsible for explaining the findings to the child. This proved a most satisfying method. The staffing over, the mother and child became the day-to-day resource persons.

At another diagnostic center the exceptional child's teacher was the appointed person, with the parent, to make sure of the fact that the jargon of the professional staff was put into understandable form for the child's comprehension. In plain talk, the child was told the facts about the impairment and what was going to be done about it. The child's role in the process was also clearly reviewed. Note that the main function of any rehabilitation team is *communication* of knowledge, one to the other, in order to execute the prescriptive plan of remediation in which all will share.

I have kept, for last, the role of the special class teacher on the rehabilitation team. If the staffing is for any aspect of the child's learning or adaptation to school, the teacher is always the central figure. It is too often the case that a child is thoroughly staffed, and plans for the future made without the teacher having any knowledge of the child until the child is ushered to her door, "Miss Jay, you have a new child. Her name is Sally."

No exceptional child should *ever* be put into a classroom and no teacher who is a real professional should accept the child without being thoroughly briefed as to the specific problem and its nature. The teacher should have full access to the staffing files and any member of the staffing committee who could answer further questions. There should be time to plan and organize an individualized, remedial, prescriptive type program *before* the child is admitted to class. This is essential for a smooth class adjustment for the teacher, the child and the other class members.

An efficient method for teacher planning and education is to always include two teachers on every educational staffing—the referring teacher, from whose class the child is coming and the special class teacher, into whose room the child will possibly be sent. The communication between the two teachers can be invaluable and will be worth the time and effort on both their parts.

Teachers, like other professionals, must receive released time for staffing. They should not be asked to come before school or after school hours. Their job is a unique one. Their classrooms are based upon individualized instruction. To write a good learning prescription they will require accurate information. *All* the information! Frustration and uncertainty on the teacher's part will reflect upon the child.

One teacher stated her case clearly when she said:

> I cannot write a specific instructional program from vague generalities. I need to know specifically what I can expect from the children, physically, mentally, and psychologically. I need to know their strengths and weaknesses. I need to know how much I can push and when to lay off. I need to know how to motivate them, how to care for them and what is important to them. Then,

> I can function in terms of my expertise as a teacher, but only then.

More will be said on this subject in the chapter on the Teacher-Counselor.

The important thing, then, is not that there *is* a staffing but *what is done with the information obtained from the staffing*. It is only when specific plans are made for the child as a result of the staffing and decisions are arrived at as to the best way to put these plans into action, that the staffing has any meaning or purpose. What is the use of hours of work-ups, the findings from which are placed in thick folders and hidden away in locked files? Nothing must be hidden or locked away from any of the members of the rehabilitation team or, like a house of cards, it will become simply a heap of meaningless symbols.

The value of a child has never been set. Each one is more valuable than any earthly possession. To lose one is somehow to lose an invaluable link which unites us all. As professionals concerned with exceptional individuals we have taken on one of the greatest responsibilities, that of helping people who have been confronted with realistic limitations which can make the process of their self-actualization more difficult, or even prevent it. With the help of those who sincerely care, each child who is disabled can discover new power, new resources, new abilities, new determination, new wonder and their own way to actualization. Without caring families, doctors, educators and therapists of all kinds, they may never do this—and we shall all suffer the irremediable loss forever!

In a manner of speaking, then, each parent, each family, each professional who does not love all humanity enough to willingly give their best for the actualization of even one individual, disabled or not, is perhaps unwittingly committing a form of murder. For in reality, we are keeping him or her from life. The knowledge gained from past mistakes does offer us the opportunity to forgive ourselves, be forgiven and thus prevent such future tragedies.

The tortured protagonist in Arthur Miller's strong drama, *After The Fall,* finds this out only after having been symbolically living a lifetime of unconscious "murders." He, like so many of us, wonders if this must go on forever. He, as we all do, seeks the necessary promise of dedication and love, to be able to answer, "No!" He says:

> But love, is love enough? What love, what wave of pity will

> ever reach this knowledge—I know how to kill? . . . That woman hopes! Or is that exactly why she hopes, because she knows? What burning cities taught her and the death of love taught me: that we are very dangerous! And that, that's why I wake each morning like a boy—even now! I swear to you, I could love the world again! Is the knowing all? To know, and even happily, that we meet unblessed; not in some garden of wax fruit and painted trees, that lie of Eden, but after the Fall, after many, many deaths. Is the knowing all? . . .

We are, none of us, without fault. We are, none of us, perfect. We cannot expect ourselves or others to be so. But the knowledge, needs, strengths and inadequacies of each specialist on the team will be vital determinants of how successful the rehabilitation will be for the person who is disabled, whose life alone, can give meaning and purpose to the process.

The knowing may not be "all" but it will be a healthy start!

Chapter 17: Counseling Disabled Persons And Their Families

A human being is not a thing among others; things determine each other, but man is ultimately self-determining. What he becomes—within the limits of endowment and environment—he has made out of himself. In the concentration camps, for example, in this living laboratory and on this testing ground, we watched and witnessed some of our comrades behave like swine while others behaved like saints. Man has both potentialities within himself; which one is actualized depends on decisions but not on conditions.

Our generation is realistic, for we have come to know man as he really is. After all, man is that being who has invented the gas chambers of Auschwitz; however, he is also that being who has entered those gas chambers upright, with the Lord's prayer or the Shema Yisrael on his lips.

VICTOR E. FRANKL
Man's Search for Meaning

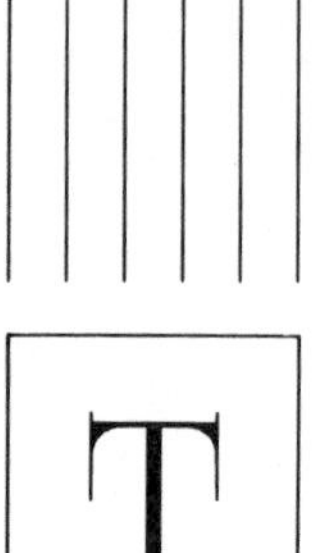

he qualities of good guidance for all human beings apply equally to those persons who are exceptional. General guidance principles and objectives will be the same. They will be concerned with the individual's personal needs, specific capacities, emotional health, intellectual functioning, social relationships and a state of continual general well-being during maturation and development.

In addition, because of the diversified nature of exceptional individuals—emotionally, intellectually and socially—there will also be some special considerations which will be required in their counseling. It has been pointed out earlier that though there may be few differences in the type of problem encountered in counseling disabled individuals, there may be a vast difference in degree. For example, the disabled are likely to have encountered more rejection, pity, or guilt from an earlier age than other children and are often required to have to deal with these for a greater duration—in fact, in some cases, for a lifetime. They have also, in several instances, been separated from their families for inordinate periods of time in hospitals and clinics. They have perhaps been involved in an emotionally unwholesome home environment, the product of parents with their own unsolved problems, who have, due to the disability, been immobilized by guilt, fear and pain. They have to undergo diagnosis, testing, evaluating and re-evaluating by a wide number of persons in a myriad of differing situations. Their disabilities have often deprived them of all sorts of normal and necessary environmental and social stimuli, which, in turn, may have prevented or distorted their normal growth and personality patterns. The resultant problems will, in most cases, be more severe, more deeply seated and multi-caused.

The specific goals of counseling the exceptional child and the parents are mainly:

★ To help the parents to see that the special child is a child first and a child with a disability second.

★ To understand the issues and facts involved in the disabling condition so as to best be able to help the child in a constructive manner.

★ To assist the parents and child to understand their unique feelings which have been aroused by the advent of a disability.

★ To aid the parents and child to accept the disability emotionally and intellectually without devaluating the individual possessing it.

★ To help the child and parents in continuing to develop their unique potentials together, and independently, toward their own self-actualization.

Counseling of the disabled will have to deal with both the giving of information (concrete counseling) and the processes involved in self-discovery (abstract counseling through feelings and emotions). It will have to consider the special physical or mental limitations of the persons who are disabled, their self-concept, their total family environment, their present integration and their total emotional and social adjustment. It will also be concerned with the disabled individual's cognitive abilities, vocational skills and occupational future. This counseling must begin as early in the child's life as feasible and continue on as long as it seems necessary, into adulthood and beyond.

The best kind of counseling for children who are born disabled, therefore, will always be family counseling. As discussed earlier, most of the formation of a child's self-concept will occur during the early years. Though this concept of self is amenable to change at any time of life, the process of forming a healthy self will never be as effortless and efficient as in the early childhood years. Counseling, therefore, begins with the family immediately upon the birth of the child who has a disability and should continue formally with them until the child is well on the way to adulthood. From then on it may become more of a process of concentrating on the individual.

Involving the family as a group, early, will have an extreme, positive effect upon the scope and need for any later counseling. It must be made clear, from the beginning, that not all the disabled or their families will require extensive counseling. This will vary, from time to time, according to need, from initial information given by a medical social worker to deep psychotherapy with a clinical psychologist or a psychiatrist. But there is no doubt that some form of counseling will *always* be indicated.

As stated earlier, family counseling should be directed toward the special child as well as to the family as individuals. In family interaction, each member with the other should examine the strengths and weaknesses as well as the special problems. It is important that problems relating to exceptionalities be isolated and studied objectively. The family should be helped to realize that such emotions as fear, hate and guilt are normal and not unique. If these emotions are not faced in honesty they can prevent them from future insights and can isolate them, one from each other, to the detriment of all. Aid should be given to each member in helping him and her to realize his and her strengths and how to use these constructively. In addition, they should be helped toward an understanding of the dynamics of change and growth, for it is these factors predominantly which will help them toward a more growing, accurate concept of self and perception of the disabled child.

Family counseling for the disabled and their families, then, becomes a cooperative relationship. Through a progressive interaction, it addresses itself primarily to information and feelings regarding disability and the resultant occurring behaviors. It encourages all family members to gain more insight into themselves and the others in the family. The goal is toward a higher, more comfortable level of action in order to deal with the disabling condition and the unique social and personal problems it may create. It helps the family to arrive at new choices, and make fresh decisions based upon viable alternatives to feelings and behaviors. It supports them in gaining the strength to assume responsibility for their decisions and to plan together for realistic and relevant courses of action which can lead to a more meaningful, joyful and productive life for all.

Of course, this can only be accomplished over a long period of time with a great deal of patient understanding and learning. Counselors cannot tell the family what to feel or do; they must allow them to find their own insights, charter their own paths, and encourage them and involve them in ego satisfying and building experiences. The family members will need praise, alternatives to behavior and, at times, strong arms to lean on or a broad shoulder on which to cry. They will need to know that the counselor cares, that they are unique individuals of worth working together cooperatively and that they are capable of working through their own problems to satisfying conclusions. This may seem a tall order for the special counselor, but in actuality, it involves the same basic understandings as for all good counseling experiences.

Counselors will be helped to accomplish this unique task if they remain flexible, aware and observant of a few basic guidelines to a humanistic approach to counseling.

Awareness of the family as people: Humans are not things. As such they must not be manipulated, controlled, or buffeted about. They are frail, easily wounded human creatures. Behind the veneer of strength, security and independence one usually finds people like most of us, somewhat confused, frightened and defensive. One will also discover some sense of dignity, self-respect and personal worth. They will not be fools, though we would often make them out as such if they do not feel, think and know what we feel, think and know.

Counselors who elect to work with disabled persons and their families must be doubly aware of these facts for, in most cases, they will find a group of people whose self-esteem has been deeply hurt. The security upon which they were building toward the future has been badly shaken. The self-fulfilling dreams of continued realization through their children have temporarily been crushed. The veneer is becoming transparent. The strength, security and independence are weakening. The confusion, the fears, the pain, are emerging dangerously close to the surface.

In most cases this is not pathology. We are not dealing with "sick" people, the immediate inference. We are dealing with people like ourselves who do a basically good job of withstanding most day-to-day anxieties and pressures but, like most of us, will momentarily reel under intense physical or psychological violence. The death of a loved one, an accident or trauma involving a family member, the sudden required readjustment, all these will momentarily shock us out of our *normal* patterns of behavior and may cause us to become disoriented. Some of modern man's most strong and respected individuals such as Dag Hammarskjöld, Mahatma Gandhi, Martin Luther King, Albert Schweitzer, have freely admitted to their psychological vulnerability to violence as human beings.

Parents of exceptional children and their families are no different. They are simply human beings. As counselors, we cannot *demand* that they be otherwise. Impatience because they do not "accept," "understand," "change," "grow up," is immature, unnatural and discloses an inhuman lack of empathy and feeling. Acceptance, understanding, change and maturity will come with time if we afford the family the respect, dignity and rights which go along with their being human.

The counselor's self-awareness: Too often, counselors forget that their jobs are to be *guides,* not *gods.* They forget that they, too, with their sophistication, wealth of knowledge, techniques, and subtle manners, are nothing more than human beings. They begin to identify with the role of *counselor,* a nebulous thing at best and a destructive thing at worst. They see themselves as omnipotent forces in behavioral change, persons with answers *for* the clients, who know what is normal and abnormal and who understand the appropriate behaviors for each category. This becomes particularly ludicrous when one learns that the highest suicide rate among professionals, at present, is among psychiatrists; or when we realize that the marriage counselor has been divorced three times. These facts have little or nothing to do, of course, with their being effective in their job as counselors but it is just a reminder to them that they, too, are human beings. They, too, have problems which seem insolvable. They, too, know fears, loneliness, even despair. These very human characteristics, if used wisely, can help them to get *closer* to their clients. It is difficult for a client to identify with a god but quite easy to do so with another, imperfect, human being.

It seems, though, that many counselors forget this simple fact and submerge themselves in god-like physical and personal distancing phenomena such as the ideal office, the piped-in semiclassical music, the comfortable furniture, the soft, well-modulated, unruffled voice and controlled manner, the answering service, the mounds of professional books, literature, degrees and honors which cover office walls, the total sanctum sanctorum atmosphere into which the troubled person is told to "relax"!

The impression conveyed by this anti-human bag of tricks is one of "I am the omnipotent one. The one who has the answers. You, poor misguided human beings, have the problems. Follow me and I'll lead you out of your maze and if you are fortunate, you can be just like I am." Good, God!

There is nothing wrong with a comfortable office, books, or professional degrees as long as counselors can rise above these and admit freely that they are human beings who are also fearful, confused, perhaps even unloved, but who want desperately to become better, more joyful and fully functioning humans as they help others to do so. It is probable that the client's problems are not their problems and therefore they will be in a position to offer them a greater variety of viable alternatives to their present behaviors. This does not make them any greater than the clients, just momentarily and in certain aspects more clear sighted.

Good counseling can take place on a stump of wood in the forest, a rock in the desert or in the client's family room. The essential factor lies in the ability of the counselor and the client to relate as people. A low pressure area must be created where one feels free to be what one is, with an accepting, respectful and flexible outlook, one toward the other. There is no room for phoniness, demanding or judging. We meet as equals.

Type of counseling: Some types of counseling are more demanding than others. They will range from simple, concrete, cognitive counseling, the giving of pure information, to the more difficult, more abstract, affective, type of counseling in which, through a study of feelings and attitudes, the clients will arrive at their own solutions. The counseling of exceptional individuals and their families will involve, at different times, both.

The family will have to be given many facts regarding the disability, limitations they may impose and the possible ramifications of these limitations as suggested by the present physical realities. It is obvious that, as the exceptional individual changes, grows, and matures, the facts will change. This suggests that even the giving of pure information will be a continuing process and that few accurate predictions can be made at any given time.

When Mary C. was born with severe spastic paralysis, the prognosis seemed dim. In fact, some suggestions were made to her parents regarding possible institutionalization. But, as Mary grew she was found to be quite intellectually precocious. Though her physique continued to present some problems, her cognitive abilities were extraordinary. She began to find alternative ways of handling even what had been suggested as permanent physical limitations. It soon became apparent that there would be very few realistic limitations that Mary would not, somehow, meet. Educational plans changed, the medical scene had to be readjusted and even now, as a student in a university, Mary is finding new, undiscovered potential for growth and development with which she must contend and with which she will need guidance.

The proper conveying of information is, in itself, not as simple a matter as it may seem. One need but ask any doctor, psychologist or educator who has ever had to inform parents that their child was functioning as a mental defective and thus would require placement in a class for mentally retarded minors! It is understandable that a counselor is often tempted, as a deeply concerned human being, to shirk the responsibilities and alleviate anxiety by essentially avoiding the problem, minimizing it or giving the parents false hopes.

It is impossible to separate facts from feelings. It is often the case that even when the terrible facts are clearly stated they are so shocking to the parents that they are actually not heard or conveniently misunderstood. Hundreds of concerned parents have confronted school counselors in utter shock and amazement with "You never told me he was retarded!" This, after having given permission at the time, in writing, allowing their child to be placed in a special program! Human behavior is a continual source of wonder to observe. The power and resources we have to avoid pain when we are not ready to handle it! There is a great art and challenge to the giving of information which cannot be minimized, especially when the information, as in the case of a disability, is so vital and so emotionally laden.

Abstract counseling is an even more complex procedure. It deals not only with the facts but with the emotional dynamics involved in the feelings which surround them. This type of counseling will take more time, require more skill, and put most of the responsibility upon the client. It is based upon the sound premise that only the clients can understand their real feelings, only they can deal with them and only they can find solutions and make decisions based upon them.

In this type of counseling, the counselor acts as a guide, but places most of the responsibility upon the client. They must work together to isolate feelings related to the problems, identify them and bring them out into the open where they can be examined and studied. Often the family feels a great deal of solace from merely being able to discuss feelings openly and together. Counselors may find themselves acting simply as corrective mirrors to make certain that each family member is perceiving the expressed feelings correctly. Feedback information helps individuals assess their feelings properly, for themselves and in a family perspective. This prevents isolation and the insensitivity that can be so destructive to many in the household.

Interactions must be analyzed. Often, by changing interactions, we can change personality, for personality is mostly a function of our social interactions.

Strengths are found within the group and plans are made to

utilize these. Each family member may vary in strengths and insights as time goes on, so each can help the other at different times. Change is not a threat to the group if it is based upon group solidarity and support.

As insights occur and feelings are seen in their proper perspective, the counselor's role becomes more one of challenging the family toward finding new alternatives. The counselor does not help them with oversolicitude and pity or false hope, but by convincing them that change occurs only in action, that they must not only instigate a plan but urge it forward into deed. This may mean that they will have to deal with specifics. For example, the mother may feel put upon, her tasks are endless, she has no time for herself or for her own continued growth. Her attitude reflects in her resentment of the child and the disability and her interaction with the total family. It may show itself in periods of frustration and outbursts of temper. If the family agrees that this is a very real problem they may set out to develop a schedule for "relief of mother." Duties will be reallocated, responsibilities will be shared and mother will get the free time she sorely needs. If a younger child feels neglected and relegated to secondary citizen status due to a disabled brother or sister, then means must be sought to give that child extra love and attention. But, the important thing is that something be *done*. Too often counseling deals with uncovering vague, nebulous, negative feelings and problems, but never moves to the point of what can be done with them. It must be remembered that insight alone is next to nothing if it does not lead to action through changes in behavior.

The total family, especially the disabled individuals, must be helped to see any distance which exists between what they say, feel and do and what actually happens. Family members may flatly state that they accept their disabled siblings, but in actuality, in many overt and covert ways, are unable to do so. The pointing out of these behaviors must be accomplished with great care and without resulting in guilt or deprecation of any individual. Whatever their behavior, it is their adjustment, but it may not be the adjustment that is most conducive to their welfare or that of the family.

Often the family is so deeply enmeshed in its feelings of helplessness and hopelessness that they are unable to deal with their problems in any form other than tears. Then, it is vital that the counselor show them that despair, depression or despondency may be a very positive impetus to change. I have heard counselors working with such parents say, "Come on, Mrs. Smith, there is no use in crying, your tears will accomplish nothing." Tears cleanse. Cleansed eyes see more clearly. Every important research states that the first response toward adjustment to disability is in some way involved in mourning. Tears are a real part of mourning. So is helplessness. So is despair. If allowed out, the tears will usually end and the process of rehabilitation will begin.

Most people in the beginning will be resistive to change, for it brings with it fear and uncertainty. We are often more comfortable with a pain with which we are familiar than attempting to change it. We fear opening a Pandora's Box of despair, about which we know nothing and which may, indeed, be worse. The counselor must show the family that any Pandora's Box brings with it enormous expenditures of psychological energies. It does not simply lie, lid on, within us. Rather the energies it demands from us to keep the lid closed can be better directed toward finding new creative solutions and feasible plans for adjustment.

Often the addition of a person with a defect in a family will bring to all of them a loss of self-esteem. The counselor may help the family to realize that this loss is only temporary, that in actuality, each member has unlimited resources for growth and development of self. The knowledge of this potential can do much toward helping the despondent individual regain a sense of self-worth and assume the responsibility for continued emotional and intellectual growth.

Abraham Maslow (1961) states that "A person is both actuality and potentiality." It is through a regaining of individual self-worth that each family member will realize that they have many alternatives to problems for the entire family. They will understand that there are many ways and many answers for common solutions. Their ways need not be the ways of other families, but may be just as valid and effective. They may often believe that there is only one right road to adjustment. It may be true there may be a right road to adjustment for one family but they are they, and as such, must discover and find their road in their way, in their time.

Since every family is unique, each factor of adjustment will have to be considered uniquely—the environment, individual values, involvement, concern, motivation, dependence, hostility, status needs, power needs, social adaptation and many others. For the counselor to approach each family with a "set of tools" or any preconceived notion of sameness is to court disaster. It is always a source of discomfort to find books in counseling or guidance which offer the *best method* for conducting an initial interview or recipes for accepting of feelings. Recipes are for the novice who needs some small feeling of security, but in the final analysis, can only be a distancing phenomenon. Rollo May (1961) states:

> Certainly it is true that students learning therapy often become preoccupied with techniques; this is the strongest anxiety allaying mechanism available to them in the turmoil fraught encounters in psychotherapy. Indeed, one of the strongest motivations for dogmatism and rigid formation among psychotherapeutic and analytic schools of all sorts is right here—the technical dogma protects the psychologist or psychiatrist from their own anxiety. But to that extent, the techniques also protect the psychologist or psychiatrist from understanding the patient; they block him off from the full presence in the encounter which is essential to understanding what is going on.

Gourmet chefs follow no recipe, but know the ingredients and understand the fundamentals of good cooking techniques. But they also know that ovens vary, that the same foods differ in sweetness or bitterness at different times, that various herbs complement certain dishes and spoil others. Good counselors are at least as flexible, subtle and artistic as the outstanding chef. They know that the real value of counseling lies in the accepting of each human encounter as unique. Carl Rogers (1939) states: "In my judgment the warm, subjective, human encounter of two persons is more effective in facilitating change than the most precise art or technique growing out of learning theory or operant conditioning." The counselor who truly realizes this is comfortable in this knowledge and not made anxious by it. Anxiety in any counseling situation arises only if counselors see their roles as all-important. The outcome of any encounter will not be fully their responsibility—it will be mostly that of the client. The counselor's job is to listen, to encourage, to offer alternatives, and to stimulate to action. It is not their job to make sure that every porridge emerges in the same manner. They must have what Carl Rogers calls "unconditional regard," a genuine concern for their clients, based upon a respect for their integrity as human beings and their ability to deal with and solve their *own* problems.

Counselors, therefore, are active listeners. They know that the essence of good counseling lies in the communication process. They are careful that they hear what is being said or ask for clarification; that when they speak they choose their words and construct their sentences carefully, for words are the source of much misunderstanding; that they use language, their major tool for communication, as a bridge for cognition and effect, not as a gulf to separate them and as a mask behind which they may hide their inadequacy.

Lastly, the counselor, like all persons, must not be afraid to fail. There are some problems that are, indeed, insoluble, at least by them. They must be willing to admit failure, to refer their clients elsewhere or to ask forgiveness of them and to try a new start. They must not expect each counseling session to be an end in itself. They must accept that they will vary in their value, but that each will be necessary as a means, that each will contribute to an eventual end. They must, as much as possible, keep their own egos out of the situation. This does not mean they do not evaluate themselves and each session but it does mean that they do not allow themselves to be seduced or wooed into feelings of grandeur. Clients who are in dire need of acceptance often become very adroit at seduction. Egos of counselors who are not aware may easily become seduced.

The converse is true, of course, and counselors may disguise their inadequacies by seducing their patients and interpreting their yielding and dependence to successful counseling. Clients must change for themselves, not for the counselor, or the relationship can, indeed, become perverted. Such permanent identification may cause the clients to become dependent and more insecure than before.

Most of all, counseling the disabled person and the parents is not a matter of *remaking* people. It is mostly concerned with trying to clarify feelings and issues which are standing in the way of their *making* of themselves. It is involved with creating for them a nonthreatening, accepting environment where they are encouraged to find, learn, and enjoy new self-affirming feelings, knowledge and behavior and put them into positive action for the good of all.

Chapter 18:

The Teacher-Counselor In The Classroom

I know a planet where there is a certain red-faced gentleman. He has never smelled a flower. He has never looked at a star. He has never loved anyone. He has never done anything in his life but add up figures. And all day he says over and over again, just like you: "I am busy with matters of consequence." And that makes him swell up with pride. But he is not a man—he is a mushroom!

ANTOINE de SAINT EXUPERY
The Little Prince

Most children who are disabled will spend their educational lives in special programs or classes. Present programs for the disabled fall mainly into five types. First, the *state schools for the disabled* for those groups of blind, deaf, cerebral-palsied children or children with other severe disabilities who are taken from home and community and sent to the large state-sponsored institutions. Second, the *segregated school,* in which all types of physically and mentally disabled children within a specified radius in a community are bused to, and educated in, a single segregated facility. The third type is a *segregated classroom.* This classroom is located within a regular elementary or secondary school and made up of children who have the same or similar defects. For example, all blind and partially-sighted children, or all retarded children, may be educated together in a regular school but these children remain in their special class with a specialist teacher for the full school day. The fourth possibility is the *integrated classroom.* In this type of program there is usually a special class in a regular school designated for a specific impairment. The children stay in this class for only a portion of the school day. Where it seems feasible, the child joins the mainstream of students for some school subjects. The retarded child may, for instance, have all academically oriented experiences in the special class but may move to other classes for physical education, shop subjects, art or music. The fifth and most sophisticated program of all is the *itinerant program.* This program is seen mainly in secondary schools, for it is believed feasible only after the child who is impaired has acquired the special skills to handle a regular school program. For instance, in the beginning it may be unavoidable that blind children remain mostly in a segregated setting until they have mastered Braille writing, typing, the use of the stylus, and other necessary special skills. They can then be placed into a regular class at their academic grade level. An itinerant teacher, trained in Braille, visits these children at specified intervals or when needed and acts primarily as a resource person for obtaining Braille books, for transcribing special materials into Braille, or for acting as a liaison for special problems between the child and the regular teacher. Aside from this, the children function normally. Programs for children with specific learning disabilities and no other obvious physical impairments are often of the itinerant teacher type.

With the sole exception of the family, no individuals will have a greater influence upon the person with a disability than the child's special teachers. It is with them that the child will learn fresh avenues and techniques for dealing with the impairment. From them the child will obtain new attitudes of hope and learn of the vast personal inner world as well as the outside world. It is the special teacher who will help the child to cross the bridge from family to the more complex social units outside. It is they who will define the new limits and requirements for school adjustment. It is they who will show the great resource of behavior available for successful learning and functioning and it is they who will continue to guide the child gently along the path to maturity. The special teachers, then, become one of the most vital forces in determining the disabled child's continued intellectual and emotional growth, development, and adjustment.

It is unlikely, of course, that there will be a special counselor assigned to each child who is disabled. Obviously, this would be impossible and, in most cases, not even necessary. Many children with disabilities, like all children who go to school for the first time, experience some home-separation anxiety but with the special knowledge and wise guidance of the teacher will soon be able to adjust. But, unlike the normal child, the intellectual and emotional needs of the disabled child will be different. In many cases they will be more acute and of an exceptional nature. It is for this reason, and this reason alone, that there is any justification for special education at all. These children have a diversity of problems. They have the usual problems of other children their age, they have some of the special problems found commonly in all disabilities and they have the problems unique to their own specific disability. They may require a special education and some group, or individual, counseling for most of their school lives. The variance in physical and mental abilities in these children is so vast that almost all of the teacher's instruction must be individualized. The degree to which adjustment counseling is necessary will vary greatly with each individual, from Mary who has had both legs amputated but is joyful, eager, and well adjusted to her wheelchair, to Tommy who has grand mal seizures and is remorseful, hostile, and withdrawn. Some children with disabilities arrive at school in such a confused, fearful, and dependent state that adjustment or learning for them is impossible. Some one-to-one type of intensive counseling is indicated for these children before any classroom learning can be achieved. Not only, then, must the teacher become involved with the learning aspect of adjustment, but, because learning is so closely correlated to emotional adjustment, and one does not occur without the other, the special teacher becomes responsible for both. In this sense the teacher is more than a teacher and more than a counselor, becoming the child's *teacher-counselor*. The teacher will be in a most advantageous position to accomplish this vital task, having almost daily contact with the child for five or six hours, seeing moments of joy and wonder and times of frustration and despair, charting the daily growth patterns, observing the struggle and evaluating the effects of the remedial efforts. It is a great responsibility and it is for this reason that special classes must be kept small. The title of "special" teacher is justifiably applied. The "specialty" is disabled children. The teacher's knowledge must be vast and include unique techniques for motivation, special skills and remediation of specific learning disabilities, perceptual retraining methods, ego-reinforcing activities, group development methods, prescriptive teaching, and methods and techniques for personality adjustment.

THE SPECIFIC ROLE OF THE TEACHER-COUNSELOR (The Cognitive Role)

Although the cognitive and affective role in educating exceptional children cannot be separated in reality, the attempt must be made for the benefit of clarification. The major cognitive requirements for the education of all children seems to be to help them to solve their unique developmental tasks on schedule as far as possible, to so individualize the curriculum as to facilitate this process, and to stress the relationship of educational competence to an overall orientation to life.

More has been written in the past several years regarding specific methods for change in classroom learning behaviors than any other area of special education (Skinner 1952; Peter 1972; Hewett 1973; Harring 1973). These works have been mostly concerned with the cognitive aspects of behavior, sometimes to the almost total disregard of affect. In some cases this disregard was intentional; in others it was included as merely one of many lesser variables which may affect learning. Regardless, the results of this study have not been without great value, for they have brought forth a renewed interest in the development and implementation of individualized instruction for exceptional individuals. They have stressed that learning and instruction is a consequence of precise behaviors which can be meticulously evaluated, carefully shaped, and accurately predicted. The crucial factor has been found to be that behavior can best be understood as it is observed through manipulation of its consequences. Although this approach to instruction works, as far as it goes, there has been some controversy as to whether such a mechanistic system is sufficient to account for the behavior of each unique human person. Nevertheless, the approach is valid in its insistence that behavior has its consequences and that these consequences, if positively rewarded, influence the probability that the same act will occur in the future, if similar environmental conditions are present. If the consequences are pleasant, the act tends to occur more often under similar conditions. If there are displeasing consequences, the act tends to occur less frequently. A teacher may then encourage or strengthen a behavior of a student by so arranging and manipulating the environment that the child experiences good things as a consequence of positive behavior. The teacher can weaken negative behavior, conversely, by changing the environment so that the learner experiences bad consequences, or no consequences at all, for negative behavior.

This, of course, is an oversimplification of what is often presented as a complex, "new" theory. In actuality, it has its base in the simple sensitivity and wisdom of the wise teacher since the beginning of time. "You can catch more flies with honey than with vinegar." "Nothing succeeds like success."

It is obvious that the effects of consequences upon future responses are not the only determinants of behavior but they are important ones for the teacher-counselor to comprehend. The effectiveness of all teachers in influencing the behavior of students will be much improved if they concern themselves with the systematic management of behavior and reinforcement of consequences.

These methods are being used and have been found successful

with various exceptional children, with the deaf, with the emotionally disturbed (Whelan 1966), with the retarded (Gardner and Watson 1969), with children who have various speech problems (Sloane and MacAuley 1968; Perkins 1962), and with most other exceptionalities.

Systemized, individualized instruction and a knowledge of the dynamics of modification of behavior are very much a part of the role of the teacher-counselor. Most of the students the teachers will be concerned with have various emotional and learning problems due to a variety of factors, from brain damage to the lack of environmental stimuli; and knowledge of the processes involved in influencing behavioral change is essential.

This process begins with a thorough assessment of each individual child. The actual testing may be done by many allied professionals, from the child's doctor to the school psychologist, but it will only be of value as the teacher is able to interpret these findings and translate them into an individualized classroom program for each child. The teacher needs to know the child's deficits as well as strengths, achievement and the level of personal and social adjustments, and also know the medical history and prognosis when this is appropriate. Only with this knowledge can a judgment be made as to the specific level at which the child is functioning maturationally and educationally in order to plan a graded, individualized course of action. Only with this knowledge can the child's value system be understood, the most effective reward reinforcements be selected and high stimulus value materials be determined.

Teacher education programs, especially in special education, have radically changed from those based upon vague generalities to those more specifically designed to offer the teacher the unique skills to interpret diagnostic material, relate this material to the child's level of functioning, plan a prescriptive program of remediation for the child, and evaluate the results of the program. Indeed, in most cases, special education teachers are prepared with a well-grounded base in education as science. But, education is also art and, as with all great artists, the teacher must not only have the tools and understand the appropriate use of them but must also have the inspiration, creativity, and insights to facilitate universal communication of this art. Thus, affect.

THE SPECIFIC ROLE OF THE TEACHER-COUNSELOR (The Affective Role)

The teacher-counselor's role is not only that of teaching the child facts and school-related learning. It has long been known that facts alone are useless, that there are actually only a few facts which have withstood the test of time. Many of us spent grueling hours, as children, learning the geography of Europe. How many times has that map radically changed? And what of scientific "facts" in the last ten years relating to medicine, biology, astronomy? Facts, or knowledge alone, are not wisdom. They may, if used efficiently, help promote wisdom, insofar as we learn from the past. But it is likely that the only true fact is *change*. Education, then, must be directed toward flexibility, adjustment, change, wonder, wisdom, and joy. It must be also concerned with the limitless, rare, sensitive person behind the facts, the affective self.

Much of what is learned regarding affect is learned in action. It is not so much talked about but experienced in action. It is a simple matter to say "I love you," for instance, but what we truly mean by that statement will only be revealed through our actions. It is obvious that what is taught in a classroom relating to affect will be generated through what goes on in the classroom, the emotional tone which permeates the group. The greatest force for setting this tone is the teacher. It is through his or her behavior that the students are most affected. They are not the only influence, for some of how they feel is affected by the attitudes of the principal and supervisors, but in their classroom they are, indeed, the major affectors. In spite of themselves, as we all do, they will teach what they are. If the teachers are free, dedicated to their own growth, and concerned with their uniqueness, they will teach their students the wonder of both. A dead or vapid teacher can only teach death.

This emotional tone is perceived by the students very early—even by the end of the first hour of the first day of class. Teacher A, for instance, starts the first class with the "rules for conduct." These are clearly spelled out on the blackboard. Or, the teacher allows the students to suggest the rules, knowing full well that they have been conditioned through past experiences, with other such teachers, to give the feedback desired. This feedback usually is expressed in what "we" don't do. "*We* don't get out of our chairs"! "*We* don't speak out unless *we* are recognized by holding up our hand," and so on, to the final "Don't."

Contrasted with this is the actual story of one of our teachers who insisted that her classroom be bare, stripped of all furniture, preplanned bulletin boards, and preset reading and science centers.

On the first day of school, when the children arrived, she greeted them from a cross-legged position on a rug at one side of an empty room. They all hesitated at seeing their new environment, having been accustomed to the usual classroom setting. "Come in and sit down," she invited them, instantly rewarding their behavior. When they had all rather confusedly found a place she said, "Boys and girls, this is *our* room. I'm Miss F. We're going to be together in this room for a whole year. I want to be happy here and I want you to be happy, too. Since it is *our* room, not *mine,* I want you to help decorate it. Outside, you will find a desk and a chair for each of you. Get one and bring it inside and set it exactly where you would like it to be."

After some coaxing, they were again rewarded for following directions. It was not really surprising that they set their desks up in rows, one next to the other, as all their previous classrooms had been structured. Miss F. smiled and said, "I'd like my desk to be right in the middle of the room, then I can be near everyone, and you won't have far to go when you need me." This, of course, necessitated a few alterations in formal structure but soon convinced the students that their teacher had really meant what she said.

The classroom, now, is like none other. She has finally convinced each child that they have a particular life space and they are entitled to do anything they wish within their life space if they respect it! Many children have now brought floor rugs, desk lamps, and flower pots for their area; others have substituted stuffed chairs for straight-backed, conventional types. The room is *theirs* to happily learn in. The emotional tone is set. It is well for teachers and administrators to note that the school does not belong to them or the superintendent, or the school board or the custodian. It is there for the children.

Since the school is the bridge between the family and society the teacher-counselor wants to keep this line of communication open. This is most satisfactorily accomplished through home visits, at best a controversial issue. One hears, "I don't have time"; "The parents aren't interested"; "It's just a waste of time"; "We all have more important things to do." There may be some truth in all of these statements but to a greater extent they are rationalizations for fear, uncertainty, incompetence, or laziness. So important is family-school communication that released time for this activity should always be offered.

The teacher-counselor who recognizes the evident value of parent-teacher communication, in the broadest sense, knows that there is just as much value in a simple *social* visit as there is in a visit laden with professional facts and figures. One mother of a retarded child explained to me her dislike of parent conferences with the statement: "She lays all this high falutin stuff on me which mostly I don't understand. It just makes me feel dumb." Is it any wonder that this mother doesn't "show up for appointments"? A school visit can be simply one in which two caring adults, each with the special child's interest at heart, relate. On the other hand, it may deal with concerns, plans for the future, classroom, or home occurrences. It is just as important that the good things about the child be discussed at these visits as those factors "*we* need to work on." This is also a favorable time to discuss what the present behavioral or learning outcomes are for the child and the possible role of the parents in reinforcing them. If the parents are asked to help—and it is hoped that they will be—then they must be given specific information, well-defined tasks and means for measuring performance outcomes. Parents, like all of us, require the necessary reinforcers. The teacher's interest, warmth, and concern is as good as any M & M! Teacher-counselors who do not use parents as at least one third of the learning team are utilizing only two thirds of their potential effectiveness.

Teacher-counselors organize their classroom environment so as to afford a certain amount of structure as well as some time for freedom, exploration, relaxation and fun. Children appreciate structure wherein they may experience some security but it must be remembered that there is danger in adhering too rigidly to any plan.

One such happening occurred in a classroom for children who were brain-damaged. During a certain period in the more or less regimented schedule a child had a grand mal seizure. The teacher, well-prepared for such an occurrence, handled the physical necessities with knowledgeable concern and efficiency. The other children were visibly shaken. As soon as the seizure was over, and the child was taken to the doctor's office, the teacher turned to the class with the statement, "All right! It's all over now. Get back to your assignment!" Needless to say, it was easier demanded than followed. This would have been an excellent time to simply stop, ignore the schedule, and discuss epilepsy. There is no greater moment for learning than when there is a need to know. Damn the schedule!

On another occasion a voluntary special assembly was called in a school for the disabled because of the surprise visit of BoBo, the Clown. One teacher would not allow her class to attend as it conflicted with her morning schedule. She did not seem to care that all things stop for children when it concerns BoBo the Clown, even her schedule!

But a lax schedule is just as disturbing for a child. A knowledge of what is expected, and when, is a security need of most of us. Perhaps a rule of thumb, well-known to the concerned teacher-counselor, is that children learn best in a relaxed, adjustable atmosphere where specific goals and the steps toward these goals are clearly stated and reinforced, but where the teacher knows that real learning does not occur by the clock.

Teacher-counselors allow some time for individual and group counseling activities. They know the value of peer group pressures and influences in determining behavior. The chapter which follows concerns itself specifically with some of these techniques, but it is also important that the teacher as counselor has some *individual, personal contact* with each child. With all else that is required, this is not an easy task to accomplish, but it is vital to good counseling. It offers children an opportunity for relating their more personal needs. It affords them the security of knowing that they will have some time alone with the teacher to use as they will. On certain days some children will have greater needs than others. The needs may take the form of academic help or just an opportunity to talk about something of special interest to the child. The old "share and tell" activity, if not abused, can offer the opportunity for all to share—but there will always be a time when what is to be shared is of a more intimate, private nature.

One teacher devised a period in which she could free herself for an hour each day while her aide took over the class. She arranged a private space behind an attractive screen where she could place two comfortable chairs. This was the place for "together time." The class was told that this was a period when they could talk with her about anything they wished. Any class member who requested a half-hour period could sign up for it in the morning by placing his or her name on the blackboard. In this way, she was able to see two children, each for a half-hour, each day. She could visit privately, every eight days, with each class member.

She related that, at first, the children felt awkward and these chats, interspaced with wiggling and giggling, related mostly to school work. Later the children used the time to discuss problems in peer relationships, home adjustments, and general growing pains. Of course, she took the liberty of "inviting" certain children to sign up, "just to get together." This experience often extended to discussions of general problem areas and concerns, common to the whole group, which could be dealt with in total classroom participation. She found that children who were disabled often had many special group problems to contend with, in addition to their own unique problems. The entire class seemed generally interested in such subjects as rejection, fear, envy, hate, sex, and development. After some time they asked to consider such special concerns as physical differences, experiences of open rejection, self-image, values, isolation, loneliness, and dating.

In one special school a fourteen-year-old boy committed suicide in the boys' toilet. He was discovered by several of his schoolmates. The situation, though obviously a devastating experience to all, was hushed up and made a taboo topic for discussion. It might have been a natural springboard for the discussion of deep-seated, real feelings. Loneliness, fear, anxiety, and pain do not vanish if we ignore them. In fact, any attempt at ignoring them simply seems to enhance them. Certainly the discussion of coping abilities and techniques, problem-solving methods, the value and the joy of life are as necessary as the algebra lesson or the latest current event!

The teacher-counselor allows some time for group social interaction, just for fun. Most disabled children are bused into and out of school and, therefore, have little time for socialization and peer group interaction. More often than not, they are strangers in their own neighborhoods and have few, if any, friends. They need the comfort and the alternatives each will afford the other. Using school time to allow children to "just talk together" may seem like a luxury, but the rewards are great. It is often through such school contacts that opportunities for weekend visitations arise and living horizons are broadened.

It is common knowledge that the traits which comprise the effective teacher have never been determined! Studies have been done in vast numbers and have succeeded only in offering vague generalities or contradictory conclusions. Even less is known about the specific role of the successful teacher-counselor. Is the firm teacher who demands quality production from students any less a good teacher than the relaxed teacher who helps the student toward quality work? Is it the difference in training, years of experience, age, knowledge of the subject area, knowledge of child development, or knowledge of exceptionalities which is the vital factor? Studies show that success in teaching is not dependent upon any of these qualities, specifically. Any quality is only as effective as the person who possesses and can communicate it.

It would be safe to say, though, that teacher-counselors need a vast knowledge of development and learning—especially as it relates to the atypical—a deep respect for the uniqueness of every living being, a sympathetic understanding of the qualities that make one human, a lack of fear of revealing themselves as people and for reaching out to others, for touching them physically and mentally. They need to have a deep respect for human potential and to be able to live their lives so as to afford themselves and others the greatest possibility for realizing it. They should have a sincere concern for the value of each individual. In other, more simple terms, they must be lovers in the broadest sense of the word.

In the book, *Love* (1973), I described the basic qualities of a lover as follows:

> To be a lover will require that you continually have the subtlety of the very wise, the flexibility of the child, the sensitivity of the artist, the understanding of the philosopher, the acceptance of the saint, the tolerance of the dedicated, the knowledge of the scholar, and the fortitude of the certain.

This is a great deal to require from a single person, but it can be a goal toward which a teacher-counselor might strive, for nothing is too good, or too much to ask, when a child's well-being is at stake. This is a great challenge, for the effectiveness and possibilities implied in the title *teacher-counselor* can never be realized in the isolated counselor's office, nor in a standard classroom. It can only be realized by the individual, through a wedding of the *best of both!*

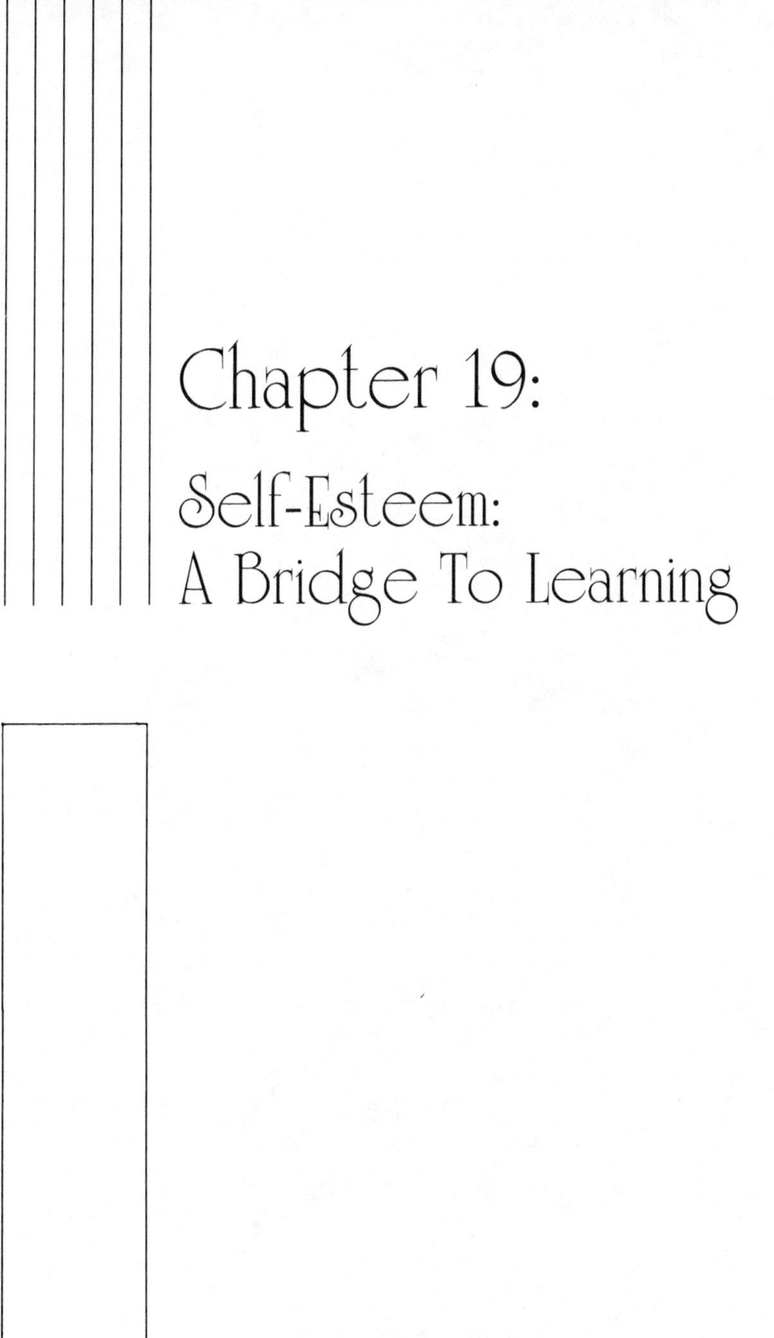

Chapter 19:

Self-Esteem: A Bridge To Learning

For years, DANIEL O'CONNOR has been involved in the process of learning best how to help others to achieve peace, joy and love in their lifetimes. This sincere desire has, through reading, study, and practice, caused him to become a growing authority in the field of personality development and spirituality and the processes involved in the sharing of the gift of being human. He is now director of Bridge Building, an urban retreat in San Francisco.

His warmth and concern are obvious. His knowledge is vast. I am indebted to him for sharing a bit of his wisdom, here, with us.

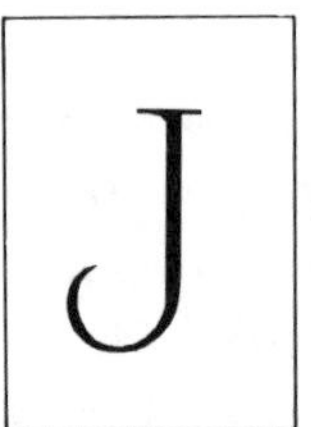

Johnny does read. He loves heroes and stories of the strong and the bold. Knights on white horses, athletes breaking world records, men who climb mountains and search for great white whales leap up to him from the pages of books. But Johnny, himself, cannot walk and probably never will.

Sally can add. She has learned to subtract and now can even get excited about doing fractions. She may grow to love dividing long numbers. But Sally cannot control her body. Her head lies limp and her arms and legs do not respond to her commands.

Johnny and Sally, along with Peter and Nancy and George and the others, listen to the wondrous deeds of athletes, doctors, and scientists. They learn of a changing world where progress is the byword. Men walking on the moon, breaking sound barriers—new agriculture bringing more food to a hungry world—musicians and dancers, poets and artists of all kinds doing what were once impossible feats. But Peter and Nancy and the others in this class cannot walk to school with their friends. They come on a special bus. They will not go home after school and play in the street. They will look out from their bedrooms or front rooms and watch while the others play. Their parents may not take them camping. They are seldom left alone in the house to explore new mysteries. They are cared for, put to bed. They live in a small protected world that seems to shrink as they grow older. They have unique and special problems.

And so, we might ask, what do the stories of heroes and the narration of great events do for *them?* What do their minds tell them? What do they feel as they look at their own lifeless arms and legs? What feelings does their dark or silent world create for them? What will they become? What great things will their bodies enable them to do? Is all that world in books a dream for them? An impossible dream? When they ask themselves, "What will I be?" "What can I do?"—is their answer, "Nothing"? or "Very little"? Is that other world for someone else? Yes, they can learn, but what do they do with their feelings of fear, inadequacy, depreciation?

What do the teachers of these children feel as they teach them about Martin Luther King's victory over fear and Neil Armstrong's giant step? Do they know what passes through the minds of their students when they tell them of the discoveries of Madame Curie and Edward Teller? The good special education teachers know. They know the children in their classes have feelings, too. They know that what they feel about themselves and others will affect their learning. They probably love them and want them to have wondrous lives. They know of the inadequacies and shame which some of the class may feel; they understand their loneliness and rejection. They may often ask themselves if they are presenting an unreal world to their students. They may question themselves if they are doing all they can to help their students to grow and enjoy their world. They may wonder what they can do to encourage, support, and inspire their students to cope with the problems which their disabilities have imposed upon them. They know that to do this they will have to enter their special world. How can they do this? "One could do worse than be a swinger of birches" is more than a line of a poem. It is meant to be the story of a life—even for Johnny. The teachers know that their work is not just to present the world—it must be a special world.

Disabled individuals may feel rejection, shame, guilt, loneliness. They may have already accepted defeat or too limited possibilities. Many disabled students will never receive the special care of a psychologist or counselor to help them heal the wounds imposed by a world that does not understand them. The classroom may be the only place where these students may learn respect for themselves and love for one another and all humans.

This chapter will deal with educating the feelings that accompany the mind on the path to becoming. It is about the findings of educators who agree that it is only through the uniting of bodies, minds, and feelings that real behavior change and learning is possible.

This chapter is concerned with beginnings more than blueprints. It is designed to suggest new possibilities and offer fresh alternatives to the dedicated teacher-counselor. It is not a *"how to,"* for the field is so vast as to make the task impossible. It is more of a *"Where to,"* a *where* to find the resources which will help the teacher to help students with the discovery of self, the development of self, and the sharing of self.

EDUCATION OF BODY, MIND AND FEELINGS

For years we called education merely "reading, 'riting and 'rithmetic." It is tempting and much easier to want to keep education in this restricted definition. Modern psychology has helped us to understand that it is not minds which are the object of education, it is *people* and the relationship of their minds and their emotions to their bodies. In some quarters there has been a debate between two kinds of education—*cognitive* and *affective*—as if somehow one can concern oneself with mind and ignore feelings. Fortunately, no such choice is necessary. Teachers of the disabled child can teach their curriculum in English, science, math, social studies and the arts, while at the same time dealing with their students' feelings. They can teach Johnny about the strength of history's heroes while they are dealing with their own personal feelings of inadequacy and isolation.

This process has been studied as a Ford/Esalen project concerning cognitive and affective education. The project was directed by George I. Brown and his associates at the University of California at Santa Barbara who developed and established the theory of *confluent education.* Dr. Brown states:

> *Confluent education* describes a philosophy and a process of teaching and learning in which the affective and cognitive domain flow together, like two streams merging into one river, and are thus integrated in individual and group learning. The term "affective" . . . refers to the feeling or emotional aspect of experience and learning. The more familiar "cognitive" refers to the activity of the mind in knowing an object—to intellectual functioning.

The report of this work is to be found in Dr. Brown's *Human Teaching for Human Learning*. It is an invaluable resource for the teacher who wishes to know the "how to" and theoretical implications of combining these "two streams." It offers valuable suggestions for the application of the theory to practice in the classroom. It would be well for teacher-counselors to familiarize themselves with confluent education. *The Live Classroom* by George Brown with Tom Yeomans and Lyle Grizzard, an Esalen book (1975), is also recommended. Other resources for confluent education include *DRICE* (Development and Research in Confluent Education) Ford/Esalen project in Confluent Education, an ongoing process that offers a number of papers and reprints, among which are *An Initial Bibliography for Confluent Education,* compiled by Jean Long (1971), an excellent listing of over 500 publications with special categorization for education for the disadvantaged, the exceptional child, mental health, etc., which focuses the material for the teacher of the disabled child; *Beyond Vibration Teaching* by John M. Shiflett, Research and Curriculum Development in Confluent Education, (Occasional paper No. 11); and *Human is as Confluent Does* by George Brown (Occasional paper No. 9). Other papers which suggest how affective education may be combined with the teaching of art, music, literature, etc., are available from DRICE, University of California at Santa Barbara.

MEETING AFFECTIVE NEEDS OF THE DISABLED STUDENT IN THE CLASSROOM

A. Assessing affective needs: The teacher of the disabled is obviously in an ideal position to observe the affective needs of the class. This assessment is of the utmost importance and is best achieved through the simple process of offering students the opportunity to speak of themselves and relate their own feelings. What is mainly required of the teacher is the ability to listen, to accept, to understand. But listening is a complex skill. It must be learned and developed.

Skills for learning how to listen are explored and developed by Dr. Thomas Gordon. Dr. Gordon calls his technique *active listening*. He explains how this ability can be developed in his work, *Parent Effectiveness Training*.

While Dr. Gordon's book is addressed primarily to the concerns of parents, the principles are easily adapted to the needs of the classroom teacher. (Dr. Gordon, himself, makes this adaptation in his Effectiveness Training Workshops. Though these workshops offer a brief but an invaluable resource designed for the teacher who has not had professional background in counseling or communications skills, much help can also be gained through reading his book.) Teachers will have no difficulty in translating these skills for listening in their own situation. For example, the teacher is asked the simple question, *How well do you listen?* and is presented with sample statements of children and asked *What feelings do you hear behind the words?*

Oh boy, only ten more days until school's out. ____________

Gee, I'm not having any fun. I can't think of anything to do. __
____

We get too much homework. I can never get it all done. What'll I do? ____________________________________

> I can do it myself. You don't need to help me. I'm old enough to do it myself. ________________

Dr. Gordon states that the first child feels glad or relieved; the second, bored or stumped; the third, defeated, or the job is too hard; and the fourth feels competent and does not want help.

Dr. Gordon asks the counselors to assess if they were close to the proper response. He wonders what we would reply to students who speak such feelings—would we allow them to speak, accept them and their feelings; or would we put up a road block to further communication by offering advice, preaching to them, or even commanding? The teacher of the disabled child will find in Dr. Gordon's techniques considerable assistance in developing listening skills as well as suggestions for activities which will foster, rather than cut off, further expression of feelings. Such skills will enable the teacher to create a classroom atmosphere of genuine openness and acceptance, an atmosphere which convinces the students that "who they are" and "what they think and feel" are as important as academic learning.

Dr. Gordon (1972) states:

> Through research and clinical experience, we are beginning to understand the necessary ingredients for an effective helping relationship. Perhaps the most essential of these is the language of acceptance.

Johnny may never have known such a relationship, a relationship based not upon fear or mistrust, but one that can help him to accept himself as a person and as a learner and convince him that he has genuine potential for limitless achievement and growth, disabled or not.

A further useful tool for the teacher wishing to develop listening skills is the book, *Teachers and Learners: The Interactive Process of Education*. In this book theories of communications are discussed and group exercises are presented and fully described.

B. The Self-Image of the Disabled Child: One of the main goals in the counseling of the disabled is to help them to develop positive self concepts. Dr. William Purkey has done much research into affect and its effect upon self-concept of learners. He describes his findings in his book, *Self Concept and School Achievement*. He states:

> Before we consider the process of building positive and realistic self-concepts in students, it is necessary to point out the need to avoid instilling negative ones. The self is remarkably conservative,

> and once a child has formed a negative image of himself, as a learner, the task of the teacher becomes extremely difficult. Therefore, the *prevention of negative self concepts is a vital first step in teaching.*

Dr. Purkey suggests that the power of the teacher to affect the self-image of the students rests upon the following factors: (1) what teachers believe about themselves; (2) what the teacher believes about the students; and (3) what the teacher does in the classroom. He makes interesting observations on all three of these aspects:

1. What the teachers believe about themselves:

   > The way the evidence points is that each teacher needs to view himself with respect, liking, and acceptance. When teachers have essentially favorable attitudes toward themselves, they are in a much better position to build positive and realistic self-concepts in their students.

2. What the teacher believes about the students:

   > Teachers . . . need to view students in essentially positive ways and hold favorable expectations. . . . the student's perceptions of the teacher's feelings correlated positively with his self-perception.

3. What the teacher does in the classroom:

   > Dr. Purkey describes six indispensable factors in teachers' attitudes—challenge, freedom, respect, warmth, control, and success.

Dr. Purkey's work suggests that it is crucial for teachers to understand the self-image of their students. To do this, they must comprehend the process of how to help them turn what might be negative images to positive ones. They must also understand how to enhance their growing self-concept in a classroom setting. Purkey's work is dedicated to answering these vital needs, and is a must for teachers of the disabled.

C. Further Resources for Exploring and Developing the Self-Image of the Disabled Student: Among the various resources that explore the importance of self-esteem and self-image of the learner the following should be especially useful: *The Acorn People* by Ron Jones (Bantam Books) develops many useful approaches for teaching students with special needs. While the following books are written with no particular group of learners in mind, their value for teachers of disabled students is not diminished: *100 Ways to Enhance Self-Concept in the Classroom* by Jack Canfield (Prentice-Hall); *Your Child's Self-Esteem* by Dorothy Briggs (Doubleday); *Building Positive Self-Concept* by Donald W. Felker (Burgess); and *Peoplemaking* by Virginia Satir (Science & Behavior Books). The literature designed to develop and enhance self image among learners has become extensive in recent years. The resources listed above will prove to be a good introduction in the field.

D. Group Interview: *Purpose:* This strategy, done in small groups, provides students with an opportunity to share on a more intimate basis than in the public interview some of their personal interests, beliefs, activities and values. It also affords the students the experience of interviewing each other.

Procedure: After the students break into groups of five to ten, one member of the group volunteers to be interviewed. Before the interview starts, group members take a minute or two to write down any questions they would like to ask the focus person. The volunteer may also write down questions to be asked and passes these to a friend. The questions should deal with interests, hobbies, family, friends, beliefs, hopes, goals in life, activities.

The students ask the focus person questions. The focus person controls the interview by calling upon various group members. The focus person has the option of not answering any question which is too personal or inappropriate by saying, "I pass." In turn, the volunteer may question group members about their purpose in asking a question before answering it. Unless there is a time limit set, the interview is over when there are no more questions or when the focus person ends it by saying, "Thank you for your questions."

The interview is to be conducted by the following ground rules which are given to the students:

1. Personal information, beliefs and values are to be shared and discussed on a voluntary basis. Please remember that there are things which all of us do not wish to discuss with others at a particular moment. This feeling should be recognized and respected by all members of the group.

2. The group interview is not the place for argument or debate. Please respect each other's right to live differently, feel differently, think differently and value differently. You may disagree with someone in the group; but try to understand their position rather than telling

them they are wrong or trying to make them change. People are more apt to change their lifestyles, beliefs, and values when and if they have different experiences, rather than when they are badgered into feeling their ideas are wrong.

E. Removing Barriers to Action: *Purpose:* Often, we find that of the seven subprocesses of valuing, the ones that are least likely to have been fulfilled are those dealing with acting on one's beliefs. Students may not be willing to take a stand, to prize their beliefs and be willing to publicly affirm them. They may have chosen their beliefs from alternatives, freely, with knowledge of the consequences, but they may be unwilling or unable to act upon them because of perceived or real barriers to action. This strategy is designed to help students identify and remove barriers to action which often block and plague their values development.

Sample Procedure: Students are asked to write at the top of a paper some action they would like to take or decision they would like to make. It should be an action which they are having some difficulty taking or which they fear to take. Then they are asked to draw a line lengthwise down the middle of the paper. On the right-hand side of the paper they list all the perceived or real barriers, both within and outside of themselves, which seem to be keeping them from acting. On the left-hand side of the paper they list steps they could take which might help remove or reduce each of the barriers. Finally, on the back of the paper, they develop a plan of action for actually removing the barriers.

This task may be done individually or in small groups, with each of the group members taking turns having the focus and receiving help from the group. The group helps in the listing of barriers to action, steps to be taken to remove or reduce the barriers, and in developing a plan of action.

This sampling may suggest to the teacher some idea of the limitless possibilities which the processes of Values Clarification can bring to the classroom and the great value it may have for the disabled student.

Psychosynthesis: It is possible that students with mental or physical limitations can be so closely identified with their disabilities that they are not able to develop other qualities and strengths which they may possess. A disabled body need not be an obstacle to the development of an able mind.

The theory and principles of Dr. Roberto Assagioli can be extremely useful in helping to establish a sense of identity within disabled individuals, especially if they are overidentified with one aspect of themselves to the detriment of the remainder of self.

Dr. Assagioli's books, *Psychosynthesis* and *Act of Will,* and the publications of the Psychosynthesis Institute describe a number of self-identification and dis-identification exercises which can help disabled students to begin to find their true selves and to dis-identify from the false or partial images which they may have imposed upon themselves due to their disability. To describe these many experiences in any detail is beyond the limits of this brief chapter. But for the interested teacher-counselor, the resources of *Psychosynthesis* are the following: Writings by Dr. Assagioli: *The Act of Will,* Penguin Books, Inc., Baltimore, Maryland, 1974; and *Psychosynthesis: A Manual of Principles and Techniques,* Viking Press, New York 1971. Among recent publications in the field of psychosynthesis one is especially useful, simply written and comprehensive: *What We May Be* by Piero Ferrucci (Tarcher Press).

CONCLUSION

This chapter is certainly too limited to do more than offer some suggestions as to the valuable resources available to teachers who are interested in helping their students toward affective development. The field of personal growth has made so many contributions to education in recent years that it is not possible to cover, in any authoritative way, all the contributions which can help the teacher.

The materials suggested are hopefully a beginning. Many of the books which have been quoted contain excellent bibliographies of other sources and resources which the enterprising teacher can easily adapt for use. They suggest ways in which teachers can create a classroom where Johnny and Sally can indeed learn about their world—but, at the same time, learn about themselves. They can suggest means of finding answers to questions with which their students must be concerned and helped.

In essence, these references can create in the special classroom an atmosphere where the learning of acceptance of self and others can overcome rejection and fear and loneliness, an atmosphere which encourages all the disabled students to grow into the whole persons they are without fear or limit.

While suggestions for techniques and the sources for them are the aim of this chapter, a word of caution is advised. Resource after resource warns that it is not so much the "technique" that is going to be effective in the educational and the emotional growth of the student, but rather teachers themselves. It is the teacher's qualities of humanity, warmth, love, acceptance and encouragement that are prime and indispensable factors for the continued growth of the child. There is no technique that can ever surpass the power of those qualities, nor any that can substitute for their absence.

Chapter 20:

A Behavioral Approach To Counseling

Many years ago, JIM LEIGH wrote me an impressive letter stating why he desired to spend his life working with exceptional children. At that time, he requested a Doctoral Fellowship to pursue his studies toward what had become a real desire for him: to help the disabled, in every way, to develop their potentials toward becoming total, productive, independent human beings.

Jim is now Associate Professor of Special Education, University of Missouri-Columbia. The field of the psychology and education of exceptional children will be richer in the future for his caring. Jim also has contributed a review of the literature (Section II, Chapter 3) to this book.

Assisting him in writing this chapter was graduate student JANE ELLIS, Department of Special Education, University of Missouri-Columbia. She has taught the learning disabled, behaviorally disordered and mentally retarded for the past five years.

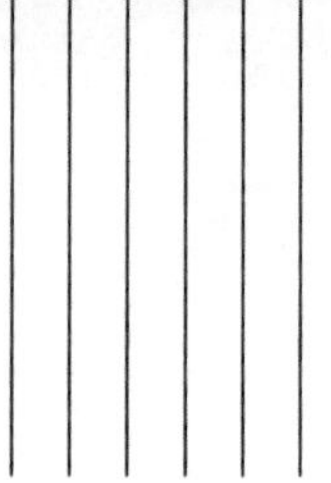

espite the obvious methodological differences which distinguish various counseling approaches, all orientations to counseling share one common characteristic—an essential focus on behavior from beginning to end. All counseling situations, from classical psychotherapy to operant behavioral therapy, are instigated when concern exists regarding an individual's behavior. A counselor's initial challenge is to identify and examine the behaviors (whether social, academic, verbal, or motor) which, because of their presence or absence, indicate a need for counseling. Moreover, the counselor must be continually sensitive to the client's behavior during the counseling process to make decisions concerning the direction and pace of the counseling activities. Similarly, all counseling situations terminate, and are judged as successful or unsuccessful, as a result of changes which occur or fail to occur in an individual's behavior.

Because of this requisite emphasis on behavior in all counseling orientations, the principles of *applied behavior analysis* are particularly well-suited for application in counseling situations. Applied behavior analysis (which is also referred to as *behavior modification* or *behavior management* in some contexts*) involves the systematic application of basic principles of learning for the purpose of establishing desirable new behaviors, changing certain existing behaviors, and eliminating undesirable behaviors. Applied behavior analysis should not be conceptualized as a discrete set of techniques which a counselor elects to use or not to use. The conditions and events which influence the occurrence of behavior are constantly operating; the counselor simply has an opportunity to control certain conditions and events in such a manner that they operate to the client's benefit rather than detriment. The remainder of this chapter contains an introduc-

*Several books and articles have been written which provide precise and detailed descriptions of applications of behavioral principles and techniques. If the brief introduction to a behavioral approach in this chapter generates curiosity or interest, there are readings suggested in the bibliography at the end of the book.

tion to the basic premises of applied behavior analysis, followed by recommendations for enhancing the effectiveness of those premises when applied in counseling situations.

BASIC PRINCIPLES OF APPLIED BEHAVIOR ANALYSIS

The first step in the behavioral approach is to identify and describe the behaviors of concern. Within the behavioral context, a behavior must be both observable and measurable. Therefore, at least two people should be able to see a behavior occur and agree on what happened. According to this definition, then, terms such as *hostility, aggression, laziness, anxiety,* and *frustration* are not behaviors. Instead, they are rather vague interpretations referring to presumed etiology or psychological conditions underlying the behaviors of concern. The behaviors which must be dealt with are observable, such as hitting, kicking, running, getting out of a chair, laughing, talking, crying, or writing.

After the behavior has been specifically identified, it is necessary to establish a *baseline.* This involves observing and recording the occurrence of the target behavior before any intervention is attempted. Baseline data provides a reference point for monitoring change in the target behavior and a means of determining the effectiveness of the intervention. The behavior is usually recorded several times over a period of days to obtain an accurate estimate of the rate of occurrence. A written record is maintained of all measurements and recordings.

Three of the simplest and most common methods of recording behavior are referred to as anecdotal recording, frequency recording, and duration recording. *Anecdotal recording* is performed by developing a written narrative account of the occurrence of a behavior, which often includes additional information regarding the environmental context in which the behavior was produced and the resulting consequences of the behavior. Anecdotal records are generally useful to the extent that the observer provides precise descriptions of overt behaviors while avoiding subjective judgments and interpretations. *Frequency recording* merely involves counting exactly how many times a behavior occurs, and is particularly useful for recording behaviors that occur very quickly or with a high rate of occurrence. *Duration recording* involves measuring how long a behavior occurs each time it is produced. These three methods of observational recording can be used separately or together in conjunction with more sophisticated techniques of measurement (e.g., *time-sampling*).

After the behaviors of concern have been identified, observed and recorded, an intervention is implemented. Although behavioral intervention is widely associated with control of the *consequences* of behavior, the effective counselor will devote equal attention to arranging the *antecedents* of behavior. Antecedents refer to the environmental conditions and events that exist immediately prior to production of specified behaviors. The physical setting of a room, schedule, materials, type of activity or task, and grouping arrangement can be designed to create the greatest probability for successful performance of the desired behaviors. The counselor can also provide highly specific cues, known as *discriminative stimuli,* concerning when specified behaviors are appropriate or expected. In an even more directive manner, the counselor can create opportunities for clients to acquire new behaviors by observing and imitating appropriate *models* of behavior provided by others.

In addition to controlling antecedents in order to influence behavior, the counselor also may arrange the events which follow certain behaviors. Such manipulation of behavioral consequences will virtually always involve, to some extent, the provision of *positive reinforcement.* In a broad sense, positive reinforcement refers to a reward or desirable consequence of a behavior. More specifically, positive reinforcement must be defined in relation to the effect it produces on the behavior it follows. If a behavior is reinforced, it will have a higher probability of continuing to occur in the future.

In order for reinforcement to produce the greatest effect, it should immediately follow the target behavior. Initially, every instance of the desired behavior should be reinforced. This *continuous reinforcement* ensures that the behavior will become firmly established. However, if a behavior occurs frequently and is reinforced each time, the reinforcer soon loses its power. Eventually, therefore, only occasional occurrences of the behavior are reinforced, through *intermittent reinforcement,* to maintain the behavior.

Generally, tangible reinforcers such as edibles, tokens, or toys are effective with young children while older children may respond more to praise, smiles and other indications of attention. If tangible reinforcers are used, they should be accompanied by a social reward. As the behavior change process progresses, tangible reinforcers can be phased out or delayed. The behavior is then maintained by social reinforcers and, eventually, by the self-reinforcement or satisfaction derived from successful performance of the newly acquired behaviors.

A very important principle to remember when using applied behavior analysis is that seemingly simple skills and behaviors which individuals are learning may seem quite complex and unmanageable to them. Even behaviors such as tying a shoelace or writing one's own name involve many difficult steps which require much effort for children to master. Counselors cannot expect disabled individuals to produce certain behaviors all at once, but instead should gradually help the individual learn the behavior through *shaping*. During behavior shaping, successive approximations to the desired terminal behavior are reinforced, so that the individual progresses step by step until he or she can finally execute the entire skill or behavior. In this way, the person experiences positive reinforcement and feedback for succeeding in small steps rather than feelings of frustration for failing to master immediately a new behavior in its entirety.

Another possible way to deal with behavior other than through positive reinforcement is by the use of *punishment*. Punishing undesirable behavior is generally much less effective than rewarding desirable behavior. Punishment refers either to the application of an undesirable or aversive consequence or to the removal of a positive consequence. For example, if children do something wrong they may be spanked or lose certain privileges or be forced to stay in during recess at school. As many parents and teachers realize, however, punishment often produces very little lasting change in a child. Unfortunately, some children receive little attention except when they misbehave and are punished by parents or teachers. In many cases, the individual attention received during punishment is rewarding enough to sustain the negative behavior. Therefore, unless the behavior is very dangerous or disruptive and must be stopped immediately, it is more effective to extinguish the inappropriate behavior by reinforcing an incompatible or competing positive behavior. Moreover, certain undesirable behaviors are amenable to extinction by merely withholding attention or inadvertent reinforcement through ignoring the behaviors.

During the entire intervention, written records should be kept of the increase or decrease in the rate of the behavior. The data may be placed on graphs or charts which provide clear, concise visual representations of the effectiveness of the intervention. These records objectively indicate whether or not the intervention strategy is working and exactly to what degree the behavior is changing. The advantage of such precise accountability has become increasingly evident as school personnel have attempted to comply with the provisions of PL 94-142 in recent years.

INVOLVEMENT OF TEACHERS, PARENTS, AND DISABLED INDIVIDUALS

The goals of counseling are not always accomplished in a specific place and time in the presence of a professional counselor or therapist. Instructing parents and teachers in the principles and applications of applied behavior analysis will add support and consistency to the counselor's efforts. With the present emphasis on mainstreaming of exceptional children, it is necessary for teachers to increase their skill in managing behavior within the classroom. Teachers often find the use of applied behavior analysis to be an effective preventive technique. Rewarding successful academic performance and task behavior may reduce the occurrence of inappropriate behaviors, allowing the teacher to devote more time to instruction and other teaching responsibilities.

Equally important is the active and essential role the parents assume in the child's progress. Unfortunately, after an initial diagnosis of an exceptional child, the child is often placed in the hands of special education teachers, remedial reading teachers, speech therapists, physical therapists, pediatricians, psychiatrists, counselors, or other highly specialized professionals, and parents sometimes feel relegated to the role of merely providing food, shelter, and clothing for their child. Many parents trained in the application of behavioral techniques, though, experience new feelings of importance and worth. More importantly, the special love and dedication of a parent combined with the skilled application of behavioral techniques often produce changes which an entire team of specialists cannot accomplish.

Perhaps the ultimate goal of counselors, parents, and teachers is to provide the disabled individual with the skills necessary to bring about change in his or her own behavior. Many individuals who have handicapping conditions, particularly adolescents and adults, clearly have the capability to understand and apply the basic behavioral premises and techniques discussed in this chapter. Since the principles of applied behavior analysis are undeniably effective, it is only logical that they be *shared with,* rather than simply *used on,* exceptional individuals who have the capacity to benefit from such knowledge and skill. Such individuals may then not only assist the counselor in working toward established behavioral objectives, but may also independently instigate positive behavioral change in themselves and others.

APPLICATION WITH OTHER APPROACHES

Even if a total behavioral approach is not adopted by the counselor, the application of behavioral principles and techniques provides a valuable supplement to virtually any counseling approach or orientation. For example, even though applied behavior analysis is not generally associated with counseling approaches concerned with attitudes and feelings, the counselor may indeed use a behavioral approach in conjunction with therapies designed to deal with the client's affective experiences. Although emotions and attitudes cannot be directly observed and measured, the concomitant behaviors associated with these feelings are amenable to intervention, which, in turn, may significantly influence emotional and attitudinal development and expression. Counselors who subscribe to a behavioral viewpoint recognize the existence and vital importance of inner subjective experiences, but do not sacrifice a practical focus on the behavioral manifestations of attitudes and feelings to time-consuming and, in many cases, useless theoretical conjecture concerning their etiology.

CONCLUSION

Finally, a behavioral approach comprises an awareness of the dignity and worth of each individual. The efforts and success of an individual are attended to and focused upon rather than his or her failures and disabilities. The exceptional individual is not viewed as "handicapped," but as a unique human being with both abilities and disabilities. Desirable abilities and behaviors are developed and disabilities are remediated directly, without the derogatory and negative implications and connotations associated with the application of labels. The environment is structured to maximize the possibilities for success, systematic strategies are employed to assist in the acquisition of positive behaviors, and the resulting successful approximation or mastery of desired behaviors is rewarded. In this sense, a behavioral approach to counseling must certainly be characterized as a humanistic orientation.

Chapter 21:

Special Concerns In Counseling The Intellectually Limited

DR. EDDIE H. WILLIAMS is a professor and Director of Graduate Studies in Special Education at the University of Southern California. Among his major interests is the psychology and education of the intellectually limited. A warm, concerned person, his knowledge is vast and practical. I appreciate his taking time from an active schedule to share in this volume.

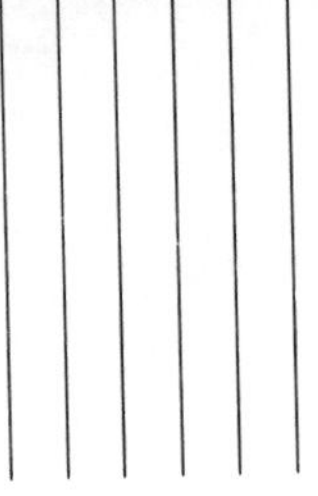

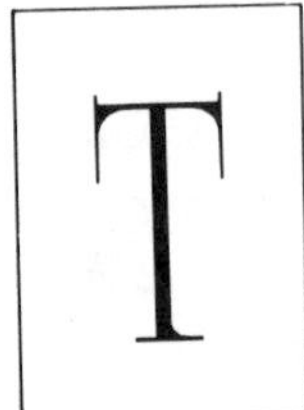

his chapter deals with the unique problems of counseling and guidance for the intellectually disabled individual from the early developmental stages through adulthood. While there are some general characteristics to be found among the intellectually disabled, these are more due to degrees of severity of their problems. Each psychological or learning characteristic attributed to intellectual disability has a wide range of levels of severity. These diversified characteristics may exist in personal-social aptitude as well as learning style and cognitive abilities. In order to fully appreciate the potential of the intellectually disabled person, each individual and his/her unique characteristics must be considered; for example, one may present extreme deficits in one dimension, such as cognition, and have very mild deficits in another area, such as social adaptability.

PARENTAL REACTION

Parental reaction to the awareness of the intellectual limitations of a child varies greatly, with such factors as personality, family stability, and family constellation being important influences. While no single reaction can be identified as "typical" several are common, such as frustration, disappointment, guilt, pain, despair, or ambivalence. The emotional reactions of parents to the awareness of their child's disability were first categorized by Roos (1963) from his work in psychological counseling of parents of retarded children. These reactions were described as follows:

1. *Loss of self-esteem*. A defect in one's child may be interpreted as a defect in one's self, particularly when a parent identifies closely with the child. Life goals may be abruptly and radically altered, including loss of the fantasy of immortality through one's children.
2. *Shame*. Parents may anticipate social rejection, pity, or ridicule and related loss of prestige. Social withdrawal may be a common consequence.
3. *Ambivalence*. The simultaneous experience of love and hatred

normally experienced by parents toward their children is likely to be greatly intensified toward a retarded child. The retarded child's relative lack of achievement and tendency toward irritating behavior are likely to be sources of continuing parental frustration. Frustration, in turn, generates anger and resentment which may lead to death wishes toward the child and feelings of rejection, typically accompanied by guilt. Inconsistent behavior, sometimes alternating between rejection and overprotection, may also be expressed.

4. *Depression.* Chronic feelings of sorrow are to be anticipated as a nonpathological reaction to having a retarded child. These parents are disappointed in their child and concerned about the future. To some, mental retardation symbolizes the child's death, and hence precipitates a grief reaction similar to that associated with the loss of a loved one.
5. *Self-sacrifice.* Some parents adopt a "martyr" attitude and sacrifice all personal pleasures for the child. The retarded child may become the focus of such parents' total interests, often to the detriment of other family members. Family disruption, including marital conflicts, may accompany this pattern. The retarded child may become the focus of mutual blame and criticism by the parents.
6. *Defensiveness.* Parents may become acutely sensitive to implied criticism of their retarded child and may react with resentment and belligerence. In extreme cases, parents may deny the existence of retardation, rationalize the child's shortcomings, and seek professional opinions to substantiate their own contention that "there is really nothing wrong" with him.

In addition to these emotional reactions to the awareness of the child's disability, it has been suggested that there is a pattern to the manner in which parents adjust to this awareness. The five stages of parental reaction suggested by Rosen (1955) regarding parents of mentally retarded children progress from the initial awareness of the problem through a level of acceptance: (1) awareness that a serious problem exists, (2) recognition of the retardation, (3) search for the cause, (4) search for a solution or cure, (5) acceptance of the problem. While these phases are arranged in a hierarchy they are not discrete and there is obviously a great deal of overlap from one phase to another with many factors influencing the degree of acceptance finally achieved. The discreteness of these categories as well as the time-bound progression through the phases should never be accepted by the counselor as an absolute. In fact there is growing evidence that parents of disabled children experience intense grieving feelings which are re-evoked on numerous occasions throughout life (Wikler, et al, 1981). Olshansky (1961) has discussed this as *chronic sorrow* which is a repeated sadness experienced by parents of retarded children. The counselor needs to be aware that, regardless of the level of acceptance on the part of parents, there will probably be periods of disillusionment, disappointment, and sadness. Olshansky has suggested that chronic sorrow is a natural rather than a neurotic reaction in that sorrow is a natural response to a tragic fact. As an intervention to the periodic crises encountered by the family over the life-span of the disabled individual a continuum of appropriate support services should be provided.

ADVOCACY AND THE PARENT'S ROLE

There have been several federal laws passed relative to the rights of handicapped persons and their parents. These include rights concerned with confidentiality of records and information, right of access to school records, due process, and right to free public education. In terms of parent involvement in the educational process, the Education of all Handicapped Children Act (PL 94-142) enacted in 1975 and fully implemented in 1980 has no doubt been the most significant. This act guaranteed access to a free and appropriate education for all handicapped children and included the following:

1. *The right to due process.* Procedural safeguards were mandated to assure due process in classification and placement in the schools. Parents are guaranteed access to school records and the right to impartial hearings regarding their child's placement. Parents are also guaranteed the opportunity for independent evaluations of their child.
2. *Protection against discriminatory testing during assessment.* This safeguard ensures that placement will not be made on the basis of a single psychometric instrument, and requires that tests be administered in the child's native language.
3. *Placement in the least restrictive educational setting.* This provision states that handicapped children should be educated in environments resembling, as closely as possible, those

in which nonhandicapped children are educated. It is intended to protect the child from the presumed detrimental effects of segregation.

4. *Individualized education programs.* Educators must prepare a written description of each child's program to ensure accountability. These programs must specify: (1) the program's objectives, (2) the services to be provided, (3) the program's schedule, and (4) the criteria used to determine the program's effectiveness (MacMillan, 1982).

The professional working with parents should review the provisions of PL 94-142 carefully and be prepared to assist parents in meeting the requirements for parental involvement. It is not realistic, however, to expect all of the frustrations, anxieties, and serious concerns of parents to disappear with the enactment of laws to protect their handicapped child's rights and assure a free, appropriate education. Even in school situations where everything possible is being done to meet these provisions, there is still basis for parental concern. The intellectually disabled individual presents a complex set of needs in both the home and school and requires a high level of cooperation between parents and professionals. Parent and teacher interaction and involvement in developing an individual education program is a good start.

Problems of Adaptive Behavior: When maladaptive behavior is found with an intellectually disabled person it is not usually the result of limited cognitive ability, but rather a product of disturbances in psychological growth. Deficits in such areas as reasoning and judgment create problems in the acquisition of a repertoire of appropriate personal-social skills which may bring about maladaptive behavior. Hutt and Gibby (1976) state:

> It is important to recognize that the maladaptive behaviors of mentally retarded children are not the primary result of their retarded intellectual capacities. Rather, they are the result of incomplete or distorted personality functions associated with mental retardation. It is of course true that the inferior intellectual capacities of the mentally retarded child make it much more difficult for him to achieve a high degree of success in many areas (such as academic or vocational areas), but intellectual factors play a secondary rather than a primary role in the production of maladaptive behavior.

Since it is disturbance in psychological growth which may lead to maladaptive behavior, the guidance and counseling approach to be used with the intellectually disabled should not be as concerned with changing basic cognitive abilities but more with providing opportunities for developing adequate patterns of adaptive behavior. It seems, therefore, that the intellectually disabled can best be helped by providing them with consistent, positive experiences and opportunities to develop personal-social skills congruent with their individual maturational levels.

COUNSELING AND GUIDANCE AT SPECIFIC STAGES OF DEVELOPMENT

Intellectual disability is usually associated with impairments in maturation, learning, and social adjustment. Individual differences among persons who are intellectually disabled are obviously very great. This makes it almost impossible to predict the patterns of maladaptive behavior which any individual will have. Certain developmental stages do, however, seem to present certain common problems associated with deficits in experience and development.

Infancy and Early Childhood: During infancy and early childhood, counseling and guidance problems are more likely to be related to interactions between parents, child, and siblings in the home. Developmental delays are not always obvious to the parents at the beginning and it is therefore difficult for the parents to predict or understand their particular child's needs. The intellectually disabled child will often show delays in speech, other motor activities such as walking, and various visual-motor functions. According to Barnard and Erickson (1976) some of the most characteristic delays seem to be in (1) not sitting up by eight months of age; (2) not walking by 15 to 18 months of age; (3) not responding to verbal commands; and (4) not using expressive language.

Maturational skills related to infancy and early childhood must be assessed in order to provide the parents with a guide to appropriate sequences of activities and experience. Developmental scales such as the *Denver Developmental Screening Test, Gesell Developmental Schedules,* and *Bayley's Scales of Infant Development* can be of great help. They provide information on a child's progress in areas such as motor, perceptual, language, personal-social, and sensory discrimination. Infant stimulation programs are available for the child with developmental delays. These include enrichment of the environment through such activities as: tactile stimulation, auditory and visual stimulation, and a wide variety of motor exercises. Barnard and Erickson

(1976) provide an excellent guide for infant stimulation in *Teaching Children with Developmental Problems.* Continual, periodic assessment of the child's developmental level is particularly important during these early stages, as small gains, while difficult to recognize, are very important in identifying readiness stages for new skills.

The disabled child may require special guidance in learning to walk, to speak, to become toilet-trained and to develop competence in self-feeding. These self-care skills are an important part of the early guidance procedures and must be individualized according to the child's developmental patterns. Consistency of approach, repetition, and environmental stimulation are important aspects to consider. Self-care skills can be broken down into a complex set of sequences of behavior, each leading to the mastery of a new function. Motor skills, for instance, are a prerequisite for other more complex self-care skills. Learning and cognitive behavior depend on the child's motor skills, i.e., ability to walk, ability to grasp and manipulate objects. The *Washington Guide to Promoting Development in the Young Child* is a comprehensive instrument providing expected tasks and suggested activities for infants and young children and covers motor skills, feeding, play, language, discipline, and toilet training. This is a particularly useful guide in working with intellectually disabled children. With this guide, developmental stages can be established quite simply by a study of the tasks the child can perform. Barnard and Erickson (1976) have developed carefully sequenced guidance procedures pertaining to self-care during the early maturational stages. These are correlated with specific behavioral tasks for reaching each new developmental level.

Cromwell (1961) has identified seven fundamental principles in the behavioral development of the intellectually disabled child. These are provided as a means of creating an environment wherein the child can develop with a minimum of emotional conflicts:

1. Positive reinforcement will increase the possibility of a particular behavioral reaction occurring. Negative reinforcement will decrease such a possibility. This means that desired forms of behavior should be praised whenever possible.
2. If the child is to develop a more goal-directed than avoidant form of behavior, then more positive than negative reinforcement should be provided. That is, more "praise" than "punishment" should be given.
3. The reinforcement should be as immediate as possible.

4. The parent is, of course, not always able to administer reinforcement whenever it is appropriate. But this does not necessarily mean that its efficiency in maintaining a particular form of desirable behavior is impaired.
5. Whenever possible, the reasons for the positive and the negative reinforcements should be verbalized to the child.
6. It is important that the parent be consistent in the administration of both positive and negative reinforcements.
7. Positive reinforcement should be administered to the child regardless of whether or not it is specific to the behavior that the child is displaying. As a result, the child learns to regard him or herself as a worthwhile person despite the particular behavior.

Later Childhood: During the school years differences between the child with intellectual disabilities and other children become more obvious and, due to social and cultural influences, bring about major problems. During this time the parents, too, may become aware of limitations which have not been noticed during the earlier developmental periods. The demands of the greater society are first manifested through the school environment. It is very difficult for the intellectually disabled child to participate in a school program without comparisons being made between his/her ability and that of peers. The parent who was able to accept delayed development and set realistic goals during the early developmental stages may be frustrated when the child is not offered the same kind of understanding and acceptance in school. For one thing it is usually impossible for the child to achieve academic success comparable to his/her age peers and the child will inevitably be given special attention, through special class placement, or differential treatment within the regular classroom. Special treatment can present additional problems, in that it may cause other children to first perceive differences between themselves and the intellectually disabled schoolmate. This often results in rejection. If children are made to perceive themselves to be different or inadequate, it may often be more "handicapping" than their intellectual disability.

Many of the child's new problems may be related to the inability to achieve academic success. During the school years this is a compounding problem since success in academic areas, such as reading, is a primary societal demand. The intellectually disabled child cannot meet this requirement on the accepted schedule. Attempts on the part of the school to remediate the situation with the pressures of special treatment can further complicate the situation.

There are also problems in the area of socialization during the school years. The socialization process of school-age children is developmental and follows a typical sequence. Children's games become more complex with chronological age and the sophistication of social nuances and innuendos increases with language development. The intellectually disabled child is always functioning at a lower mental age than chronological-age peers and often has difficulty comprehending subtle language usage and the rules of games. This may additionally complicate the situation and deny him/her the necessary socialization and interaction in play and peer group activities. Opportunities must be afforded which are cross-aged and heterogeneously grouped, as opposed to those which are locked into strict chronological age bands, if the child is to receive the much needed social understandings.

Adolescence: The adolescent years are difficult for all young people and are particularly confusing, frustrating, and traumatizing for the intellectually disabled. Socialization is at the peak of importance. Acceptance by peers and membership in the group become most vital for the development of a positive self-concept. It is not uncommon for the intellectually disabled to have severe adjustment problems at this point. Part of this is due to the fact that they are interacting with peers in an easily noticeable, unacceptable manner. Socialization skills may be limited and the nuances of peer group language and jokes may escape them.

During puberty the increased sexual drives and development of secondary sexual characteristics present additional problems for the intellectually disabled. Physiological changes create psychological problems for most people during puberty; however, the intellectually disabled individual is less likely to possess the ability for understanding these phenomena. They often do not have the ability to read and comprehend material about biological functions and physiological changes and may not have other sources for acquiring this information. Rapid development, or lack of development, of secondary sexual characteristics often brings about conflicts in developing a self-image. This is particularly true when there is a wide discrepancy between mental and chronological ages.

With adolescence, many parents become concerned about the sexual behavior of their children. The mildly intellectually disabled adolescent usually will not differ in sexual development and inclinations from others in his/her age group. Because of their intellectual limitations, some of the children become impulsive and may show poor judgment in their interpersonal relationships. These children must be educated regarding sexuality and maturing social relationships.

Many families need the opportunity to explore their fears and concerns about the adolescent's sexuality, as well as specific advice upon which they may build their educational plans.

Although sexual "acting out" and other such adjustment problems during adolescence do not occur in any greater frequency with the intellectually disabled than with the rest of the population, when they do occur, the mechanisms for coping with them are more often inadequate. Maturity, judgment, reasoning have an influence on behavior. The level of intellectual functioning plays an important part in how the individual deals with sexual development. The "significant others" in the adolescent's environment also influence his/her behavior during this period. For instance, if parents deal with masturbation in a punitive manner during childhood, the adolescent may view all sexual urges in a negative manner. The individual may develop feelings of guilt and a low self-esteem. Of course, sex education for the intellectually disabled has to be individualized, according to the person's level of intellectual functioning, interest or concern, experience, and emotional maturity.

During adolescence it is particularly important for the intellectually disabled to be provided with activities that allow for social interaction with peers. Heterosexual relationships may be difficult to establish through usual school contact so whenever possible an effort should be made to involve the adolescent in community recreational programs. Special abilities can often compensate for disabilities, and help the individual gain social acceptance. Any asset, such as ability to dance, athletic ability, a hobby, or musical ability, which the adolescent has for social success should be cultivated as much as possible.

In addition to personal and social problems during adolescence there are other concerns which require guidance and counseling. Guidance in setting realistic goals and aspirations for vocational training and future employment becomes necessary. If an adolescent is not provided this training in high school, the counseling and guidance role is greatly increased. It may then be necessary that the person be referred to community agencies which provide vocational training and rehabilitation. This is of the utmost importance for a smooth transition from adolescence to maturity, from dependence to independence.

Adulthood: The counseling and guidance needs of the intellectually disabled adult vary greatly according to the degree of disability as well as to previous educational opportunities, vocational aptitude, personality, and social adjustment. Smith (1971) has indicated that the major needs of the intellectually disabled adult are for love, belongingness, recognition by others, usefulness, praise, and the opportunity to be meaningfully involved in a task. It is often difficult to structure the environment of the adult in order to provide for these needs; consequently, community services must be available through a variety of agencies. In order to maintain an adequate standard of living and meet the aforementioned needs, the adult usually needs advisement in such areas as legal assistance; sex information including family planning, contraception, and voluntary sterilization; vocational training and employment; recreational activities; management of finances; public assistance and services available; family relationships; and child care.

In adulthood most people prefer to leave their parents' home and create their own life styles, compatible with their unique interests and needs. The intellectually disabled quite often have these inclinations and the majority of the mildly disabled can make this transition without much problem. The degree of disability is obviously the major consideration in planning for this transition in living arrangements. The development of half-way houses and community residential centers for small groups of adults has provided opportunities for trial experiences which may eventually lead to independent living for many intellectually disabled adults. Even after independence is established, the adult may need assistance in selecting appropriate living arrangements and in maintaining an adequate standard of living. The factors which relate most closely to this independence are social-adjustment skills. The intellectually disabled adult needs an opportunity to develop socialization skills leading to self-confidence through supportive, nonthreatening interactions. Traits such as cooperation, initiative, maturity in self-control, and judgment, while not necessarily acquired incidentally, can be gained through repetitive, reinforcing experiences. The major counseling and guidance function at this level is to provide services which lead to maturity in social adjustment and independence in living.

If the adult is totally dependent, an important consideration in the counseling and guidance process is the arrangement for life-long care and supervision. Parents, and others providing care, need supportive counseling, as well as advisement, in making decisions about residential placement when they may be no longer able to provide care and supervision.

CONCLUSION

Counseling and guidance with the intellectually disabled is a unique, life-long process requiring continual supportive care, understanding, and encouragement. This process involves little, if any, of the usual short-term, therapist-client interactions, but rather an individualized, developmental approach wherein realistic goals are met through positive experiences. The problems of intellectual disability relate directly to delayed development which means that the guidance process must be concerned with activities which allow individuals to grow and gain independence in keeping with their aptitude and abilities. This process is continuous throughout life and always involves experiences which lead from dependence to independence. This begins with early developmental tasks in infancy and proceeds through adult self-sufficiency in vocational success and social adaptation. The tasks vary greatly through the process, though the basic concepts remain the same, that is, realistic goals, positive experiences, support, and encouragement.

Chapter 22: The Disabled Are Also Sexual

It is a great honor to have DR. SOL GORDON contribute his expertise to this volume. Dr. Gordon is a professor of Child and Family Studies at Syracuse University. He is also a much-sought-after lecturer and an important author. (A partial bibliography of his related publications appears at the end of this book if the reader desires more specific and detailed information relating to general sex education and sexuality.) But most of all, for our purposes, Dr. Gordon is an international authority in the field of sexuality relating to the disabled individual in our society. He is a controversial figure. One may agree or disagree with his ideas, as can be seen from reading this chapter. But there is no controversy in the fact that Dr. Gordon is a much needed and respected pioneer in the area of aiding disabled persons to realize their rights to full and satisfactory sexual lives.

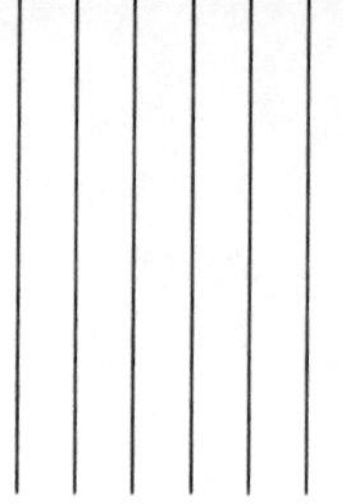

erhaps, as a start, we should acknowledge that people who have disabilities are entitled to full, responsible sexual expression. Many individuals find it difficult to accept the normal sexual desires and impulses of disabled persons; they wrongfully (perhaps unconsciously) assume that since they are limited in certain physical or mental aspects, they must be limited in most other areas as well.

The following represents some ideas about sexuality that seem to me important to consider before we deal with sexuality of others. In some instances it is not so important that we agree with these ideas as it is that these stimulate discussion and thought. We might agree, however, that people who repress sexual ideas and feelings probably transfer these attitudes to others (whether consciously or unconsciously). The function of facilitating adjustment in these areas will be greatly enhanced by our own personal liberation from noncommunication about sex. The best thing that could result is an understanding of our own sexuality and how this understanding can create and influence healthy feelings in others.

People used to think (and some still do) that sex could be sublimated (propelled into "higher channels" without direct expression) by being creative, athletic, doing charitable work or becoming a priest. In the case of the disabled, the additional distractions of limited physical or mental abilities supposedly erase any remnants of sexual interest.

My view is that postpubescent sexuality can only be

Expressed
Repressed
Suppressed

but it cannot be sublimated!

The people who are really in trouble are those who *repress* significant aspects of their sexuality. Repressed sexuality can produce, among other results:

★ Psychosomatic illnesses
★ Immaturity

★ Revulsion in response to natural functions of the body
★ Meanness
★ Obsessive-compulsive neurosis
★ Fear of homosexuality
★ Castration fears
★ Failure to achieve orgasm.

ROAD TO SUCCESS

Those of us with long-standing experience with disabled people and their parents have come to realize that a person's eventual adjustment to the mainstream is, in general, less related to the nature of the handicap and academic success or failure in school, than it is to self-image, ability to socialize and be productive.

It is a hard fact of our society that having a physical or mental limitation entails no special privileges. The special classes, schools, counselors, and programs generally available do not really compensate for the difficulties involved. Some people realize the dilemmas and are willing to help, but most of the population avoid the problems of the disabled.

Many people seem to operate on the false belief that the less exceptional children know about sex, the less likely they will be sexually irresponsible. Some educators protest that they have enough trouble teaching reading and arithmetic. Why get into "sensitive" issues? And yet, these individuals experience the same physical and emotional changes that "normal" children do, as well as the anxiety which often accompanies adolescence. Thus, disabled persons must cope with all the emotional conflicts of their "normal" counterparts in addition to those produced by their disabilities.

The question is not whether we should have sex education for the disabled, but whether we consider "educational" the information they receive from sexploiting popular media, pornography, myths from gutter discussions, graffiti in our public school bathrooms, and premature and sometimes involuntary sexual experiments. Exceptional youth must be taught about love, conception, contraception, and venereal disease. They, too, must be able to discuss sexuality in the context of mature decision-making and moral dilemmas. They must learn that it is wrong to risk premarital pregnancy, wrong to risk getting venereal disease, and wrong to have sexual relations for exploitation purposes. They must know that masturbation can be healthy but that, at times, it can be inappropriate if not done privately or if done compulsively.

Yet we need not request professionals alone to respond to this urgency for sex education. We need to consider that some of the best education is done by so-called "unqualified" people. I have not noticed that teachers, nurses, or doctors are, in general, especially good sex educators. We have, perhaps, overstated the importance of expertise, when what counts the most is attitude and good will.

Although sex educators have a tendency to present information in a scientific and, unfortunately, obscure fashion, we need not adhere to such narrowness. Moreover, the topic *sex education* includes more than the issues of reproduction, sexual intercourse, or the differences between male and female. The term covers all areas which have to do with human sexuality, including our attitudes, our feelings, our behavior, and the way we relate to ourselves and others. Therefore, it is important to understand several things that happen to our children, disabled or not, in their early years if we are to help them develop positive attitudes regarding their sexuality, themselves, and others.

Sexual pleasure is not just confined to stimulation of the genitals, but many of us believe that all pleasant physical contact is related to sex. This is true even of babies who learn about the pleasures of physical contact through early touching and fondling. Parents stroke, kiss, and cuddle babies and they respond with affection. Obviously infants are learning even though they do not yet talk. They will use this early learning later in life. What they learn about love, affection and physical contact will affect their sexual attitudes and behavior when they become biologically ready.

WHEN DOES A CHILD LEARN ABOUT SEX?

Many of our sexual feelings and attitudes are determined before the age of five. Much of what any child, including the disabled child, learns about sexuality comes from the general atmosphere of her/his family. How do *they* show affection? Do they touch each other? Do they express their feelings freely?

For instance, toilet-training before children are ready can create feelings of self-doubt, guilt and shame that could trouble them for the rest of their lives, although they probably will not even be aware of the cause. If they have an "accident" and are punished or told that they are "bad" or "dirty" when they are not capable or old enough to control elimination they may become seriously (and honestly) confused, so that they feel anxious, guilty and inferior.

This is also true when children begin to discover and explore their own bodies. If we slap their fingers when they play with their genitals, but coo and smile and comment on how cute they are when they play with their toes, they will be confused and may associate their genitals with feelings of guilt and shame.

No one expects a baby who is barely old enough to walk, talk or know where the bathroom is to be anything but innocent and carefree. When children are old enough to go to the bathroom on their own, we can teach them not to touch their sex organs in public just as we can teach them not to suck their thumbs.

Nudity in the home is a natural introduction to sexual differences and sexuality. Children will let their parents know when modesty dictates privacy (by closing the door, asking to bathe alone, etc.). By the same token, adults have a right to their own privacy, and most children can accept that their parents want to be alone sometimes.

Giving the correct names for parts and functions of the body early is important too. It is just as easy to teach a small child *penis* as it is *ding-a-ling;* or *bowel movement* or *b.m.* instead of *poo-poo* or *vagina* instead of *privates*. When we talk with children, we should be receptive to their language, although we should supply proper terms. The time to discuss sex is whenever the topic comes up—when a child asks a question (not later) or when it comes up in a discussion. Don't postpone sex talks for one all-inclusive session.

Mothers often worry whether they can talk with their sons; fathers wonder if they can talk with their daughters. Parents—single parents included—should understand that it is not prescribed that the male talk to the male and the female, the female. If both parents are unable to share the responsibility, then the parent who is most comfortable with his or her sexuality should speak with the children. Similarly, professionals must free themselves to counsel clients of either sex.

But what about the child who hasn't asked, or the teenager who may need help now? It is difficult to be frank with them if we have never talked with them before about sex. But even if we are uncomfortable, we should not withhold the opportunity to communicate. It may be easier to hand them a book, but we must remember that communicating with them is as equally important as the printed information. If we are embarrassed, perhaps we can start by acknowledging our discomfort. Something to this effect may be helpful to us: *It's not easy for me to talk about sex, but there's no reason to be ashamed of sexual feelings or thoughts—everybody has them. I may have been brought up with different ideas about sex, but it would still be good if we could both discuss it.*

COUNSELING ABOUT SEXUAL BEHAVIOR

Some disabled young people isolate themselves, perhaps because they feel incapable of any "normal" relationships, or they believe no one could really care for them. It may be necessary to gently urge these youngsters to become involved in events and to seek companions. Anything that makes them feel better about themselves and more comfortable with other people will help. Sleep-away or day camps, creative activities with others (arts and crafts), volunteer companions (community agencies, colleges and universities are especially helpful), anything that can promote a sense of *achievement* and togetherness is advisable. This might include, initially, arranging group dates on occasions, and talking over their apprehensions so they understand that their feelings are experienced by nearly everyone at first. Getting out, even if it is gently forced, can be a good way to develop socialization skills. It might be well to convey to the disabled person that some people *choose* not to marry or have children because it is not right for them—but this does not prevent them from making friends and leading socially active lives.

Some youngsters whether disabled or not will experiment with sex despite society's prohibitions. The question then becomes whether to risk pregnancy, forbid the child to socialize anymore (or allow only closely supervised activities), start the daughter on birth control (pill, intrauterine device, or injection), or prepare the son for use of the condom. In this case, the child's maturity and ability to understand must be considered; there may be a danger of pregnancy even if there are no dates or formal get-togethers. If one is legitimately worried that the child will "get into trouble" and is sure that he or she is not likely to change from this position, then birth control or sterilization may make relationships less threatening. Certainly it is impossible to supervise someone every minute and trying to restrict the child's actions entirely will deprive him or her of much needed physical and mental stimulation.

MENTAL RETARDATION

Some people are so seriously retarded that they cannot be expected to manage sexual experiences without being sexually exploited. In these instances, the advice of a professional is desirable. If it is generally agreed upon, sterilization may be a fair solution for these children's safety and well-being. Some humanists and religious leaders may raise moral objections to the procedure, but it must be understood that some retarded youngsters are incapable of saying *No*. No one has a right to bring a child into this world for a life of abuse, neglect, and exploitation.

Many retarded persons are capable of, and interested in, sexual intercourse but do not know how. They may be comfortably taught with the use of photographs and discussions describing the positions and techniques involved. There should be no moral objection to this, as explicit marriage manuals have existed for ages, and are numerous today. The healthy expression of sexuality and building a relationship of affection and tenderness may be the greatest comfort and learning experience in the life of a retarded person. Those who scoff that the retarded are not capable of meaningful relationships and responsibilities do not know of what they speak.

With patience and repetition retarded persons will learn what they need to know. Some parents, for instance, complain that their retarded youngsters insist on exposing themselves or masturbating in public. This can embarrass the parents socially and cause other children to taunt the offender. Yet, any children who use the toilet by themselves can be taught to masturbate only in private.

As mentioned earlier, one of the great fears surrounding the sexuality of the retarded relates to their vulnerability. Since some are gullible and may do whatever is asked of them, they can be easily exploited. It is not uncommon that the retarded, who do not know any better, are used sexually by other children and adults. The retarded who have early or irresponsible sexual experiences are those who know the least about sexual values and behavior, conception, contraception and venereal disease. We can help prevent these incidents by helping these youngsters to understand what to expect. This is very closely related to explaining what forms of physical expression are appropriate; stress that sex with a stranger, acquaintance or friend should not be agreed to, even if the person is "very nice."

Although retarded children are much more frequently victims, they may display similar aggressive sexual behavior. Retarded children may initiate sex or feel the bodies of other boys or girls. This is not uncommon in classes or in public groups. Retarded persons do not often understand the seriousness of this behavior or its impact on others. Parents or teachers should gently but firmly explain that their actions are inappropriate and they must not touch people who do not want to be touched. Some form of punishment may be indicated if they cannot understand that this behavior may get them into trouble. The problem may be that they have no other outlet for sexual energies and no interests or exercises to occupy their time, they may not have proper social skills or may have a low opinion of themselves and see this as an opportunity to be recognized. Whatever the reason, understanding and patient teachers and parents may help toward the necessary behavioral changes.

Parents of the retarded sometimes feel it is appropriate to play it safe and structure their child's activities only with members of the same sex. They do this in fear of heterosexual contact and pregnancy (some retarded make no connection between sex and pregnancy). Then these same parents are surprised and anxious when they discover homosexual experiences going on. It has been proven in prisons and institutions that people who do not have access to their preferred sex partners tend to adapt themselves to whomever is available. Hence, organizing a male's life only with other boys or a female's only with other girls (especially in adolescence) may be encouraging homosexuality. At certain points in their lives people prefer the companionship of members of their own sex; but when different interests develop and no opposite sex relationships can be formed, the homosexuality may continue.

DATING

Most adolescents develop an interest in dating—funny, but it is usually either too early or too late for the parents' tastes. Through interactions with other teenagers in class and activities, a disabled person is very likely to want to date as other teenagers do.

Young people usually have far more experience in relating to members of their own sex, and, at first, may feel threatened and nervous with members of the opposite sex. The physically impaired, in particular, often worry that their braces, artificial limbs, wheelchairs, awkward body movements or speech may cause them to seem unattractive, and lead to rejection. Double dates and group activities are easier in the beginning and provide the opportunity to learn how to relate better with girls or boys. Whether they are school friends, workshop or job acquaintances, neighbors or whatever, these warm-up experiences can help reduce between-the-sex tensions. Being with other people requires a certain degree of self-confidence for anyone.

There are certain things all people can and should do to keep in shape and looking nice. Grooming, manners, proper clothing, can all help. Beyond these, there is a psychology of *feeling* attractive. We must help disabled individuals to realize that some people will find them ugly, others won't care, and still others will think they are beautiful no matter what. When we love and care for someone, physical appearance is not nearly as important as inner depth and a unique self.

Most disabled teenagers are not emotionally prepared for the intimacy and involvement of sexual relations. Since they may already be concerned about their mental or physical state, they may be more susceptible to emotional upset and the resulting insecurity and anxiety stemming from unsatisfactory or guilt-ridden sexual thoughts and experiences.

ADULT SEXUALITY

Adult partners, one or both of whom may be disabled, need to be very sensitive to each other's needs and desires, and to be understanding if special procedures must be followed: adjusting a catheter, removal of braces or artificial limbs, different positions for comfort. They may have to be more imaginative in their sexual affairs than the average person.

Our society and media have placed tremendous emphasis on the man-woman relationship, with sexual intercourse as the fullest expression of their sexuality. The implication is also that if people are not enjoying frequent, intense orgasms, they are hung-up and unfulfilled. It is time to correct these generalizations and mistaken impressions. The only rules for one's sexual expression are that it should be voluntary, enjoyable and non-exploitative. Beyond this, individuals should be comfortable with whatever satisfies them.

If people who have disabilities are satisfied with sex once a month, they should not be bothered by statistics that state the average couple has sex 2.3 times each week. If intercourse is difficult or impossible, but other forms of physical closeness are enjoyable, this is all right too. No positions or techniques are any better than others if an individual does not think so, nor must sex last for a certain amount of time, nor is an orgasm necessary every time (or any time).

There are a very few disabled people who are incapable of virtually any sexual expression. Many feel sexual in their minds, but do not know how to translate the feeling into behavior. A word of caution: some impaired individuals are indeed able to enjoy sex in some form, but have convinced themselves that they can't. This is when professionals, doctors or trusted friends, ministers or parents can be most helpful. Things are not likely to get better if impaired individuals keep their needs bottled up inside because they feel unable to communicate with any of us.

MARRIAGE...

As youths mature, they (and their parents) may begin to seriously consider the possibility of marriage. Contrary to several beliefs, many disabled people marry and adjust very well to their situations. Others, just like any group of people, never wish to marry. Of course, some want to marry but are afraid they cannot. If disabled persons think they will never marry because of the nature of their limitations, they may gain hope if encouraged to see the film *Like Other People,* about two individuals with cerebral palsy who fall in love and marry. The film has some beautiful scenes which illustrate that an inability to find a mate is not always related to an impairment but rather more to problems of personality and self-image.*

Some young people feel sorry for themselves and decide in advance that nobody will ever love or marry them. This becomes a self-fulfilling prophecy: nobody will love us unless we let them and unless we love ourselves. In any case, personal preferences are important. Not everyone need be married. More and more people are proving that the single life is a valid one.

Some parents insist, as an absolute prerequisite, that their offspring be capable of financial independence before undertaking marriage. This is an important consideration. These parents may rightfully not wish to support the marriage for years. If at least one partner is employable, this may not be a problem. Yet,

---

*Available for rental through Perennial Films, 477 Roger Williams, P.O. Box 855 Ravinia, Highland Park, IL 60035.

if neither can work, and if their families had planned on supporting their children anyway, sharing the expenses of providing for a couple, instead of two individuals, can be a wise decision and even save money. Marriage gives many disabled individuals a great feeling of independence as long as some agreeable arrangements can be worked out.

The success of a marriage certainly depends on more than adequate finances. It is imperative that each person feel emotionally mature enough to deal with the other person's problems and the problems they share. This usually involves responsibility and work: cleaning, dishes, repairs, shopping, laundry, cooking, etc. When people live with each other, the sharing of these "little" things can become the focus of major disagreements. They must be helped to understand that much of married life is similar to unmarried life: unexciting routine.

Parents should support the marriage of their exceptional children for the right reasons. They may want to get their disabled child out of the house, they may be tired of caring for him or her, or they may want their family to appear "normal." But if these are the only reasons for encouraging their marriage, they may be advocating a relationship and future life that can be disastrous for the child. Marriage for the disabled can help prevent great loneliness. It may allow for the development of shared interests at compatible levels and for fulfilling sexual expression. In-laws and new relatives often introduce increased social interaction and learning situations. But a marriage can also create more extreme problems.

...AND CHILDREN

For some, no reasons other than personal preferences exist in deciding whether or not to have children. It is a simple matter of the couple communicating their desires. For others, however, there are external considerations.

Children for the disabled sometimes becomes an emotionally charged subject. They may want a child, but doctors and parents may insist that their child would probably not be cared for adequately or that the baby may be born disabled. No one can be sure of this until the opinion of a genetic counselor is obtained.

People often marry with romantic ideas about parenthood. They imagine the joys of cuddling and feeding their infants, giving them their love and raising healthy and intelligent children to adulthood. These are creative, worthwhile goals, but they are not so easily realized. Children are also a lot of work, a great expense, and emotionally demanding. What is important is how individuals relate with children, and if they are able to provide adequate care for a child. This can be easily observed if they are asked, for example, to do several weeks of volunteer work at a nursery or day care center before making a decision.

It has been shown that marriage for the disabled is often more successful without children. The additional burden of children often proves too much of a strain. Children of some retarded parents, born normal, may become retarded as they grow and develop, due to insufficient care and stimulation. It is difficult for a retarded girl or boy to understand the implications of what it means to have and care for their baby. They are often more concerned with their present pleasures and satisfactions, and have a difficult time determining future problems.

In some cases voluntary sterilization (vasectomy for the male or tubal ligation for the female) can be a viable, even desirable alternative for severely disabled couples who are *certain* they want no children. This decision should be considered permanent, as there is no guarantee it will be reversible. On the other hand, if children are desired at some future time and conventional contraceptive methods are difficult or unwieldy, then a contraceptive injection called *Depo-Provera* may be another alternative. The injection renders a woman infertile for 90 days with no further precautions.

An unplanned, unwanted pregnancy can entail exceptional problems for the disabled. They may simply not be capable of enduring the rigors of pregnancy or caring for the child. Abortion in these cases may be an alternative. This decision should be carefully considered in the context of personal, moral, and religious beliefs. Important to consider in this decision is the question of who will care for the child once born.

SOME GENERAL PRACTICAL SUGGESTIONS

How does one who has been an insignificant source of sex education for disabled persons become a significant source? Answer: Come across as being "askable." Once you reveal that you are open to discussion, the questions will be asked.

Here are a few practical suggestions:

★ Leave booklets on sex, birth control, venereal disease, etc., around, giving the message that you are interested.

★ Never ask, *Do you have any questions about sex?* The reflexive response is *No.*

★ If questioned, don't use meaningless jargon. It is confusing and the kids are not interested. Sex talk should be straightforward.

★ Don't assume you are making yourself clear in your explanations. It is very important to listen to the individual's responses. They will tell you if you are communicating.

Undoubtedly, you can think of many ways to make yourself available and askable.

SOME GENERAL COMMENTS

1. People with special needs, as all people, should have free access to information on sexuality.
2. Masturbation is normal. It is an expression of sexuality no matter how frequently it is done or at what age. It becomes a compulsive, punitive, self-destructive behavior largely as a result of guilt, suppression, and punishment.
3. All direct sexual behavior should be in private. (Recognizing that institutions and hospitals for the retarded, mentally ill and delinquent are not built or developed to ensure privacy, the definition of what constitutes privacy in an institution must be very liberal; bathrooms, one's own bed, the bushes, basements are private domains. This is also true in the individual's own home.)
4. Anytime a physically mature girl and a boy have sexual relations, they risk pregnancy.
5. Unless they are clear about wanting to have a baby and the responsibility that goes with child-rearing, both the male and female should use some form of birth control. (Individuals of any age must not be led to believe that everyone wants and must have babies in order to be "normal.") Birth control services and genetic counseling should be available to all who need and desire it.
6. Until individuals reach a certain age—perhaps 18—society feels they should not have intercourse. After this they decide for themselves.
7. Adults should not be permitted to use children sexually.
8. In the final analysis, sexual behavior between consenting adults (regardless of mental age) and whether it is homo- or hetero-, should be no one else's business, providing

there is little risk of bringing an unwanted child into the world.

The following additional factors need to be considered:

1. We need greater acceptance of abortion as a safe, legal alternative to bringing an unwanted or severely disabled child into this world.
2. Voluntary sterilization can be a desirable protection for some individuals who can function perfectly well in a marriage if there are no children.

In essence, what is needed for people who deal with exceptional individuals is for them to begin to show some honesty, courage, and integrity in facing squarely the issues of human sexuality for—accept it or not—the disabled are also sexual.

Note: This chapter is based on work by the author extensively elaborated and documented in the following publications: *The Sexual Adolescent* (1979 revision), Duxbury Press, North Scituate, Massachusetts; *Love, Sex and Birth Control for the Mentally Retarded—A Guide for Parents* (1979 revision) with Winifred Kempton and Medora Bass, Planned Parenthood, 810 Seventh Avenue, New York, New York; *Sexual Rights for the People...Who Happen to Be Handicapped,* Center on Human Policy, 216 Ostrom Avenue, Syracuse, New York; and *Facts About Sex for Today's Youth* (1983), Ed-U Press, Fayetteville, New York. All of Sol Gordon's publications are available from Ed-U Press, P.O. Box 583, Fayetteville, New York 13066.

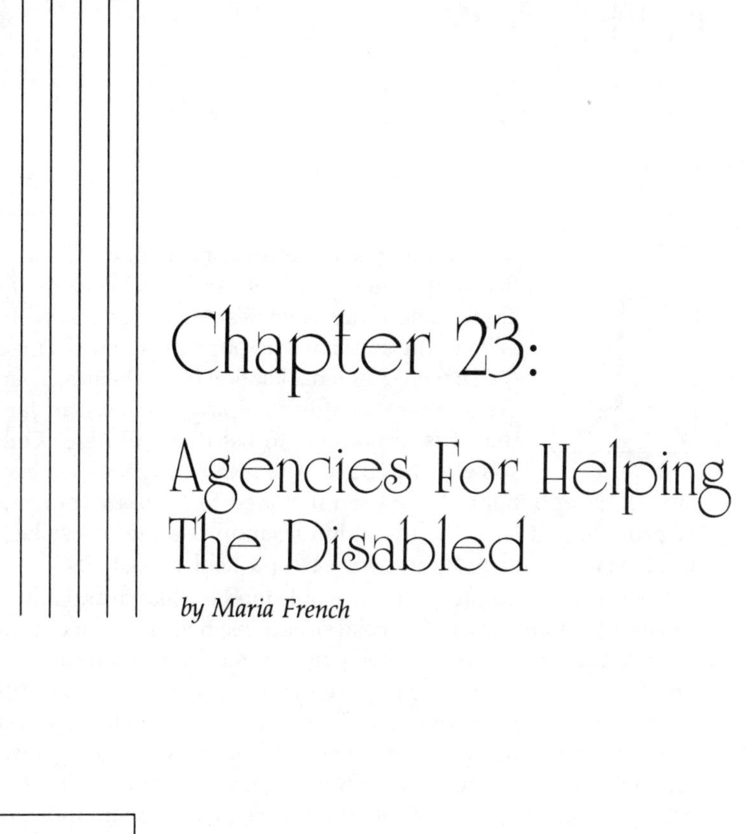

Chapter 23:

Agencies For Helping The Disabled

by Maria French

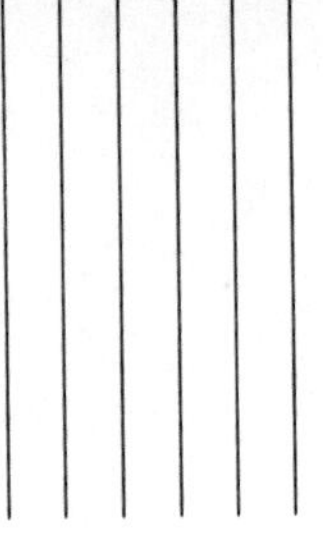

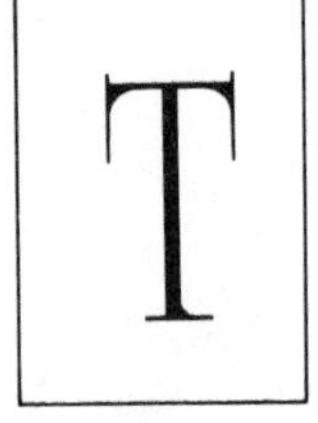

hough it may sometimes appear so, disabled individuals, their families, and teachers are not alone. There are agencies, public and private, all over the country who hope to help them meet the challenge of rehabilitation of disabilities. There are so many of these helping agencies, in fact, that it is impossible to list them all here. Only some of the larger, better-known agencies in each area of exceptionality have been included to serve the purpose of providing at least the initial information relating to available local services and programs for each particular disability.

The services and programs available tend to change and adjust constantly, according to financial situations, needs and/or criteria of each agency. Therefore, each agency may vary its functions, procedures, and eligibility requirements from regional to county to state to federal programs. This makes it difficult to detail specific service information. Hence a brief description follows for the four major agencies offering general services: The Department of Vocational Rehabilitation, The Department of Social Services (Office of Health and Human Services), The Social Security Office, and the Regional Centers funded through the Department of Developmental Services.

The main concern of the State Department of Rehabilitation is to aid the disabled individual to become a self-supporting, independently functioning and productive member of society. Its first function is to determine whether the individual's impairment is of sufficient magnitude to warrant eligibility to the program. This is determined by a battery of tests—physical, mental, and occupational—as well as a series of counseling interviews. If the disabled meet certain specific eligibility requirements, the second function becomes that of helping them to determine future feasible and practical goals. When these goals are agreed upon the rehabilitation process is begun. This may include extensive occupational training, personal and occupational counseling, schooling, medical treatment, provision for appliances (ramps, electric wheelchairs, hand controls, crutches), and anything necessary to aid the individual to achieve the determined goals.

If the individual is not eligible and/or feasible for a Vocational Rehabilitation Program, there may be the alternative of regional center services and/or programs. The regional centers service those individuals with cerebral palsy, mental retardation, epilepsy, autism, developmental disabilities, or any other similar incapacitating neurological impairment. To be eligible for services, the impairment needs to be of such a degree that it interferes with attendance at regular schools, participation in vocational training and/or job or living situations. On the basis of assessment, physical examination, and diagnostic evaluation, an individual program plan is developed for each client and case management. Purchased or otherwise provided services may include room and board, daytime programs, emergency services, services necessary for maintaining clients in their own homes, developmental training essential for preventing deterioration or maintaining progress, and basic health care.

The regional center and the Department of Vocational Rehabilitation often combine services in order to provide a more complete program for the disabled client. Services provided may vary from client to client and from state to state. The regional center can begin to provide services from the time of birth, while the Department of Vocational Rehabilitation begins to provide them when the individual is ready to explore vocational alternatives and/or higher education. The State Department of Rehabilitation is under the United States Department of Education. The central offices where one can write for information regarding the latter described services, as well as those under Social Security, are:

United States Department of Education
400 Maryland Avenue, S.W.
Washington, D.C. 20201

Bureau of Rehabilitation
666 11th Street, N.W.
Washington, D.C. 20200

United States Department of Health
and Human Services
300 Independence Avenue, N.W.
Washington, D.C. 20200

Social Security Administration
3244 Pennsylvania Avenue, S.E.
Washington, D.C. 20200

Social Security makes it possible for the disabled to have some kind of income and medical benefits if they are not able to obtain or maintain employment. The Social Security Income Program

(SSI) allocates money for food, living expenses and needed house modification. In-Home Supportive Services (homemaker-chore) are provided under Department of Social Services, as part of Social Security. The medical benefits come through Medicare or other state medical programs. To be eligible, one has to establish financial need, as well as being able to show that the unique physical disability is a deterrent to having any type of regular income. With this aid, county and/or university hospitals can be approached with regard to specialized needs or services dealing with any specific disability.

The person with a disability who is turned down by any of the programs outlined thus far, i.e., Department of Rehabilitation, Regional Center, SSI, In-Home Supportive Services, etc., has the right to appeal. Each departmental program or service has its own process or client advocate type person to aid and inform as to the right, steps, and procedures involved.

All states have several colleges, universities, hospitals and school districts. These can be excellent sources for more local help. Most of these institutions have specialized clinics or teaching programs for the study of exceptional children and adults. These clinics are usually well prepared to offer direct help or to serve as knowledgeable referral agencies. They are an inexpensive and well-prepared recourse.

Some cities like Los Angeles and San Francisco have Centers for Independent Living or similar services that provide information and needed support for community integration and functional participation. The following list of National Agencies has been organized according to the disability they serve. The agencies listed under *Orthopaedic Limitations* and *Agencies Offering Specific Services* offer general aid and information to any individual regardless of impairment.

NATIONAL AGENCIES

Arthritis: *The Arthritis Foundation,* 115 E. 18th St., New York, New York 10003.

Asthma (Respiratory disorders): *CARIH* (National Jewish Hospital), 3800 E. Colfax, Denver, Colorado 80206; *Tuberculosis and Respiratory Disease Association,* 1670 Beverly Boulevard, Los Angeles, California 90026.

Autism: *National Society for Children and Adults with Autism,* 1234 Massachusetts Ave., N.W., Suite 1017, Washington, D.C. 20005-4599.

Behavioral Disorders: *Children's Behavioral Services,* 6171 W. Charleston, Las Vegas, Nevada 89158.

Cerebral Palsy: *California Association of Neurologically Handicapped Children,* P.O. Box 604, Main Post Office, Los Angeles, California 90053; *United Cerebral Palsy Association, Inc.,* 66 East 34th Street, New York, New York 10016.

Communication Disorders: *The Council for Exceptional Children,* Division for Children with Communication Disorders, 1920 Association Drive, Reston, Virginia 22091; *American Speech, Language, and Hearing Association,* 10801 Rockville Pike, Rockville, Maryland 20852.

Deaf: *Alexander Graham Bell Association for the Deaf,* 3417 Volta Place, N.W., Washington, D.C. 20007; *National Association for the Deaf,* 814 Thayer Ave., Silver Springs, Maryland 20910; *Helen Keller National Center for Deaf and Blind Youths and Adults,* 111 Middleneck Rd., Sands Point, New York 11050; *John Tracy Clinic for the Deaf,* 806 W. Adams Blvd., Los Angeles, California 90007.

Diabetes: *American Diabetes Association,* 2 Park Ave., New York, New York 10016.

Epilepsy: *Epilepsy Foundation of America,* 4351 Garden City Drive, Suite 406, Landover, Maryland 20785.

Gifted: *The American Association for Gifted Children,* 15 Gramercy Park, New York, New York 10003; *The Council for Exceptional Children (CEC),* 1920 Association Drive, Reston, Virginia 22091.

Heart: *American Heart Association,* 1615 Stemmons, Dallas, Texas 75207.

Learning Disabilities: *Association for Children with Learning Disabilities,* 4156 Library Rd., Pittsburgh, Pennsylvania 15234.

Leukemia: *Leukemia Society of America, Inc.,* National Headquarters, 800 Second Ave., New York, New York 10017.

Mental Illness: *Health Services and Mental Health Administration,* Maternal and Child Health Services, Suite 739, Parklawn Building, 5600 Fishers Lane, Rockville, Maryland 20852; *National Institute of Mental Health,* 5600 Fishers Lane, Suite 15C17, Rockville, Maryland 20857.

Mental Limitations: *American Association on Mental Deficiency,* 5101 Wisconsin Ave., N.W., Suite 405, Washington, D.C. 20016; *National Association for Retarded Citizens,* 2501 Ave. J, Arlington, Texas 76011; *National Association of State Mental Retardation Program Directors,* 113 Oronoco St., Alexandria, Virginia 22314.

Multiple Sclerosis: *National Multiple Sclerosis Society,* 205 E. 42nd St., 3rd Floor, New York, New York 10017.

Muscular Dystrophy: *Muscular Dystrophy Association of America, Inc.,* 810 Seventh Avenue, New York, New York 10019.

Myasthenia Gravis: *Myasthenia Gravis Foundation, Inc.,* 225 Park Avenue South, New York, New York 10003.

Orthopaedic Limitations: *International Center for the Disabled,* Rehabilitation and Research Center, 340 East 24th Street, New York, New York 10010; *The National Easter Seal Society for Crippled Children and Adults,* 2023 W. Ogden Avenue, Chicago, Illinois 60612; *United Way of America,* United Way Plaza, Alexandria, Virginia 22314; *U.S. Department of Health, Education, and Welfare,* Bureau of Education for the Handicapped, Washington, D.C.

Ostomy: *United Ostomy Association, Inc.,* International Office, 2001 W. Beverly Boulevard, Los Angeles, California 90057.

Paraplegia: *National Spinal Cord Injury Association,* 369 Elliot Street, Newton Upper Falls, Massachusetts 02164.

Parkinson's: *The Parkinson's Disease Foundation,* William Black Medical Research Building, 640 West 168th Street, New York, New York 10032.

Polio: *The British Polio Fellowship,* Bell Close, West End Road, Ruislip, Middlesex, HA 4 6LP, England.

Visual Disorders: *American Association of Workers for the Blind, Inc.,* 206 W. Washington Street, Suite 320, Alexandria, Virginia 22314; *American Foundation for the Blind,* 15 West 16th Street, New York, New York 10011; *American Printing House for the Blind,* P.O. Box 6085, Louisville, Kentucky 40206; *National Association for the Visually Handicapped* (for partially sighted), 305 East 24th Street, New York, New York 10010; *Association for Education of the Visually Handicapped,* 206 North Washington Street, Alexandria, Virginia, 22314; and 1604 Spruce Street, Philadelphia, Pennsylvania 19103; *Blind Veterans Association,* 1735 De Sales Street, N.W., Washington, D.C. 20036; *The Library of Congress,* Division for the Blind and Physically Handicapped, 1291 Taylor, N.W., Washington, D.C. 20542; *Recording for the Blind, Inc.* (RFB), 215 East 58th Street, New York, New York 10022.

AGENCIES OFFERING SPECIFIC SERVICES AND GENERAL INFORMATION

For products and equipment aids as well as computerized information: *The ABLEDATA System,* National Rehabilitation Information Center, 4407 Eighth Street, N.E., The Catholic University of America, Washington, D.C. 20017.

National: *American Public Health Association,* 1015 Fifteenth Street, N.W., Washington, D.C. 20036; *American Alliance for Health, Physical Education, Recreation and Dance,* 1900 Association Drive, Reston, Virginia 22091; *Center for the Study of Evaluation,* Dissemination Office, 145 Moore Hall, UCLA School of Education (Graduate), University of California, Los Angeles, California 90024; *Closer Look* (information), Box 1492, Washington, D.C. 20013; *Demonstration and Research Center for Early Education,* Information Office, George Peabody College, Box 151, Nashville, Tennessee 37205; *Education Commission of the States* (services and information), Handicapped Children's Education Project, 300 Lincoln Tower, 1860 Lincoln Street, Denver, Colorado 80295; *Rehabilitation International,* 432 Park Avenue South, New York, New York 10016; *Social Security Administration,* Bureau of Disability Insurance, 6401 Security Boulevard, Baltimore, Maryland 21235.

State: *Federal Information Clearinghouse for Exceptional Children,* 1920 Association Drive, Reston, Virginia 22091 (to request information about government involvement in areas desired); *The President's Committee on Employment of the Handicapped,* 1111 20th Street, N.W. Rm #636, Washington, D.C. 20036.

My thanks to the California State Department of Rehabilitation, SEIMC-University of Southern California, and everyone who provided information and addresses.

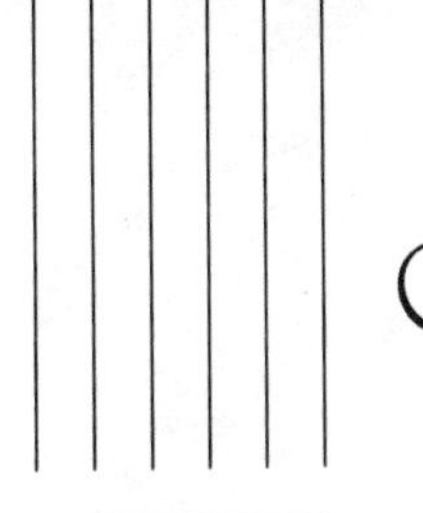

Section VI:

The Challenge For Tomorrow

Chapter 24: Tomorrow's Challenge

(With Betty Lou Kratoville)

Existence is beyond the power of words to define:
Terms may be used
But are none of them absolute.
In the beginning of heaven and earth there were no words,
Words came out of the womb of matter;
And whether a man dispassionately
Sees to the core of life
Or passionately
Sees the surface,
The core and the surface
Are essentially the same,
Words making them seem different
Only to express appearance.
If name be needed, wonder names them both:
From wonder into wonder
Existence opens.

LAO TZU
The Way of Life

s we stand back and survey tomorrow's challenge for the disabled, we are often utterly daunted by the magnitude of the task at hand. Disabled children are everywhere — neglected, hungry, dirty, ill, abused, and prejudiced against. Although good people of great heart attempt to ease the plight of these youngsters, their well-intentioned efforts touch the lives of only a comparative few. Our country, it is true, has played a considerable part in compassionate, international endeavors, sharing its wealth of materials, money, research, and human resources. Yet we cannot rest on laurels which are clearly insignificant compared to the all-encompassing need. As humanitarians, we are responsible for all people and we must not tolerate the loss of even the smallest fragment of human potential.

PRIORITY: AWARENESS

Strong, effective movements such as "The International Year of the Disabled" sponsored by the World Health Organization, the removal of many architectural barriers in our environment, federal, state and local programs of education and rehabilitation reveal an emerging awareness of the needs of the disabled.

Strong support has come from a number of professional groups such as the Council for Exceptional Children, the American Speech and Hearing Association, the Alexander Graham Bell Association for the Deaf, the Epilepsy Foundation of America, and others. We can applaud the dedication of organizations founded by parents — the Association for Children and Adults with Learning Disabilities, the National Association for Retarded Citizens, the Feingold Association, and their counterparts. If for no other reason, these groups can be commended for the consciousness raising they have accomplished. In addition, they have fought and lobbied for legislative changes — changes that have greatly altered and improved the quality of life for the disabled.

Recently, a number of professional and parent associations pooled their resources by forming coalitions to block the federal government in its attempt to rescind some important programs earlier designed and implemented for the disabled. It is no small challenge to take on the federal government — but take it on they did — and they won!

In a sense, the untoward direction that the U.S. Department of Education was endeavoring to take, while initially threatening and demoralizing, became a significant unifying force. For the first time these groups, as they worked together to defeat a common foe, grew in awareness of one another and of the populations they were committed to serve. Advocates of the blind worked side by side with advocates of the mentally retarded and the learning disabled and others. Single special interest groups became a force of cohesive special interests; signifying the strength that comes in united rather than fragmented purpose and direction.

Most exciting of all, in recent years, the disabled themselves have found their own voice, have become aware of their own strengths. No longer willing to sit quietly by as objects of pity and a few token charitable crumbs, they have joined forces to insist on their rights as individuals and citizens of worth and dignity. Their efforts have been stimulating to witness. But they constantly need to continue to strengthen their ranks with allies. Counselors everywhere are charged to join this clarion cry and to benefit from the insight they will gain through close association and shared endeavors.

PRIORITY: RESEARCH

While awareness of the needs of the disabled is indeed abroad in the land, let us hastily add that it is too little, and not yet truly focused. We still tend to think more of remediation than of prevention. Although a limited amount of research is underway, funding for this research can only be labeled as inadequate if not downright pathetic. We cannot look to the future with high hopes if we continue to deal with results rather than causes. This can be likened to putting a bucket under a leaky faucet to collect the water. Emptying the bucket periodically may keep the water from spilling over, but it will not be dealing with what is essential — the cause of the leaky faucet! Through research, some "leaky faucets" have been permanently repaired — polio, retrolental fibroplasia, phenylketonuria — and others have been at least partially stunted — epilepsy, diabetes, cerebral palsy. The miracle of medicine has brought us organ transplants. The marvels of technology have provided prosthetic devices that have freed many disabled persons from total or partial confinement. An explosion of knowledge in prenatal care and prevention of birth defects has done much to diminish the pain of mental retardation, deafness, and other potentially debilitating disorders. This life-saving research must continue and it will only continue if we help everyone to understand its value and impact through long-range awareness. Perhaps more than simple awareness is needed; outrage, clear and well-directed, may be the key. But medical research alone cannot provide all of the answers. So much needs to be studied, pondered and better understood: self-concept as it relates to the disabled, the role of social and cultural barriers and values, the spread effect of disability, the dynamics of acceptance and change, the phenomenon of "mourning," the relationship of specific motivational forces, learning theory, and much more. These are topics of high priority sitting in wait for the eager researcher. The continued lack of information on these critical areas of concern, results in counseling work with disabled individuals being based often on observation, feelings, and guesswork. Not a very intellectual nor sound approach to behavior. Research is expensive.

Perhaps austerity has its place in certain private and public endeavors, but never — *never* — can it be extolled as a virtue when the prevention of life disabling conditions lies within our grasp.

PRIORITY: SPECIAL EDUCATION

It was once said by an outstanding pioneer in the field of special education that the goal of persons working with disabled children should be "to work themselves out of a job." A superb goal — yet special educators need not be threatened by it, for that day is not close at hand. They do, however, need to feel challenged by the fact that special education has never been, nor is it now, as "special" as it was once envisioned.

This lamentable fact will persist as long as school boards and administrators are more concerned with constructing buildings and adjusting budgets than educating all children, as long as educators continue to hide behind methods, materials, meetings and paperwork rather than looking at individual children, as long as counselors are more involved in labeling evaluation techniques than in the human person, as long as funds unwisely allocated or hoarded govern the quality and quantity of services for the disabled.

Federal legislation now mandates that children be placed in the "least restrictive educational setting." At the time of its passage, this legislation was hailed as the answer to much past injustice. It meant that many of the disabled would now be mainstreamed — with all of the benefits that mingling with non-disabled peers implies. It is good legislation. Indeed, it can be called legislation with a heart. Yet the effectiveness of the mandate has been challenged by professionals and parents alike. And with good reason, for it will continue to be less than fully effective until mainstream teachers truly welcome disabled children into their classrooms. They will have to embrace the opportunity to enrich the lives of these youngsters, and view this as a means of enriching their own lives and the lives of the "normal" children in the "regular" classroom. Physical integration has little or no value unless accompanied by psychological acceptance. No one is better trained or suited for this responsibility. These children are not disabled for only the few hours each day they spend in the regular classroom. They are disabled twenty-four hours a day, and their education must be reality oriented to reflect this truth. Equally important, these are not only disabled individuals, these are individuals with a disability who are people first and have a need to be valued and enjoyed like all individuals. Herein, we as counselors can play a critical role.

Finally, the self-defeating idea that special education is too costly continues to permeate the field of education. How can this be? We have only to balance the cost of educating single disabled individuals, of readying them for employment, of allowing them to become tax-paying citizens against the cost of supporting them for the rest of their lives, in or out of an institution, to realize how fallacious is this premise. Disabled children, housed for a lifetime in an institution, will cost more than one hundred and fifty thousand dollars. It would take less than half that amount to educate and counsel them in their own home and community. And the investment would be returned and multiplied as they grew into well-adjusted, self-supporting, contributing adults. Added to this must be the priceless consideration of human potential, dignity and happiness, all of which are squandered and lost when we are not permitted that precious inalienable right: to make our own contribution to our own success in our own way.

Special educators should never have to beg, should never have to justify the extra expense of their programs. How can we place a monetary value on a human being?

PRIORITY: WHY LABELS?

It is often the labels we place on the impaired that create their problem! How many retarded children have been limited by our labels and I.Q. scores? How many emotionally disturbed children have we created by using "acceptable school conduct" as the measuring stick for normal behavior? How many problems of all sorts do we create by calling individuals names? "Johnny is lazy." "Johnny is a daydreamer." "Johnny is uncooperative." Add to this the findings of a test battery! Johnny may be a perfectly great little kid. He may draw a beautiful tree or sing like a lark, but suddenly he is lost in a miasma of negative, judgmental labels.

Labels, used to simplify and facilitate communication, can just as easily destroy it. Labels can convey status (gifted) or create value judgments (learning disabled) or cause a world of confusion. The word "exceptional" is a case in point. Educators know what they mean when they use it. To a noneducator, it may have two distinct definitions. It can mean both "forming an exception" and "better than average." It is not uncommon for us to say, "I work with exceptional children," whereupon the layperson, in all innocence, assumes that we work with gifted children.

Still, we are stuck with words, and until we can find a more efficient means of conveying ideas we must learn to be as precise and consistent as possible in their use. We hear someone refer to a retarded child, and we wonder whether or not we are speaking of the same kind of child. There is only one way we will ever know that we are seeing each child as more than a label. It is when we desire to communicate with another regarding that child, and we continually ask, "What else?" until we have enough facts to see the child as "Peter" or as "Jane," unique, complicated, and precious.

PRIORITY: ATTITUDES

Unenlightened, prejudicial attitudes bring daily untold suffering to the disabled and their families. The horror and embarrassment of being stared at, ridiculed, or singled out have been described over and over again. How to stop it? At our very doorstep stands our vast public education system. As mentioned before, the underlying philosophy of the current mainstreaming movement—i.e., "normal" children would learn much about their disabled peers as they shared the classroom experience — has, to a degree, worked. These children will providentially, one day be voting and taxpaying citizens with refreshingly new attitudes regarding disability. Why should not the PTAs and the in-service planners take on the formidable challenge of enlightening and educating the adults within that same school setting? Here, they could be invited to change attitudes along with their children.

In understanding lies the greatest hope for change. Ignorance produces fear. Fear works as a dynamic force toward distancing, segregation, and the perpetuation of even deeper prejudice and misinformation. Full and total acceptance of "differentness" will never be achieved until people everywhere have been convinced that it is not the disability that produces most handicaps — but their attitudes toward disability. It cannot be said too often: A healthy adjustment for the disabled is much more related to the attitudes toward them than to their disabilities. It is naive to believe that a disability is automatically followed by an onslaught of emotional problems. Emotional problems are created by ignorance, indifference, intolerance, and injustice.

To effect attitudes we must consider the following: (1) The disabled are no more like one another than are all blue-eyed people or all left-handed people. Each disabled person is unique and different. Therefore, to generalize about the disabled as a group or class is unsound and untenable. The only important consideration will be the persons, themselves, their personal adjustment, and the response they receive from others. (2) As a general rule, disabled individuals neither crave nor need oversolicitude, pity, or special considerations. They have the same needs of people everywhere. (3) The attitudes of the disabled are widely varied and closely correlated with the treatment they receive from those with whom they are interacting. Therefore, positive interactions will bring about positive change. (4) The disabled want to assume responsibility for their own lives. They recognize the necessity of competition but need assurance that normal rewards will result from their abilities and productivity. (5) The disabled want to be free and independent. It is up to us to provide them with every possible free choice and independence.

PRIORITY: SOCIAL CHANGE

It is difficult to bring about change in the lives of the disabled unless and until we are willing to consider equally compelling needs in the world's social structure. In this great, rich country of ours—and in other countries, rich and poor—literally millions of children and adults live in abject poverty, suffer from chronic hunger, and are prey to insidious diseases which render them psychologically and physically unfit. Knowledge of child growth and development, nutrition, and basic medical care does not reach into the dark corners they are forced to inhabit. They are often unaware of normal preventative hygiene, free medical clinics or social agencies to which they can apply for guidance.

Because of this, even in a so-called "enlightened" America, most of our children are not immunized against preventable diseases. One million infants are born each year to mothers who receive inadequate or no health care during pregnancy and delivery. So the ranks of the disabled grow ever larger.

We who have the sophistication are responsible for disseminating knowledge, not only to other professionals in lectures, literature, and national conferences, but directly to the masses. Our voices must be heard on city streets, germ-filled ghettos, rat- and roach-infested tenements as well as on the floor of national and state legislatures. Of course, this will mean leaving our classrooms, our paneled offices, our immaculate headquarters, and getting our hands dirty, risking rejection and discomfort. But would it not be worth it if we could prevent even one child from spending a lifetime as a disabled person?

PRIORITIES AND CHALLENGES FOR COUNSELORS

The future of the disabled will surely hold more promise than the present if professionals in the field of guidance are willing to accept the unparalleled role that they can play, beginning with identification of exceptionality through the processes of remediation and/or rehabilitation.

The process must literally begin at the hospital bedside and continue through what may be a long and complex rehabilitation maze, as it must be immediately and fully recognized that this will be an ongoing process. Counseling goals are complex for they must deal with the *intellectual* content, which will include the type and extent of the disability, its probable cause and the facilities and services available for its rehabilitation. It will also include the *emotional* content in which the attitudes and feelings of the involved individuals will be fully explored and dealt with.

In most instances, these families will already be reasonably well-integrated, functioning people. Their primary need, therefore, is for practical, basic knowledge about how to deal with the special problems they will face now that a disabled child has become an integral part of their lives. These early days are critical and much stress will be alleviated if families are gently and wisely counseled at once, if they are offered a plan of immediate action, and if they are left with at least a modicum of hope.

Among the greatest service the counselor can offer, after compassion and warmth, is that of referral agent. Parents have been frustrated almost into madness in their search for services, many of which are denied them because of professionals' feelings of autonomy. This may be easily observed in the many federal, state, and community agencies, all with similar concerns but working independently. At times, these agencies even compete against one another. The need for integrated services is a vital one. Counselors and parents should work together to initiate actions that will alter this wasteful and confusing situation.

PRIORITY: A FINAL REMARK

We will have met the counseling challenge for the future when *all* educational facilities are special; when *all* teachers are special educators seeing all students as exceptional and respecting them as such; when *all* citizens in our society are more concerned with the inner worth of all individuals than their outward appearance; when we are no longer frightened by uniqueness and differences but see these, rather, as a positive hope for growth and survival.

We will have met the challenge for the future when we cease being threatened or overwhelmed by the enormity of the challenge and when each *one* of us assumes responsibility for making tomorrow at least a bit better than today.

We will have met the challenge for the future when there is no need for books such as this one, except as an historic document of an unenlightened age.

We will have met the challenge for the future when it is no longer "we" (the "wise") counseling "them" (the "unfortunate"), when a more perfect union has been achieved, and "we" and "they" can share — in equality and harmony and joy — our efforts to elevate a difficult human condition through love and existing truth.

Acknowledgments

I have debts to be acknowledged: to Maria French, my friend, who insisted the work be completed, to Joan Winchell, my niece, who cleared away the day-to-day necessities of home and office for a summer so that the work could be possible, to Patti Stancil and Ginger Finley who spent hours deciphering and typing my work as it was written, to Rick Finley, the Holcomes and the Clausens who helped me to find the right environment for work, and to Gigi and Don Sanders who supplied the "enchanted cottage" on the mouth of the Smith River where the work was completed.

In addition, I wish to acknowledge the many disabled children and their parents, whom I have known and grown to love over the past twenty-three years, for it is they who have given me the material upon which this work is based. And, lastly, my thanks to the Slacks, Charles, Peter and Barbara, my publishers who felt it was worth the printing, and my editor, Donna Carpenter, who made it printable.

Bibliography

GENERAL BIBLIOGRAPHY

BOOKS

Assagioli, Roberto: *The Act of Will.* New York, The Viking Press, 1973.

Axline, Virginia: *Play Therapy.* New York, Ballantine Books, 1969.

Binswanger, Ludwig: *Being in the World.* New York, Basic Books, 1965.

Brown, Christy: *Down All The Days.* New York, Stein, 1970.

Brown, Christy: *My Left Foot.* New York, Simon and Schuster, 1955.

Brutten, Milton; Richardson, Sylvia; Mangel, Charles: *Something's Wrong With My Child.* New York, Harcourt Brace Jovanovich, Inc., 1973.

Buck, Pearl: *The Child Who Never Grew.* New York, John Day Co., 1950.

Burton, Robert: *Anatomy of Melancholy.* New York, Farrar and Rinehart, 1927.

Buscaglia, L.F.: *Love.* New Jersey, SLACK, Inc., 1973.

Cooper, David: *The Death of the Family.* New York, Random House, Inc., 1970.

Cruickshank, W.M. (Ed): *Psychology of Exceptional Children and Youth,* 3rd edition. New Jersey, Prentice-Hall Inc., 1971.

Farber, N.: *Mental Retardation: Its Social Context and Social Consequences.* Boston, Houghton Mifflin Co., 1968, pp. 152-176.

Frankl, Victor: *Man's Search for Meaning.* Boston, Beacon Press, 1962.

Ginott, Haim G.: *Between Parent and Teenager.* Macmillan Co., 1969.

Gordon, Sol: *Sexual Rights For The People Who Happen To Be Handicapped.* Syracuse, New York, Syracuse University, 1974.

Harring, Norris (Ed): *Behavior of Exceptional Children.* Columbus, Ohio, Charles E. Merrill Co., 1974.

Heisler, Verda (Ed): *A Handicapped Child In The Family: A Guide For Parents.* New York, Grune and Stratton, 1972.

Hewett, Frank: *The Emotionally Disturbed Child in The Classroom.* Boston, Allyn and Bacon, Inc., 1968.

Howes and Moon: *Man, The Choicemaker.* Philadelphia, Westminster Press, 1973.

Johnson, R.C. and Medennis: *Child Psychology: Behavior and Development.* New York, John Wiley and Sons, Inc., 1964.

Jourard, Sidney: *The Transparent Self* (revised edition). New York, D. Van Nostrand Co., 1971.

Jung, Carl: *The Portable Jung: (The Stages of Life).* New York, Viking Press, 1971.

Kazantzakis, Nikos: *The Saviors of God.* New York, Simon and Schuster, 1960.

Korzybski, A.: The role of language in the perceptual processes. *In* Blake, R.R.; Ramsey, G.V. (Eds): *Perception — An Approach to Personality,* New York, Ronald, 1951.

Laing, R.D.: *The Politics of Experience and The Bird of Paradise.* New York, Penguin Books, Pantheon, 1967.

Lao, Tzu: *The Way of Life* (Walter Bynner Trans.). New York, Capricorn Books, 1944.
Lee, D.D.: A linguistic approach to a system of values. *In* Newcomb, T.M.; Haatley, E.L. (Eds): *Reading in Social Psychology*, New York, Holt, 1947.
MacGregor, R., et al: *Multiple Impact Therapy With Families*. New York, McGraw Hill Co., 1964.
Maslow, Abraham: *In* May, Rollo (Ed): *Existential Psychology*. New York, Random House, Inc., 1961.
May, Rollo, et al: *Existential Psychology*. The American Orthopsychiatric Association, Inc., New York, Random House, 1961.
Michelle: *I Am Present*. San Francisco, Private Printing, 1969.
Miller, Arthur: *After The Fall*. New York, Viking Press, 1964.
Nichols, Peter: *Joe Egg*. New York, Grove Press, 1967.
Nietzsche: *The Portable Nietzsche*. New York, Viking Press, 1954.
Ornstein, Robert: *The Psychology of Perception*. San Francisco, W.H. Freeman and Co., 1972.
Otto, Herbert (Ed): *Human Potentialities: The Challenge and The Promise*. St. Louis, Green, 1968.
Otto, Herbert; Mann, John: *Ways of Growth*. New York, Viking Press, 1968.
Park, Clara C.: *The Siege*. An Atlantic Monthly Press Book, Boston — Toronto, Little Brown and Company, 1967.
Perkins, William: *Speech Pathology*. St. Louis, C.V. Mosby Co., 1971.
Peter, Laurence J.: *Prescriptive Teaching*. New York, McGraw Hill, 1965.
Pinero, Arthur: *The Enchanted Cottage*. Boston, Balken Co., 1925.
Rogers, Carl: *Clinical Treatment of the Problem Child*. Boston, Houghton Mifflin Co., 1939.
Rogers, Carl; Stevens, B.: *Person To Person: The Problem of Being Human*. New York, Pocket Books, 1973.
Roosevelt, Eleanor: *You Learn By Living*. New York, Harper & Row, 1960.
Russell, H.; Rosen, V.: *Victory In My Hands*. New York, Creative Age Press, 1949.
Saint Exupery, Antoine de: *The Little Prince*. New York, Harcourt, Brace and World, Inc., 1943.
Sartre, Jean Paul: *Being and Nothingness*. New York, Philosophical Library, 1956.
Satir, V.M.: *Conjoint Family Therapy*. Palo Alto, California, Science and Behavior Books, Inc., 1964.
Sears, R.P.; Maccaby, G.E.; Levin, H.: *Pattern of Child Rearing*. New York, Harper and Row, 1957.
Skinner, B.F.: *The Technology of Teaching*. New York, Appleton-Century-Crofts, 1968.
Sloane, H.N.; MacAulay, B.D. (Eds): *Operant Procedures in Remedial Speech and Language Training*. New York, Houghton Mifflin Co., 1968.
Solzhenitsyn, Aleksandr I.: *The Gulag Archipelago*. New York, Harper and Row, 1973.
Stone, L.J.; Church, J.: *Childhood and Adolescence: A Psychology of the Growing Person*. New York, Random House, 1973.
Strong, E.K. Jr.: *Changes of Interest With Age*. Stanford, California, Stanford University Press, 1931.
Telford, C.W.; Saurey, J.M.: *The Exceptional Individual*. New Jersey, Prentice-Hall Inc., 1967.

Van Dusen, Wilson: *In* Rogers, C.; Stevens, B. (Eds): *Person To Person.* New York, Pocket Books, 1973.

Wharf, B.L.: Science and linguistics. *In* Newcomb, T.M.; Hartley, E.L. (Eds): *Readings in Social Psychology.* New York, Holt Inc., 1947.

Whelan, J.R.: The relevance of behavior modification procedures for teachers of emotionally disturbed children. *In* P. Knobber (Ed): *Intervention Approaches In Educating Emotionally Disturbed Children.* Syracuse, New York, Syracuse University Press, 1966.

White, R.W.: *The Abnormal Personality.* New York, Ronald, 1948.

Williams, Tennessee: *The Glass Menagerie.* New York, Random House, 1945.

Wright, Beatrice A.: *Physical Disability — A Psychological Approach.* New York, Harper and Row, 1960.

PERIODICALS

Banish, R.: Explanations offered by parents and siblings of brain-damaged children. *Exceptional Child* 27:286-291, 1961.

Barker, L.S.; Schoggen, P.; Barker, R.G.:The frequency of physical disability in children: a comparison of three sources of information. *Child Development* 23:216-226.

Barker, R.G.: The social psychology of physical disability. *Journal of Social Issues* (4)225-38.

Barker, R.G.; Wright, H.F.: Midwest and Its Children: the Psychological Ecology of an American Town. Evanston, Illinois, Row and Peterson, 1955.

Behrens, M.L.: Child Rearing and the Character Structure of the Mother. *Child Development* 25:225-238, 1954.

Bell, R.Q.: A reinterpretation of the directions of effects of socialization. *Psychological Review* 75:81-95, 1968.

Bell, R.Q.: Stimulus control of parent or caretaker behavior of offspring. *Developmental Psychology.* 1971, pgs. 63-72.

Bettelheim, Bruno: *The School Review.*

Cousins, Norman: A Case For Hope. *Saturday Review of Literature,* December 26, 1970.

Cowen, E.L.; Underberg, R.D.; Verrillo, R.T.: The development and testing of an attitude to blindness scale. *Journal of Social Psychology,* 1956.

Farber, B.: Effects of a Severely Mentally Retarded Child on Family Integration. Monographs of the Society for Research in Child Development, serial no. 71, 24(2), 1959.

Fitzgerald, D.C.: Success-failure and TAT reactions of orthopedically handicapped and physically normal adolescents. *Journal of Personality* 1:67-83, 1950.

Gardner, J.M.; Watson, L.S., Jr.: Behavior modification of the mentally retarded: an annotated bibliography. *Mental Retardation Abstracts* 6:181-193, 1969.

Hebb, D.O.: On the nature of fear. *Psychological Review,* 53:259-276, 1946.

Hess, R.D.; Shipman, V.: Early blocks to children's learning. *Children* 12:189-194, 1965.

Johnson, W., et al: A study of the onset and development of stuttering. *Journal of Speech and Hearing Disorders* 7:251-257, 1942.

Mussen, P.H.; Barker, R.G.: Attitudes toward cripples. *Journal of Abnormal and Social Psychology* 39:351-355, 1944.

Ontar, G.R.: Classification of Speech Directed at Children by Mothers of Different Levels of Education and Cultural Backgrounds. Paper presented at meetings of the Eighteenth International Congress of Psychology, 1966.

Osborne, J.G.; Wageman, R.M.: Some operant conditioning techniques and their uses in schools for the deaf. *American Annals of the Deaf* 114:741-743, 1969.

Ray, M.H.: The Effect of Crippled Appearance on Personality Judgment. Master's thesis. Stanford University, Stanford, California, 1946.

Rusk, H.A.; Taylor, E.J.: Employment for the disabled. *Journal of Social Issues* (4):101-106, 1948.

Sapir, E.: Conceptual categories in primitive languages. *Science* 74:578, 1931.

Schaefer, E.S.: A home tutoring program. *Children,* March-April, pp. 59-61, 1969.

Schaffer, H.R.; Emerson, P.: Patterns of response to physical contact in early human development. *Journal of Child Psychology and Psychiatry* 5:1-13, 1965.

Shere, M.O.: An Evaluation of the Social and Emotional Development of the Cerebral Palsied Twin. Unpublished doctoral dissertation, University of Illinois, Ann Arbor: University Microfilms, publication no. 9140, 1954.

Solnit, Stark: Mourning and the birth of the defective child. *Psychological Studies of the Child* 16:523-537, 1961.

Stratton, A.J.: Patient's concepts of tuberculosis: observations and implications. *Newsletter for Psychologists in Tuberculosis,* 4:38-43.

CHAPTER BIBLIOGRAPHIES

CHAPTER 3: Counseling The Disabled and Their Parents: A Review of the Literature
James Leigh, B.S., M.S. and Susan Marshall, B.S., M.Ed.

Abramson, P.R.; Grovink, M.J.; Abramson, L.M.; and Sommers, D.: Early diagnosis and intervention of retardation: A survey of parental reactions concerning the quality of services rendered. *Mental Retardation.* 15:28-31, June 1977.

Anderson, K.A.: The "shopping" behavior of parents of mentally retarded children: The professional person's role. *Mental Retardation.* 9(4):3-5, 1971.

Anderson, K.A.; Garner, A.M.: Mothers of retarded children: Satisfaction with visits to professional people. *Mental Retardation.* 11(4):36-39, 1973.

Anthony, W.A.: The physically disabled client and facilitative confrontation. *Journal of Rehabilitation.* 36(3):22-23, 1970.

Bowe, F.; Razeghi, J.A.: Enabling the disabled through career counseling. *Vocational Education.* 54:44-47, October 1979.

Bricklin, P.M.: Counseling parents of children with learning disabilities. *The Reading Teacher.* 23(4):331-338, 1970.

Brolin, D.; Gysbers, N.: Career education for persons with handicaps. *Personnel and Guidance Journal.* 58:258-262, 1979.

Burggraf, M.Z.: Consulting with parents of handicapped children. *Elementary School Guidance and Counseling.* 13:214-221, February 1979.

Christensen, B; DeBlassie, R.R.: Counseling with parents of handicapped adolescents. *Adolescence.* 15:397-407, Summer 1980.

Connolly, C: Counseling parents of schoolage children with special needs. *Journal of School Health.* 48:115-117, February 1978.

Davidson, P.O.; Schrag, A.R.: Factors affecting the outcome of child psychiatric consultations. *American Journal of Orthopsychiatry.* 39(5):774-778, 1969.

DeBlassie, R.R; Cowan, M.A.: Counseling with the mentally handicapped child. *Elementary School Guidance and Counseling.* 10:246-253, 1976.

Dembinski, R.J.; Mauser, A.J.: What parents of the learning disabled really want from professionals. *Journal of Learning Disabilities.* 10:578-584, November 1977.

Fellendorf, G.W.; Harrow, I.: Parent counseling: 1961-1968. *The Volta Review.* 72(1):51-57, 1970.

Gardner, J.; Ransom, G: Academic reorientation: A counseling approach to remedial readers. *The Reading Teacher.* 21(6):529-536, 1968.

Gowan, J.C.; Demos, G.D.: *The Guidance of Exceptional Children.* New York, David McKay Company Inc., 1965.

Gumaer, J; Myrick, R.D.: Behavioral group counseling with disruptive children. *The School Counselor.* 21:313-317, 1974.

Huber, C.H.: Parents of the handicapped child: Facilitating acceptance through group counseling. *Personnel and Guidance Journal.* 57:267-269, January 1979.

Humes, C.: School counselors and PL 94-142. *The School Counselor.* 25:192-195, 1978.

Humes, C.W.: A novel group approach to school counseling of educable retardates. *The Training School Bulletin.* 67(3):164-171, 1970.

Kameen, M.C.; McIntosh, D.K.: The counselor and the individualized education program. *Personnel and Guidance Journal.* 58:238-244, 1979.

Keirn, W.C.: Shopping parents: Patient problem or professional problem? *Mental Retardation.* 9(4):6-7, 1971.

Kronich, D.: Educational and counseling groups for parents. *Academic Therapy.* 13:355-359, 485-489, January-March 1978.

Lewis, J.: Effects of group procedure with parents of mentally retarded children. *Mental Retardation.* 10(6):14-15, 1972.

Lombana, T.H.: Guidance of handicapped students: Counselor inservice needs. *Counselor Education and Supervision.* 19:269-275, June 1980.

Love, L.R.; Kaswan, J.; and Bugental, D.E.: Differential effectiveness of three clinical interventions for different socioeconomic groupings. *Journal of Consulting and Clinical Psychology.* 39(3):347-360, 1972.

Marshall, N.R.; Goldstein, S.G.: Effects of three consultation procedures on maternal understanding of diagnostic information. *American Journal of Mental Deficiency.* 74(4):479-482, 1970.

Maynard, P.E.; Warner, R.W.; Lazzaro, J.A.: Group counseling with emotionally disturbed students in a school setting. *Journal of Secondary Education.* 44(7):358-365, 1969.

McDavis, R.T.; Nutter, R.N.; Lovett, P.: Counseling needs of handicapped students and their parents. *The School Counselor.* 29:232-238, January 1982.

McDowell, R.L.: Parent counseling: The state of the art. *Journal of Learning Disabilities.* 9:614-619, December 1976.

Millman, H.L.: Minimal brain dysfunction in children — evaluation and treatment. *Journal of Learning Disabilities.* 3(2):34-40, 1970.

Morgan, S.B.: Team interpretation of mental retardation to parents. *Mental Retardation.* 11(3):10-13, 1973.

Nathanson, R.: Counseling persons with disabilities: Are the feelings, thoughts, and behaviors of helping professionals helpful? *Personnel and Guidance Journal.* 58:233-237, 1979.

O'Connell, R.A.; Golden, J.M.; and Semonsky, C.J.: Which adolescent stays in group psychotherapy? *Adolescence.* 7(25):51-60, 1972.

Opirhory, G.; Peters, G.A.: Counseling intervention strategies for families with the less than perfect newborn. *Personnel and Guidance Journal.* 60:451-455, April 1982.

Ottens, A.J.; Ottens, A.: Crisis intervention as a model for counseling retarded students. *The School Counselor.* 29:200-225, January 1982.

Parker, L.G.; Stodden, R.A.: Preparation of counseling to serve special needs students. *Elementary Guidance and Counseling.* 16:36-41, October 1981.

Perosa, L.M.; Perosa, S.L.: School counselors' use of structural family therapy with learning-disabled students. *The School Counselor.* 29:152-155, November 1981.

Prescott, M; Hulnick, R.: Counseling parents of handicapped children: An empathic approach. *Personnel and Guidance Journal.* 58:263-266, 1979.

Prescott, M.R.; Iselin, K.L.W.: Counseling parents of a disabled child. *Elementary School Guidance and Counseling.* 12:170-177, February 1978.

Radin, N.: The impact of a kindergarten home counseling program. *Exceptional Children.* 36(4):251-256, 1969.

Ray, J.S.: The family training center: An experiment in normalization. *Mental Retardation.* 12(1):12-13, 1974.

Seitz, S; Hoekenga, R: Modeling as a training tool for retarded children and their parents. *Mental Retardation.* 12(2):28-31, 1974.

Sinick, D.: Career counseling with handicapped persons. *Personnel and Guidance Journal.* 58:252-257, 1979.

Sonnenschein, R.: Parents and professionals: An uneasy relationship. *Teaching Exceptional Children.* 14:62-65, November 1981.

Stephens, W.: Interpreting mental retardation to parents in a multidiscipline diagnostic clinic. *Mental Retardation.* 7(6):57-59, 1969.

Taylor, W.F.; Hoedt, K.C.: Classroom-related behavior problems: Counsel parents, teachers, or children? *Journal of Counseling Psychology.* 21(1):3-8, 1974.

Vance, H; Finkle, L.; and McGee, H.J.: Group counseling with mentally retarded persons. *Personnel and Guidance Journal.* 56:148-152, 1977.

Wikler, L.; Wasow, M.; and Hatfield, E.: Chronic sorrow revisited: Parents versus professional depiction of the adjustment of parents of mentally retarded children. *American Journal of Orthopsychology.* 51:63-70, January 1981.

Williams, D.M.L.; Darbyshire, J.O.: Diagnosis of deafness: A study of family responses and needs. *Volta Review.* 84:24-30, January 1982.

Wolraich, M.L.: Communication between physicians and parents of handicapped children. *Exceptional Children.* 48:324-329, January 1982.

Wyne, M.D.; Skjei, P.: The counselor and exceptional pupils: A critical review. *Personnel and Guidance Journal.* 48(10):828-835, 1970.

Yura, M.T.; Zuckerman, L.; Betz, M.I.; and Newman, S.S.: Parent involvement project. *Personnel and Guidance Journal.* 58:290-292, December 1979.

SECTION V: THE COUNSELOR MEETS THE CHALLENGE

CHAPTER 19: Self-Esteem: A Bridge to Learning
Daniel E. O'Connor, B.A., M.A.

Axline, Virginia Dibs: *In Search of Self.* Ballantine Books, New York, 1964. *Play Therapy.* Ballantine Books, New York, 1969.

Axline, Virginia Dibs: *Play Therapy.* Ballantine Books, New York, 1969.

Brown, George I.: *Human Teaching for Human Learning.* New York, Viking Press, 1971.

Gordon, Dr. Thomas: *Parent Effectiveness Training.* New York, Peter H. Wyden, Inc.

Gorman, Alfred H.: *Teachers and Learners: The Interactive Process of Education.* Boston, Allyn and Bacon, 1969.

Lewis, H.R., and Streitfeld, H.S.: *Growth Games.* New York, Harcourt Brace & Jovanovich, Inc., 1970.

Punkey, Dr. William: *Self Concept and School Achievement.* Englewood Cliffs, New Jersey, Prentice Hall, Inc., 1970.

Raths, L.E.; Harmin, M.; Simon, S.: *Values and Teaching.* Columbus, Ohio, Charles E. Merrill, 1966.

Schutz, William: *Joy.* New York, Grove Press, Inc., 1967.

Simon, S.; Howe, L.W.; Kirschenbaum, H.: *Values Clarification.* New York, Hart Publication Co., Inc., 1972.

Stevens, John O.: *Awareness.* Bantam Book, 1973.

CHAPTER 20: A Behavioral Approach to Counseling
James Leigh, B.S., M.S. and Jane Ellis, B.S., M.Ed.

Bandura, A.: *Principles of Behavior Modification.* New York, Holt, Rinehart, and Winston, 1969.

Becker, W.C.: *Parents are Teachers: A Child Management Program.* Champaign, Illinois, Research Press Company, 1971.

Berkowitz, B.P.; Graziano, A.M.: Training parents as behavior therapists: A review. *Behavior Research and Therapy.* 10:297-317, 1972.

Blackman, G.J.; Silberman, A.: *Modification of Child and Adolescent Behavior* (3rd ed.). Belmont, California, Wadsworth, 1980.

Brown, D.G.: *Behavior Modification in Child, School and Family.* Champaign, Illinois, Research Press Company, 1972.

Byrne, R.H.: *Guidance: A Behavioral Approach.* Englewood Cliffs, New Jersey, Prentice Hall, 1977.

Deibert, A.N.; Harmon, A.J.: *New Tools for Changing Behavior.* Champaign, Illinois, Research Press Company, 1970.

Goodwin, D.L.; Coates, T.J.: *Helping Students Help Themselves.* Englewood Cliffs, New Jersey, Prentice Hall, 1976.

Groden, G; Cautela, J.R.: Behavior therapy: A survey of procedures for counselors. *Personnel and Guidance Journal.* 60:175-180, 1981.

Hawkins, R.P.: The functions of assessment: Implications for selection and development devices for assessing repertoires in clinical, educational and other settings. *Journal of Applied Behavioral Analysis.* 12:501-516, 1979.

Hall, R.V.: *Behavior Management Series. Part I: The Measurement of Behavior. Part II. Basic Principles. Part III. Applications in School and Home.* H. and H. Enterprises, 1971 (Box 3342, Lawrence, Kansas 66044).

Hayes, S.C.; Rincover, A; Solnick, J.V.: The technical drift of applied behavioral analysis. *Journal of Applied Behavioral Analysis.* 13:275-285, 1980.

Holland, C.J.: An interview guide for behavioral counseling with parents. *Behavior Therapy.* 1:70-79, 1970.

Jones, V.F.: Humanistic behaviorism: A tool for creating healthy learning environments. *Journal of School Psychology.* 15:320-328, 1977.

Krumboltz, J.D.; Krumboltz, H.B.: *Changing Children's Behavior.* Englewood Cliffs, New Jersey, Prentice Hall, 1972.

Krumboltz, J.D.; Thoresen, C.E.: *Behavioral Counseling: Cases and Techniques.* New York, Holt, Rinehart and Winston, Inc., 1969.

Krumboltz, J.D.; Thoresen, C.E.: *Behavioral Counseling Methods.* New York, Holt, Rinehart and Winston, 1976.

Lovitt, T.C.: Notes on behavior modification. *Journal of Special Education.* 15:34-36, 1981.

Martin, G.; Pear, J.: *Behavior Modification: What is it and How to do it.* Englewood Cliffs, New Jersey, Prentice Hall, 1978.

Meichenbaum, D.: *Cognitive-Behavior Modification: An Integrative Approach.* New York, Plenum Press, 1977.

Mikulas, W.L.: *Behavior Modification: An Overview.* New York, Harper and Row, 1972.

Nelson, R.O.; Hayes, S.C.: The nature of behavioral assessment: A commentary. *Journal of Applied Behavioral Analysis.* 12:491-500, 1979.

Panyan, M.C.: *Behavior Management Series. Part IV: New Ways to Teach New Skills.* H. and H. Enterprises, 1972.

Patterson, G.R.; Gullion, M.E.: *Living With Children: New Methods for Parents and Teachers.* Champaign, Illinois, Research Press Company, 1971.

Reese, E.P.: *The Analysis of Human Operant Behavior.* Dubuque, Iowa, William C. Brown Company Publishers, 1966.

Rosenbaum, M.S.; Drabman, R.S.: Self-control training in the classroom: A review and critique. *Journal of Applied Behavioral Analysis.* 12:467-485, 1979.

Sanders, M.R.; Glyn, T.: Training parents in behavioral self-management: An analysis of generalization and maintenance. *Journal of Applied Behavioral Analysis.* 14:223-237, 1981.

Shelton, J.L.; Meyer, E.M.: Catch them being good: Training parents as behavioral engineers. *School Counselor.* 25:110-115, 1977.

Smith, J.M.; Smith, D.E.P.: *Child Management: A Program for Parents and Teachers.* Ann Arbor, Ann Arbor Publishers, 1966.

Sulzer-Azaroff, B.; Mayer, G.R.: *Applying Behavioral-Analysis Procedures With Children and Youth.* New York, Holt, Rinehart and Winston, 1977.

Sulzer, B; Mayer, G.: *Behavior Modification Procedures for School Personnel.* Hinsdale, Illinois, Dryden Press, Inc., 1972.

Tharp, R.G.; Wetzel, R.J.: *Behavior Modification in the Natural Environment.* New York, Academic Press, 1969.

Valett, R.E.: *Modifying Children's Behavior: A Guide for Parents and Professionals.* Belmont, California, Fearon Publishers, 1969.

Wahler, G.R.; Fox, James J.: Setting events in applied behavior analysis: Toward a conceptual and methodological expansion. *Journal of Applied Behavioral Analysis.* 14:327-338, 1981.

Walker, J.E.; Shea, T.M.: *Behavior Modification: A Practical Approach for Educators.* St. Louis, Missouri, C.V. Mosby, 1980.

Watson, D.L.; Tharp, R.G.: *Self-Directed Behavior: Self Modification for Personal Adjustment.* Monterey, California, Wadsworth, 1977.

Watson, L.S.: *Child Behavior Modification: A Manual for Teachers, Nurses and Parents.* New York, Pergamon Press Inc., 1973.

Wolf, M.M.: Social validity: The case for subjective measurement or how applied behavioral analysis is finding its heart. *Journal of Applied Behavioral Analysis.* 11:203-214, 1978.

CHAPTER 21: Special Concerns in Counseling the Intellectually Limited
Eddie Williams, Ed.D.

Barnard, K.E.; Erickson, M.L.: *Teaching Children with Developmental Problems.* St. Louis, C.V. Mosby Company, 1976.

Hutt, M.L.; Gibby, R.G.: *The Mentally Retarded Child.* Boston, Allyn and Bacon, Inc., 1976.

MacMillan, D.L.: *Mental Retardation in School and Society.* Boston, Little, Brown and Company, 1982.

Olshansky, S.: Chronic sorrow: A response to having a mentally defective child. *Social Casework,* 43:190-193, 1962.

Roos, P.: Psychological counseling with parents of retarded children. *Mental Retardation,* 1:345-350, 1963.

Rosen, L.: Selected aspects in the development of the mother's understanding of her mentally retarded child. *American Journal of Mental Deficiency,* 59:522, 1955.

Smith, R.M.: *An Introduction to Mental Retardation.* New York, McGraw-Hill, 1971.

Wikler, L, Wasow, M; Hatfield, E.: Chronic sorrow revisited: Parent vs. professional depiction of the adjustment of parents of mentally retarded children. *American Journal of Orthopsychiatry,* 51(1):63-70, 1981.

CHAPTER 22: The Disabled Are Also Sexual
Sol Gordon, Ph.D.

BOOKS

Ayrault, E.W.: *Sex, Love and the Physically Handicapped.* New York, Continuum Publishing, 1981.

Blacklidge, V.: *Sex Education for the Mentally Retarded.* San Leandro, California, Mental Retardation Service, 1968.

Blum, G.; Blum, B.: *Feeling Good About Yourself.* Feeling Good Associates, 507 Palma Way, Mill Valley, California 94941, 1981.

Cornelius, D.A.; et al: *Who cares? A handbook on Sex Education and Counseling*

Services for Disabled People. (2nd edition), Baltimore, Maryland, University Park Press, 1982.

Featherstone, H.: *A Difference in the Family — Living With the Disabled Child.* New York, Penguin Books, 1981.

Gordon, S.; Scales, P.; Everly, K.: *The Sexual Adolescent.* Belmont, California, Wadsworth, Inc., 1979.

Johnson, W.R.; Kempton, W.: *Sex Education and Counseling of Special Groups: The Mentally and Physically Handicapped, Ill and Elderly.* (2nd edition), Springfield, Illinois, Charles C. Thomas, 1980.

Kempton, W: *Sex Education for Persons With Disabilities That Hinder Learning: A Teacher's Guide.* Planned Parenthood of Southeastern Pennsylvania, 1220 Sansom Street, Philadelphia, 1975.

Pattulo, A.: *Puberty in the Girl Who is Retarded.* New York, National Association for Retarded Children, 1969.

Robinault, I.P.: *Sex, Society and the Disabled.* Hagerstown, Maryland, Harper and Row, 1978.

PERIODICALS

Gordon, S: Love, sex and marriage for people who have disabilities. *The Exceptional Parent,* December 1976; pp. 18-21.

Gordon, S.; Snyder, C.: Family life education for the handicapped. *The Journal of School Health,* 50(5):272-274, 1980.

Gordon, S.; Snyder, C.: Family life education for the handicapped. In A.D. Spiegel; S. Podair; and E. Fiorito (Eds): *Rehabilitating People With Disabilities Into the Mainstream of Society.* Park Ridge, New Jersey, Noyes Medical Publications, 1981.

Gordon, S.: Sexuality and the disabled. *Australian Journal of Sex, Marriage and Family,* 2(4):157-164, 1981.

PAMPHLETS

Dickman, I.R.: *Sex education for disabled persons.* New York, Public Affairs Committee, 1975. (Pamphlet #531)

Gordon, S.: *Sexual rights for the people . . . who happen to be handicapped.* Syracuse, Center on Human Policy, 1979.

Gordon, S.; Kempton, W.; Bass, M.: *Love, sex and birth control for the mentally retarded.* Planned Parenthood of Southeastern Pennsylvania, 1979.

McKee, L.; Blacklidge, V.: *Sexuality and socialization. A book for parents of people with mental handicaps.* (Available from Ed-U Press, P.O. Box 583, Fayetteville, NY 13066.)

FILMS

All Women Have Periods
Feeling Good About Yourself
Like Other People
These People

All of the above films are available from Perennial Education, Inc., 477 Roger Williams, P.O. Box 855, Ravinia, Highland Park, IL 60035.

SUGGESTED READING

For Information and Human Understanding
(Of course there are many more — add your own!)

AMPUTATION

Baker, Louise: *Out on a Limb.* New York, McGraw-Hill Book Co., 1946.
A well-written, deeply feeling work, well worth pondering for its information as well as its philosophy.

Russell, Harold: *Victory In My Hands.* New York, Creative Age Press, 1949.
A very human document of value to all, but especially to those who must adjust to an impairment later in life.

APHASIA

McGinnis, M.: *Aphasia Children.* Washington, D.C., Volta Review, 1963.
A fine introduction to aphasia in children, with a wealth of information.

Barry, Hortense: *The Young Aphasic Child.* Washington, D.C., Alexander Graham Bell Assn. for the Deaf, Inc., 1961.
A valuable source of information for the remediation and classification of a complex problem.

Myklebust, H.: Aphasia in children — Language development language pathology. *In* Travis, L. (Ed): *Handbook of Speech Pathology.* New York, Appleton-Century-Crofts, 1957.
A classic explanation, practical and useful. A good initial presentation.

Perkins, William H.: *Speech Pathology.* St. Louis, C.V. Mosby Co., 1971.
A bit technical for the layman, but a valuable up-to-date resource for all speech and language problems.

AUTISM

Park, Clara C.: *The Siege.* An Atlantic Monthly Press Book, Boston, Little, Brown and Co., 1967.
A beautiful, well-written, informative true story of a family's struggle to understand their autistic young family member.

Rimland, Bernard: *Infantile Autism.* New York, Appleton-Century-Crofts, 1964.
A classic in the field; beautifully written and highly informative — a must.

BLIND AND PARTIALLY SIGHTED

Caufield, Genevieve: *The Kingdom Within.* Evanston, Illinois, Harper and Row, 1960.
A fine uplifting book reflecting a strong mind and sound emotions. It will be of help to all.

Lowenfeld, Berthold: *Our Blind Children: Growing and Learning With Them.* Springfield, Illinois, Charles C. Thomas, 1964.
A classic in the field of visual impairment which will always be one of the most important books in the area of exceptionalities. An "oldie" but good and *not* dated.

Bryan, Dorothy: *Guide For Parents of Pre-School Visually Handicapped Children.* Springfield, Illinois, Office of Public Instruction.
Practical suggestions for parents raising a visually impaired child. It covers attitudes, eating and sleeping habits, mobility, and school readiness.

Cutsforth, T.D.: *The Blind in School and Society* (2nd ed). New York, American Foundation for the Blind, 1951.

A fine book — another classic in the field — well written and documented. A great resource.

CEREBRAL PALSY

Brown, Christy: *Down All The Days.* New York, Fawcett World, 1971.

A moving, exquisite, fictionalized document concerning the inner feelings, trials, joys, wonders of growing up brilliant with cerebral palsy.

Killia, Marie: *Karen.* Englewood Cliffs, New Jersey, Prentice Hall, Inc., 1952.

A moving true story of a young girl with cerebral palsy who has a message for us all.

Cruickshank, William M.: *Cerebral Palsy: Its Individual and Community Problems.* Syracuse, New York, Syracuse University Press, 1966.

A professional presentation of cerebral palsy that has much information about the etiology, educational planning for, and remediation of problems encountered in cerebral palsy.

Finnie, Nancie: *Handling the Young Cerebral Palsied Child At Home.* New York, Dutton and Co., 1970.

A good practical guide for parents who have a child with cerebral palsy from birth to five years of age. Hints on feeding, bathing, toilet training and general care.

DEAF

Myklebust, Helmer R.: *Your Deaf Child: A Guide for Parents.* Springfield, Illinois, Charles C. Thomas, 1960.

A classic guide that offers parents a plan for working with and aiding in the development of their hearing disabled child.

Tracy, S., et al: *If You Have a Deaf Child.* Urbana, University of Illinois Press, 1965.

Good for mothers of preschool deaf children. Deals with language, hearing aids and home management.

John Tracy Clinic: *Correspondence Course for Parents of Little Deaf Children.* Los Angeles, John Tracy Clinic.

An internationally known program for training *parents* to work with their preschool deaf children. Great!

DIABETICS

Vanderpoel, S.: *The Care and Feeding of Your Diabetic Child.* New York, Frederick Fell, Inc., 1968.

A practical and helpful guide for raising your diabetic child.

BEHAVIOR DISORDERS

Burch, Claire: *Stranger in the Family — Guide to Living with the Emotionally Disturbed.* Indianapolis-New York, Bobbs Merrill Co., Inc., 1972.

A book which deals with some of the home problems of disturbed individuals as well as the possible problems of interrelationships with professionals.

Dupont, Henry: *Educating Emotionally Disturbed Children.* New York, Holt, Rinehart, Winston Inc., 1969.

An excellent book of readings dealing with life space interviewing, techniques of learning theory, psychoeducational processes, evaluation and research.

Long, N.J.; Morse, W.C.; Newman, Ruth G (Eds): *Conflict in The Classroom.* Belmont, California, Wadsworth, 1965.

A book of classic readings in the field of behavior problems of children and young people. Outstanding and readable.

Milton, O.; Wahler, Robert G.: *Behavior Disorders.* Philadelphia, Pennsylvania, J.B. Lippincott Co., 1973.

A book of readings for parents and professionals who want to discover an over-all view of some of the more theoretical aspects of behavior disorders.

Smith, Bert: *No Language But A Cry.* Boston, Beacon Press, 1964.

A real "feeling" book written by a truly knowledgeable human being. She outlines advantages and disadvantages of programs and ways of helping the disturbed back into meaningful, useful lives.

GIFTED

Gallagher, J.J.: *Teaching the Gifted Child.* Allyn and Bacon, 1964.

A fine guide to understanding, and working with, the gifted.

Gold, M.J.: *Education of the Intellectually Gifted.* Columbus, Ohio, Charles E. Merrill, 1965.

A highly acclaimed work which covers the field of the gifted in a most readable form.

Torrance, E.P. (Ed): *Creativity: Its Educational Implication.* New York, John Wiley.

An excellent look at the creatively gifted. Some fine suggestions for helping to encourage creativity.

INTELLECTUALLY LIMITED

Murray, Mrs. Max A.: *Needs of Parents of Mentally Retarded Children.* Arlington, Texas, National Association for Retarded Children, 1972 (pamphlet).

A fine publication with a vast amount of information for anyone interested in working with and gaining a better understanding of the intellectually limited.

Katz, Elias: *The Retarded Adult at Home: A Guide for Parents.* Seattle, Special Child Publications, Inc., 1970.

A rare presentation of some of the considerations and information necessary for living with a retarded adult in the home.

Flanigan, P.J.; Baker, G.R.; La Follette, L.G.: *An Orientation to Mental Retardation.* A Programmed Text. Springfield, Illinois, Charles C Thomas, 1970.

A basic book which includes overviews of development, special programs, vocational information, and services available for the retarded.

Buck, Pearl S.: *The Child Who Never Grew.* New York, John Day Co., 1950.

A moving true story of a mother's adjustment to her exceptional child. Written by one of America's great writers and outstanding women.

Kirk, Samuel A.; et al: *You and Your Retarded Child* (2nd ed). Palo Alto, Pacific Books, 1968.

A great book for any parent faced with the challenge of a retarded child. Full of knowledge, wisdom and plain good sense.

Barnard, K.E.; Powell, M.L.: *Teaching the Mentally Retarded Child.* St. Louis, C.V. Mosby Co., 1972.

An excellent book for parents as "teachers" of the young intellectually limited child.

LEARNING DISABLED

Lewis, R.: *The Perceptually Handicapped Child.* California Association for the Neurologically Handicapped Children, Los Angeles, California 90053, P.O. Box 604.

Problems of perception explained in laymen's terms.

Kratoville, Betty Lou: *Happiness Is A Thing Called Learning.* Houston, Texas, Association for Children with Learning Disabilities.

A wise and witty (as well as informative and well written) true story of a mother and her learning disabled child as they grow together.

Brutten, Milton; Richardson, Sylvia; Mangel, Charles: *Something's Wrong With My Child.* New York, Harcourt Brace Jovanovich, Inc., 1973.

A valuable guide for parents striving to understand and help their learning disabled child.

Myers, Patricia T.; Hammill, D.D.: *Methods for Learning Disabilities.* New York, John Wiley, 1969.

A technical but invaluable book that discusses, in a brief but thorough manner, the major theories involved in the diagnosis and remediation of learning disabilities.

SPEECH AND LANGUAGE DISORDERS

Johnson, W.: *Speech Handicapped School Children.* New York, Harper and Brothers, 1956.

One of the best and most readable books on speech and language disorders of children and adults.

Wood, Nancy E.: *Language Disorders in Children.* Chicago, National Society for Crippled Children and Adults, 1959.

A classic in the field of language disorders. Well written and outstanding as a source book.

GENERAL SOURCES

Buscaglia, Leo F.: *Leo Presents the Parents (Hotline for Parents).* Houston, Texas Association for Children with Learning Disabilities, 1972.

The author and four parents express their views on some considerations dealing with being a part of the remediation of exceptional children.

Buscaglia, Leo F.: *Love as a Behavior Modifier.* Houston, Texas Association for Children with Learning Disabilities, 1970.

A speech delivered by the author relating to affect, and human growth and development.

Des Jardins, Charlotte: *How to Organize An Effective Parent Group and Move Bureaucracies.* Chicago, Illinois, Co-ordinating Council for Handicapped Children, 1971.

A fine, informative, well-planned pamphlet which helps parents form meaningful groups to aid exceptional children.

Dunn, Lloyd M. (Ed): *Exceptional Children In The Schools.* New York, Holt, Rinehart, Winston, Inc.

Tops for a discussion of different types of exceptionalities: the etiology, remediation, and needed educational modifications.

Haring, Noris G.: *Behavior of Exceptional Children.* Columbus, Ohio, Charles B. Merrill Publishing Co., 1974.

A fine general book on exceptionalities. Excellent source book.

Kirk, Samuel A.: *Educating Exceptional Children.* Boston, Massachusetts, Houghton Mifflin Co., 1973.

An updated classic which is a readable must for anyone desiring information regarding various exceptionalities and school programs concerned with their remediation.

Kronick, D. (Ed): *They Too Can Succeed.* San Rafael, California, Academic Therapy.

Techniques and ideas for working with disabled children compiled by four mothers who speak from experience. A must!

Wright, Beatrice: *Physical Disability — A Psychological Approach.* New York, Harper and Row, 1960.

Another "oldie" but a real classic that is an invaluable source for all professionals and lay persons who want a well written, highly technical work on disability as a psychological phenomenon. Outstanding!

Copyright acknowledgments

The author is grateful to the following publishers for permission to reprint excerpts from selected materials as noted below:

Victor E. Frankl, *Man's Search for Meaning.* Boston: Beacon Press, 1962.

Doris Peel, To Be Spoken Sadly. *The Christian Science Monitor.* The Christian Science Publishing Society; copyright 1972; reprinted by permission, all rights reserved.

Verda Heisler, *A Handicapped Child in the Family: A Guide for Parents.* New York: Grune & Stratton, 1972; reprinted by permission.

Antoine de Saint-Exupery, *The Little Prince.* New York: Harcourt Brace Jovanovich, Inc., 1968.

Eleanor Roosevelt, *You Learn by Living.* New York: Harper & Row, 1960.

Clara Park, *The Siege.* Boston: Little, Brown and Company, 1967.

Rollo May, *Existential Psychology.* New York: Random House, Inc., 1961.

L. Joseph Stone and Joseph Church, *Childhood and Adolescence: A Psychology of the Growing Person.* New York: Random House, Inc., 1973.

Tennessee Williams, *The Glass Menagerie.* New York: Random House, Inc., 1945.

Christy Brown, *My Left Foot.* New York: Simon & Schuster Inc., copyright 1970; reprinted by permission.

Sol Gordon, *Sexual Rights for the People Who Happen to be Handicapped.* Reprinted by permission.

Elizabeth Boyden Howes and Sheila Moon, *Man the Choicemaker.* The Westminster Press; copyright 1973; used by permission.

Pearl S. Buck, *The Child Who Never Grew.* New York: The John Day Company, 1950.

Arthur Miller, *After The Fall.* New York: Viking Press, Inc.

Index

A

B

C

D

E

F

G

H

I

J

K

L

M

N

O

P

R

S

T

U